T0365721

'Why,
When I Was A Kid...'

autobiographical ramblings

James R. Palmer Jr.

Order this book online at www.trafford.com
or email orders@trafford.com

Most Trafford titles are also available at major online book retailers.

© Copyright 2005 James R. Palmer Jr.
All rights reserved. No part of this publication may be reproduced, stored in a retrieval
system, or transmitted, in any form or by any means, electronic, mechanical, photocopying,
recording, or otherwise, without the written prior permission of the author.

Print information available on the last page.

ISBN: 978-1-4120-6510-8 (sc)

Because of the dynamic nature of the Internet, any web addresses or links contained in
this book may have changed since publication and may no longer be valid. The views
expressed in this work are solely those of the author and do not necessarily reflect the
views of the publisher, and the publisher hereby disclaims any responsibility for them.

Any people depicted in stock imagery provided by Getty Images are models, and such images are
being used for illustrative purposes only.
Certain stock imagery © Getty Images.

Trafford rev. 10/23/2020

 www.trafford.com

North America & international
toll-free: 844-688-6899 (USA & Canada)
fax: 812 355 4082

Contents

4

Forward

We live in fast paced, hectic society which seems far removed from the less complicated days of the recent past when life wasn't really all that easy in some ways. For all those kids who survived the 1930's, 40's, 50's, 60's and 70's, the stories of my 'good ole days' as written on the pages of this book may strike a familiar chord. After all you have survived without all the modern technology and before the lawyers and government regulated our lives for our own good. First, we survived being born to mothers who smoked and/or drank while they carried us. They took aspirin, ate blue cheese dressing and didn't get tested for diabetes. Then after that trauma, our baby cribs were covered with brightly colored lead-based paints. We had no child proof lids on medicine bottles, doors or cabinets and when we rode our bikes, we had no helmets, not to mention the risks we took hitchhiking. As children we would ride in cars with no seat belts or air bags. Riding in the back of a pick-up on a warm day was always a special treat. We drank water directly from the garden hose and not from a bottle. We shared one soft drink with four friends from one bottle and no one actually died from this. We ate cupcakes, bread slathered with butter and jam, and drank soda pop with sugar in it, but we weren't overweight because we were always playing outside! We would leave the house in the morning and play all day, as long as we were back when the porch lights came on. No one was able to reach us all day long and we were okay! We would spend hours building our go-carts out of scraps and then ride down the hill only to figure out that we forgot the brakes. After running into the bushes a few times, we learned to solve the problem. We didn't have Playstations, Nintendo's, X-Boxes, video games...no 99 channels on cable or satelite, no video tape movies, no surround sound, no cell phones, no PC's, no internet or chats rooms. We had friends and we went outside and found them! We fell out of trees, got cut, broke bones and teeth and there were no lawsuits from these accidents. We made up games with sticks and dirt clods and ate worms. And although we were told it would happen, we did not put out very many eyes, nor did the worms live in us forever. We rode bikes or walked to a friends's house and knocked on the door or rang the bell, or just walked in and talked to them! Little League had tryouts and not everyone made the team. Those who didn't had to learn to deal with disappointment. Imagine that! The idea of a parent bailing you out of trouble if we broke the law was unheard of. They actually sided with the law! This generation has produced some of the best risk takers, problem solvers and inventors ever! We had freedom and failure, success and responsibility and we learned how to deal with it all without going to the shrink every five minutes. If you are one of the above, congratulations! Kind of makes you want to run through the house with scissors, doesn't it?

This book was originally written as a series of short stories about my childhood, in an attempt to give my children and posterity a few glimpses into my life. In addition to those stories, I have added some well polished hunting stories and others just to add a little flavor. Hopefully, the stories may be of enough humor or interest to encourage others to read this as well. Some of these stories may seem foreign to a city kid since the setting for most is rural farms and the mountains, but plain old country folk like myself surely will have something in common with a lot of these tales. Some skeptics (mostly jealous brothers) may argue that these accounts have been embellished and are not totally accurate as compared to their versions of the same stories, but one should remember that they were much younger than I at the time most of these events occurred, giving them less credibility. I must assure the reader that though some of these stories have been told many times and have become rather "polished" through the years, every effort has been made to be as accurate and truthful as possible. No attempt has been made to arrange the stories in any sequence or chronological order, except to intersperse my personal favorites in strategic locations to keep the interest of the reader throughout the entire volume.

I have led a very normal life and for the most part it has been a pleasant experience. Sure there have been a few storms and strife, but the Lord has blessed me with a great family and faith in His goodness and mercy. I'm sure that everyone has had similar experiences, and reading this book may bring some good memories of childhood experiences to the surface. Some of the stories included here are of a rather personal nature and took a great deal of energy and emotion to put into words. I hope you feel a portion of this emotional roller coaster as you peruse the enclosed pages!

Introduction

Why, When I Was a Kid...

Remember when you got the speech from your dad or grandpa that always started with the preface, "Why, when I was a kid....."? You would fold your arms and roll your eyes back into your head as you listened impatiently to the boring speech that sounded more like a bunch of baloney than reality. "Why, when I was a kid, I had to walk ten miles to the school bus, uphill both ways! The grass was greener, the sky was bluer and the snow was deeper!" "Duh!" I would think to myself. "You were shorter then too!" I would say sarcastically, in an attempt to refute the 'deep snow' portion of the stories.

The Crotchety Old Man skit from the old Saturday Night Live television show was always funny to me because it was so much like what we used to hear all the time. Billy Crystal in his old man costume would say, "Why, when I was a kid we were so poor that we would use baking soda for toothpaste! And we liked it! We would walk ten miles just to get to the one-roomed school house! And we liked it!" he would say in his best crotchety old man voice. I would sit and watch and laugh and laugh, all the while realizing, now that I had gotten much older, that there really was some basis of truth to those old stories. Maybe they had been embellished a bit, but those old folks really did have it tough compared to our generation.

9

Now that I am approaching mid-life, I find myself giving that same great speech to my children and nieces and nephews. They have it soft compared to folks my age! (The cycle continues!) There really are some fantastic things that happened to me in my normal boring life in the country. This book is an attempt to pen some of those memories into a compilation of stories that may sound something like a session with the Crotchety Old Man.

Maybe I should have named this book, 'Believe it or Not, Stories of Truth from a really crotchety old man.' I believe I may have figured out why the old man was so crotchety! Whenever he tells a story, it seems so fantastic, that no one believes it, even though it really did happen. Such has been my life. "You know how you can tell if Uncle Jim is lying, don't you?" my skeptics will spout. "He moves his lips!" they say and then laugh mockingly, not knowing that they speak in total ignorance of the real truth.

So, as you venture through the pages of this book, please understand that I am telling the truth, the whole truth and nothing but the truth! Why, when I was a kid, I really did have to walk a mile uphill both ways to the school bus! I remember when the winter was so cold that the monkey bars on the swing set grew feathers to keep warm. I remember walking a mile to milk the cow that would give five gallons per milking, and having to walk back home the full mile, carrying the full bucket, before and after school each day (we rented pasture & milking facilities). When I was a kid, we would have only one pair of clothes for the whole school year, and we liked it! I remember when wheat burgers were our staple diet during some lean times and Smack Ramen noodles were a delicacy. I remember changing my younger sibling's diapers with those old stained cloth diapers instead of disposable. Being the oldest boy in a family of 13 kids, I remember when sharing a bed had a whole different meaning than it does now that I'm married. I remember when the snow was so deep that it was up to my dad's chest, and when it was so cold that it was more than 20 degrees below zero for more than two weeks at a time. I remember stuffing old newspaper into our hand-me-down pack boots just to keep our feet from freezing and used socks on our hands to keep warm. Why, when I was a kid, the snow was deeper, the sky was bluer and grass was greener! We had it tough! And we liked it! And that's the truth!

The Big Fish

My internal alarm clock rang like an over-zealous rooster as I rolled onto the floor out of my side of the bed that was shared with a younger sibling. The morning had finally come! The waking sun had not yet peeked over the horizon as I stumbled into my worn out Converse high tops with the broken laces. My quiet ramblings were the only sounds that stirred in the quiet country home.

I had intentionally planned this early morning excursion to the Posey Valley ditch, with great anticipation and hopes of catching The Big Fish. The many previous tries had ended with defeat and disappointment and had conditioned my hopes of that day. I wanted that Big Fish!

The cold morning mist caressed my face and washed away the remaining sleepiness as I picked up my old dilapidated fishing pole and headed down the hill through the dew soaked grass to the big hole below the bridge. My breaths came in short gasps as I fought to control my anticipation. As I approached the bridge through the chin-deep-timothy, I slowed to calculate which strategy might work to capture the old brook trout which lay beneath the old wood bridge.

The emerging sunbeams danced off the water as I scanned the shadows of the big hole below the bridge for any signs of the monster fish that had previously thwarted my many attempts to end it's long life. I fumbled through my green tattered creel to find the new Royal Coachman Bucktail fly that would be the latest attempt to fool my arch enemy.

"Who would win today?" I thought as I tied the fisherman's knot to the fly, then double checked the knot that was tied to the handle of my short white pole. I had learned to stream fish without a reel, by necessity, and had learned that by tying the line to the handle and then threading it through the eyelets, I could hold the slack with my left hand and could short cast to reach most of the little fish-filled pools of the local streams and ditches. I could hear the quiet peaceful ripples of the ditch water as I started my methodical belly crawl to the bridge. "I can't blow it this time," I thought to myself as I continued my stealthy crawl through the pollen laden grass towards my goal.

Careful not to make noise or vibrations, I snuck to the edge of the bridge and let out a controlled sigh as my fly slipped into the dark water at the head of the deep pool below the bridge. The water immediately boiled with activity as the huge, multi-colored, mother-of-all-fish, clamped down on the size-eight, hand tied Royal Coachman. My pole felt like it would shatter as I carefully tugged the fat fish onto the bridge. I didn't even notice the pain of the splinters as I scrambled to dive onto the fish in order to prevent it's desperate attempts to return to the cold water below. I thought my heart would burst as I lifted the plump fish to inspect it's sizable proportions and admire it's beautiful iridescent colors. WOW! What a fish! I quickly scooped up my creel and worn out pole and without even taking the fish off the hook, I started for home. I couldn't wait to share this long awaited triumph with the world!

As my size-seven, soggy tennis shoes slogged across the kitchen floor, I squeaked out in a breathless, exultant voice , "Mommy I finally caught him! I got him!" My red, freckled face, beamed from ear to ear as I handed my 15 inch prize to the chef. The Big Fish had met his match!

Dirt Clods and Aspen Trees

"**B**ombs away!" I yelled as the slender aspen tree bent toward the ground and then flipped quickly back upright as I dropped giggling to the ground. "Give it a try! It's really a blast!" I yelled up to my, more timid neighbor. The trick was to climb to the top of the skinniest tree you could find, and then swing way out, while grasping the tip and releasing your legs. The supple saplings would bend almost to the ground without breaking, giving us a free ride to the bottom. "Yippeeee!" I yelled as the ground rushed up to meet me for the second time.

The large, thick grove of aspen trees, green with the newest leaves of springtime, stood shimmering in the spring breeze near our garden space, as I bent to pluck another pigweed from the corn patch. I gazed at the inviting trees, daydreaming of the shade that the tall trees must offer, as another muddy drop of sweat rolled off my forehead and into my squinting eye. The sun was at about the eleven o'clock position, as my youthful mind began to be bored with the difficult task at hand, and became distracted by happier thoughts. "What if we climbed up...." My thought was suddenly brought back to reality, by the whiny voice of my sister yelling, "Git back to work you guys, or we'll get into trouble!" She was the more obedient type and for some reason was always very motivated to do what she'd been asked to do. I ignored the interruption and gazed at the tall money trees. We always called them money trees because of the coin shaped leaves that constantly rustled in the wind.

The neighbor boy showed up at the garden gate carrying a sling shot, and that was it! I slid under the fence, like an old tom cat on a hot summer night, and headed for the cool shade of the tall trees. "I'll finish the corn patch later!" I yelled over the fence to my frustrated sibling, who stood with jaw clenched and hands on her hips glaring at me and my younger brothers. We started out goofing around with my friend's new sling shot, but for some reason began shimmying up the white barked trunks of the slender money trees. "Hey, check this out!" I hollered to my friend as I swung wildly back and forth in the tree tops. It wasn't long before he had joined me, and we started to bang against each other in sort of a contest to see who could stay aloft. I swung too wide on the next pass and felt the ground rushing up to meet me as I continued to cling tightly to the tree trunk. We continued our antics, which looked something like a cross between a smoke jumper and a ballet dancer, until one of us picked a tree that was more brittle than before. The tree top snapped, sending my friend to the ground with a thud. "Uugghh!" I heard my neighbor grunt, as he hit the ground with enough force to knock most of the wind from his lungs. "I'm tired of climbing trees anyway," I exclaimed as I swung to the ground for the final, "Bomb's away!"

We moved up the hill toward the drainage ditch that Bill Wise had dug for my father. The deep ditch was still uncovered and offered a wonderful play ground for the gang of butch-headed, sunburned boys. The clods of dried white clay, that lay mixed with the rich black dirt on the ditch banks, caught our eye and we began to fling them at each other, like little miniature bombs. "Pppkkkkkkk!" we would sputter, making the sound of a little bomb going off. The clods would turn into little white poofs of dust upon impact, making them perfect for our little war games. We would shuttle back and forth down the maze of drainage ditches, hiding, then popping up to throw the white powdery clods at our enemy. My little brothers always seemed to be on the other side, since they were smaller than I and wouldn't argue much about the way the teams were split up. They would always duck and dodge the exploding clods until one of them caught it in the head and went off crying to mom. "They're softer than the black walnuts we used last time!" I reasoned, trying to get them to stay at the fun war game. "Youuuu whooooooo!" mom would yell in a high-pitched voice at the top of her lungs, when it was time for supper or evening chores. We dropped our handful of clods and ran for the kitchen. The aspen trees and dirt clods would have to wait for another day! The smell of Mom's home cooking wafted through the evening breeze as my dirty bare feet churned up the dust while I trotted off toward the house.

Cow and the Pitch Fork

Ann Boerner was a sweet little old lady that lived down at the end of a quiet country lane in the little town of Halfway Oregon. She had lived alone in the old house for as many years as anyone could remember, caring for herself even at her advanced age. The grayed wood siding on the dilapidated old homestead revealed the fact that it had not seen any attention for quite a few years, though it was still straight and well kept for the most part. Some of the outside maintenance items had been too much for the tiny aging women, and she had come to rely more on outside help. My father had been around to help her with some of the heavier chores and in exchange she had allowed us to keep our family milk cow in her overgrown pastures. The cow had finally given birth to her new calf which caused her to produce much more milk than the calf could consume, requiring a twice-a-day milking.

Through the eyes of a young five-year-old boy, the well-beaten paths between her back porch and the old barn seemed like dangerous overgrown jungles. I returned recently and drove by the old house which is still standing, and realized that it hadn't been as far to the barn as I remembered. Things seemed much bigger then. I would often accompany my father to her home to help with the wood chopping and the milking duties and would always receive some sort of treat from my older friend. The small amount of work I did was often rewarded this way, which kept me coming back on a regular basis. I was too young to really be of much help, but Ann always made me feel like I had moved mountains and she was so grateful. On one such occasion, just after the cow had given birth, I had gone around the rear of the barn to fetch up the cow and calf to entice her to enter the milking stantion in the old barn. My father had disappeared into the darkness of the musty smelling barn to prepare the milk room for the cow.

As I rounded the corner of the barn, the surprised young mother cow glared at me defiantly, quickly identifying me as a threat to her cute new born. She started after me with head down and nostrils flaring. Instantly turning tail to retreat, I ducked around the corner of the wood-sided barn, sprinting for safety with the cow in hot pursuit. (For those readers who don't understand the gravity of this situation it is important to point out that many people have died as a result of being charged and trampled by an angry mother cow. Savvy cow hands never turn their backs on a new mother while tending to a helpless newborn.)

My young legs began to tire as I started the second lap around the barn, still trying desperately to shake my demon pursuer. The terror I felt must have been evident from my piercing screams, because my dad soon emerged from the shadows of the milk room with a pitch fork in hand. The maddened Guernsey was about to overtake me when I heard a sickening thud and heard the cow bawl and turn away from me. The pitch fork had found its mark in the skinny ribs of the mad cow, sticking briefly, then falling to the ground. The puzzled mother shook her slobbery snout with anger, realizing that she hadn't the stomach for tangling with the large man who wielded the sharp-pointy-thing and returned quickly to her panicked youngster. I darted into the door of the barn to safety, happy that my father had responded so quickly. I breathed a sigh of relief, knowing that my dad was the strongest man in the world and would always protect me. Things did seem a little bigger then, but after all, perception is reality!

Monster In The Milk Barn

My younger brothers constantly blame me for their phobia of the dark, reciting an incident when I made them walk to the fence in our back pasture in the dark to tie a rag to the fence as proof that they had been there. Two of my brothers, who are now grown men with families, still claim to be permanently scarred from this incident. I try to explain to the wimps that they were already scared of the dark, and that I didn't make them that way. If this type of trauma truly could make you scared of the dark then why didn't I develop this phobia from the following described incident?

The family milk cow named Bossy, normally would be waiting at the barn door for the evening milking, but for some reason she was nowhere to be found. As the daylight faded and total darkness fully enveloped us, my sister and I continued the search, which led us to the bottom of the lower 40 acres that had become a tangle of thorn brush. Finally, the reflection of the cow's eyes in the beam of the weakening flashlight betrayed her hide-out. We rounded her up and headed her for the barn. Our procrastination often led to this type of scenario, where we were out in

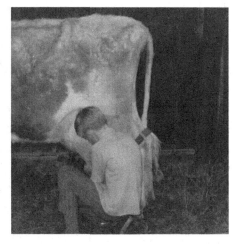

the old barn after dark. With no electricity in the old panel-sided barn, we became adept at balancing the flashlight between our knees as we stripped the fat-rich milk from the gentle jersey. The barn, equipt with two simple wooden stantions, had panels on two sides and wood boards on the other two sides. There was a small hole at the bottom of the wood wall on the west side of the barn, through which the pussy-eyed barn cats would travel back and forth when we showed up to milk. I had seen this hole but not paid much attention to it until this evening.

My father, who had grown a full length beard in order to appear as an extra in the movie "Paint Your Wagon" which was being filmed on Eagle Creek several miles from our home, had decided to come to the barn to see if everything was okay. I was by now in my normal posture, cuddled up to the cow with my head in her flank, flashlight tucked between my knees, milking like a wild man so that I didn't have to spend more time out in the dark. I always had the cow securely hobbled, mostly so that I could attach her swinging tail to the hobbles. The manure soaked fly swatter was pretty disgusting when it smacked you on the side of the face! Anyway, I digress. Back to the story.

My dad thought it would be a good idea to wait until the last possible moment to reveal his presence in the door of the dilapidated milk parlor. Since I was engrossed in my project, with the noise of the squirting milk hitting the pail, I didn't hear anyone approaching. When my dad came through the opening into the faint light of my flashlight, he let out a roar that sent me into instant panic. In total terror, I spun sideways on my one-legged milk stool with the dexterity of a cat, and shined the beam of the flashlight at the direction of the noise. What I saw in the eery light of the dim flashlight, was a large, hairy, kid-eating-monster! With eyes as big as pie plates, I fell backwards off the stool while emitting a girlish squeal, continuing my rotation until I landed on my knees facing in the same direction I had started. It was at that exact moment that I realized that the hole in the side of the barn looked larger than I had previously remembered and certainly was large enough for a nine-year-old boy to fit through. I darted underneath the startled, hobbled bovine and dove through the hole with plenty of room to spare. I must have been halfway to the house before I came to my senses and realized that the monster was just my father. I sheepishly returned to my stool and resumed my chore with still-trembling-hands.

Contrary to the flawed theories of my city-slicker-brothers, I was not permanently scarred by this event and have spent many nights in the woods alone in the dark. I can't think of a time when I have been more startled though. Maybe that monster in the milk barn scared the phobia right out of me!

Log Cabin Lillian

"Who's this?" came the sweet, quiet, query on the other end of the line. "It's your favorite grandson!" I stated assuringly. "Oh, Jimmy!" came the swift reply with a little giggle attached. I had been using that line for years until Grandma Pope had finally given up protesting that I was only one of her favorites. Now she would just admit it by acknowledging me by name. Proof of the fact that I had successfully brainwashed her, came one day when my younger sibling Thane, had called and made the same statement. "It's your favorite grandson!" he said. "Jimmy!" she had emphatically declared. He then had sheepishly admitted that he was someone other than the favorite grandson and had moved quickly on to other conversation. He finally admitted this to me some years after the actual event and we laughed together knowing that our sharp witted little grandma had that way of making each of us feel like the favorite one.

Born, Grace Lillian Nelson, at the dawn of the 20th Century, (Sept. 21, 1906) to Mary Ann and Isaac Nelson in Aitken County, Minnesota, her earliest recollections often recited to me through the years, were of their wilderness home there. She would describe how her family had homesteaded this parcel of treed land, struggling to build a rudimentary log cabin there and had scratched out a meager living. "Log Cabin Lillian" was the name that I would dub her later in my life after hearing her recite the story of those early days once again. One of my favorite activities as a youth and as an adult, was to sit around the little round kitchen table in their humble abode and listen carefully to Grandpa and Grandma Pope narrate their memories of life. With Grandpa sitting at his spot with his back to the wall, with his elbows on the cleared table, and Grandma perched on her pillow in the chair to his left, she would pull out one of her many knitting projects, and the stories would begin. This petite woman, born with congenital hips making her appear somewhat shorter than the normal person, had led anything but a normal life. I'm sure she thought that she had never done anything out of the ordinary, but I always sat there for hours, listening intently, enthralled by the fascinating life that she had led. Though plagued with much economic adversity, living through the grueling days of the Great Depression and suffering the tragic loss of her first born son at five years of age, her resilience and tenacity were often revealed as she would talk of these hard times as though they were truly "The Good Ole Days."

With only a hint of sadness, never bitterness, she and grandpa would give a detailed account of much of these hard times…, and of the good times. I was never sure if the sadness was on account of the trials of life they had endured, or that they were sad that these days were long past. There seemed to be a sense of longing to stay connected to those fading memories. Occasionally when the conversation would turn to topics of a more tender nature, I could detect a slight twinge of remorse for acts done, or events that occurred, which could have had a more pleasant outcome had things been different or alternative action taken. This burden, which really is the seasoning of wisdom that life provides as we age, has only seemed to motivate her to go on living.

As she sat in her favorite restaurant the other day with me and other members of the family, while celebrating her 98th birthday, someone started the chorus of the familiar "Happy Birthday" song and we all chimed in heartily. When it came to the part where you say their name, I inserted the words, "Happy Birthday, dear Log Cabin Lillian…, Happy Birthday to you!" She smiled shyly from all the attention and began to choke-up with emotion. Tears came to her eyes as she took the time to thank everyone and assured us that she really did love us. Though she didn't need to say it for us to feel her affection, it was good to hear it again for the billionth time. "That's my favorite Grandma!" I thought affectionately to myself, and I'm her "favorite grandson!"

Faith of a Child

Sometimes, when tuning a radio to a certain station, one finds that it is not a clear signal, making the reception seem scratchy or intermittent. I have oftentimes thought that this analogy is somewhat like the thoughtless prayers that some well intentioned Christians have repeated over and over again with little thought or emotion attached to them. I wonder if such insincere babbling is received on God's end like the scratchy or intermittent radio signals. In contrast, I would bet that he hears the innocent pleadings of a sincere child, loud and clear. One day my young four-year-old child expressed his heart-felt thanks "for the trees that make the air we breathe." That innocent prayer of thanks reminded me of a childhood experience that really taught me the value of communicating with a higher power.

We lived on a forty-acre farm situation on a hill bordering a large section of National Forest near the tiny town of Jim Town, which now was nothing more than a store and a service station. The little old one-room school house adjacent to the little town, had been converted into the church that we attended regularly. The road from the church to our home on the hill, was several miles long, stretching in a straight line up the long hill and around a sharp corner to our heaven on earth. My older sister and I anticipated the return of our father, who had gone to haul a little storage building home from the Hell's Canyon Dam Project which had just been completed. We had waited and waited at the top of the long hill, straining our eyes to look the long distance down the road as far as our young eyes could see.

After several hours of impatiently waiting, we decided that we would start walking down the road in order to meet up with our father sooner.

I'm not sure that I remember exactly how old I was, though it seems to me that I was younger than eight at the time. I was one year younger than my sister, being born on her birthday, the day after Christmas. We trudged down the long country road without encountering any traffic along the way. By the time we reached the old school house, which was a familiar landmark to us, the sky had darkened with the threatening clouds of a summer thunder storm. Lightning began to crack around us and the wind began to whip stinging debris at us, as we ran quickly to the cover of the church entryway. We sat huddled together on the step of the empty, little church as the thunder boomed loudly around us. The next loud crack came simultaneous with a huge gust of wind that toppled a nearby power pole.

Since we were scared out of our wits, and with no one around crazy enough to be out in a storm like that, we had decided that our only option was to kneel right there on the sidewalk and offer up a plea to Heavenly Father, since it was he who could control the weather and just must have forgotten that we were out there in it. We knelt together, holding hands, and pleading with the Father to make the violent storm cease, or to at least give us some peace and assurance that we would be safe. The faith of a child did not go unnoticed! He must have heard us loud and clear, because it seemed as if the storm stopped immediately and a peaceful calm feeling came into our hearts. I'm not sure how we got home because I don't remember that part, but I do remember being convinced that I somehow had a direct line to my Father in Heaven and that he really would listen if I was in trouble and needed help. Some may argue that it was a coincidence that the storm blew over just at the exact time of our little prayer, but those same skeptics probably have their radio tuned to the wrong station! The faith of a child is a sweet and powerful thing! Wouldn't it be a great if we could remain untainted by the world?

Broken Arm

I lay stunned on the cold crusty snow of the slick driveway, carefully taking inventory of each injured body part. "Are you all right?" came the stupid question from the thrilled onlookers. "No! I'm not okay!" was my swift, annoyed reply. I groaned in pain while rolling over onto my stomach to attempt to stand up. My head throbbed with pain from the impact of the violent crash which had left it's mark on my bruised and bloody forehead. Wincing with pain, I touched the fat, bloody lip that now protruded farther from my pouting face. "I think my arm is broke!" I muttered, rising to my knees on the icy surface of the steep driveway.

Just a few short minutes ago, I had been healthy and happy, speeding down the driveway on my runner sled from the house to the bottom of the hill near the creek. I would start at the house and travel down around the icy corner, across the culvert at the wide irrigation ditch, then down the steep incline past the main bridge at the creek. I had done this exhilarating run several times while my siblings and father watched. "Start up the hill higher!" suggested my father, knowing of my thirst for more speed. "The crusty snow will hold you and you'll really be moving by the time you hit your normal starting point." he explained helpfully. The deep snow had been plowed from the long driveway, leaving huge balls of now-frozen-hard snow heaped up on the sides of the roadway. Up to this point the frozen snow banks had served to keep me on the luge-like sled run down the winding driveway.

"Yippeeee!" I yelled with glee as I whizzed past my cheering audience

24

who stood at my normal starting point. The rushing cold air nearly took my breath away as I rapidly picked up speed and headed into the big sweeping corner of the curve. The little Red Flyer skidded as the momentum carried me sideways, threatening to throw it off the normal track. "Ohhhhh nooooo!" I exclaimed out loud, while fast approaching the looming ice berg ahead of me. I leaned hard to the right, scraping my elbow and knee on the icy rough surface of the road, desperately trying to regain control and almost falling off sideways. "I'll never make the corner!" I thought to myself.

The huge solid ice ball came directly at me, and I slammed headfirst into the frozen mass of dirty snow. I barely had time to raise my arm for protection as the sickening impact nearly sucked the life out of me. I had smashed into the cement-like snow bank at a high rate of speed, splatting on the glazed hard surface like a juicy bug on a windshield. It wasn't until that exact moment, that I realized how hard the snowballs really were.

"Uughh!" I grunted as the tremendous force of the impact knocked the wind out of my lungs and seemed to render me unconscious for a brief period of time. I now lay writhing in pain, worried that there would be long term affects from this accidental crash. I finally struggled to my feet, at the relief of the onlookers who felt a slight twinge of guilt for goading me into trying the higher starting point that had been the cause of my demise.

The doctor at the Medical Clinic sixty-miles away, shook his head with affirmation that the arm was truly broken, and began wrapping the arm with some new-fangled casting material that looked sort of like fiberglass. The attention that the new white cast created almost offset any disappointment that I had in not being able to perform my normal activities for the next several weeks. I learned to shoot the Jabar hook rather well while sporting the dingy cast at my basketball practice. The newness wore off quickly as the itching began in places under the cast that couldn't be reached with a bent wire hanger, but I healed quickly and soon returned to the sledding hill, maybe a bit more cautious…but not much!

Don't Touch The Bacon!

The kids of today don't have any idea how spoiled and sedentary they have become compared to our generation. Now I realize that my father said the same thing about us, and his father probably said the same thing, but it really is true. Even though television had been invented by then, (contrary to what my children tease me about), we didn't spend much time in front of it like the kids of today. We had other more fun things to do like catching frogs, fishing, hiking, exploring or horseback riding. Even the long winters were spent outside sledding and fort building.

One summer my two younger brothers and I decided to travel the nine-mile distance to Pine Lakes, which is a trio of crystal clear, turquoise blue lakes nestled at the foot of the jagged Red Mountain. Situated at the south side of the Eagle Cap Wilderness, the lakes offered us youngsters a virtual fishing paradise. Though the beautiful and colorful native brook trout of those high elevations never get much longer than 10-12 inches, they are plentiful and hungry. The high lakes always seemed more attractive to us than more local fishing holes, since the fish were so plentiful and we could only get there once or twice during the summer lay-off from school. I was about 14 or 15 years old and my two brothers were about 10 or 11. We packed up our tattered second-hand backpacks, kissed our mother goodbye and rushed up the trail toward our lofty goal as fast as our young legs could carry us. We would usually return home from such trips when we ran out of food, which was never longer than 5 or 6 days at a time. This particular trip was to be the ultimate, since we had splurged and brought along a large

26

pack of bacon to supplement our usual bland meals, consisting mostly of Top Ramen noodles.

We arrived at the heavenly destination in record time and hurriedly set up our wimpy little pup-tents, in order to stake our claim to the prime campsite on the north side of the larger-of-the-three lakes. We had been there many times before and had repeatedly chosen this particular spot in the pristine alpine basin, mostly because someone had left a large metal grate there that we could use for cooking fish. Our little aluminum pans could barely fit the small pan sized fish anyway and when we were able to use the rusty grate to roast the fish, we didn't have to wash our pans. After an evening of fishing and story telling, we retired to our cramped quarters for the night, exhausted but happy.

The heat of the morning sun woke us from our deep sleep and we stumbled groggily from the warm cocoon of our mummy bags. After rubbing the sleep from our eyes, we began the chore of cooking breakfast. By the time I had emerged from my purple pup tent, my brother, Kim had already started the fire and had carefully laid his portion of the raw bacon strips side by side in his small pan. As we approached the warm crackling fire, I noticed the roll of 'important papers' as we called them, tucked under Kim's boney elbow. "Hope everything comes out OK!" we cackled as he waddled up the hill, obviously intent on taking care of some serious business. "Don't forget to do the paper work!" we taunted. As he disappeared up the hill to his private wilderness retreat, we began to yell wildly, "your bacon is burning! Your bacon is burning!" His uncomfortable scamper back to the fire had left him with unfinished business and revealed to him that his bacon had only just begun to simmer.

"Leave my bacon alone!" he hissed crossly, as he labored back up the hill. The earlier waddle had evolved into a painful saunter that almost looked like something out of a John Wayne movie. Just as he disappeared into the cover of the short alpine spruce trees, we mimicked our earlier chant, "Your bacon is burning! Your bacon is burning!"

Being raised in a family of 13 kids had conditioned him to protect his portion of food like a lion cub on a fresh kill. We giggled as he yelled something about "killing us till we were dead" and began his agonizing ramble back down the hill to his 'still-raw' slab of home grown bacon. "Keep yer filthy hands off my food!" he threatened. "I mean it! Don't touch my bacon!" he emphatically howled. Before he could crest the top of the small hill for the third time, his spattering bacon had began to blacken. "Your bacon is burning!" we seriously lamented. "Oh shut up! You better not touch it!" he countered. "No, really, it really is burning this time!" we yelled helpfully. By this time his space-aged, official-Boy-Scout-mess-kit was totally engulfed in flames as the explosive bacon grease was being consumed by the intense fire. "Do you want us to take it off the fire?" we yelled towards his secluded latrine. "I told you not to touch my bacon!" he screamed from his hide out. "Okay! But don't forget we warned you!" we giggled with triumph.

The relieved look on his face immediately turned to anger as he tossed the now-reduced roll of toilet paper into his open pack and realized that we had been telling the truth. Our cries of wolf had duped him into believing that his bacon was still just beginning to simmer as it was when he left it. "Why didn't you stupid guys take it off the fire?" he lamented, as he held the remnants of his charred breakfast aloft. The heat of the intense grease fire had totally melted his aluminum fry pan into something that closely resembled the pile that he had just left in the woods. The long handle was the only portion of the pan that had escaped unscathed. Howls of laughter filled the air as we held our aching sides and rolled on the ground uncontrollably. "Don't touch my bacon!" we mimicked as he stomped off towards the lake, mumbling something under his breath about the advantages of being an only child.

Brownie and the Pony Herd

H is slick, brown coat glistened in the sun as the tall thoroughbred raced across the field frantically whinnying and squealing like a rank stud that has caught wind of a new mare in heat. Brownie was the newest addition to our little herd of ponies, but had quickly assumed the lead role in the pecking order of the small band of misfits. My sister had been saving her meager earnings until she had enough money gathered to purchase the large and beautiful horse, not realizing that he would be too much to handle for a young inexperienced girl. His hot temperament had been more than most of us were willing to deal with, so he rarely got ridden and often remained as the loner in the large field while we rode the other ponies. This particular day was no exception and he raced wildly back and forth across the field, distraught at the prospect of being left alone again.

My father had slowly gathered a herd of misfit ponies for us to ride, most of which were given to him by the previous owners because of some physical disorder or personality flaw. Some of the little hay-burners where tall and lanky, others short and squatty with pot bellies and split hooves. One of them we had dubbed Pickle because of his dapple-grey color, that when viewed in the right light, had sort of a green hue to it. His habit was to spin in circles after the rider had mounted until he would get so dizzy that he would fall down, spilling the rider to the ground. He would lay there until he caught his breath and would do the stunt all over again. We never did get to ride that darn pony! Another tall painted pony named Sundown, had come to us as a wheezy, foundered plug that looked like he was on his last leg. After riding the heck out of him, he snapped out of it and became a very good horse, which is another story that I will tell somewhere in this book. Anyway, to say the least, this remuda was a sorry lot, but we thought highly of most of them and rode them all over the hills. That's where I learned to ride well, since we mostly rode bareback because we only had the one saddle that had come with Brownie.

One day while attempting to catch our desired mounts for the day, we had cornered them along the south fence of the lower pasture when Brownie had decided that he would stop us from taking away his pasture mates. He rushed into the middle of the pack of ponies with teeth bared and

ears laid flat to his head, scattering our unkept mounts like leafs in an October wind. I screamed for the younger boys to "look out!", but it was too late. The mean, agitated horse grabbed for the nearest of the scrambling kids, biting him hard on the shoulder, then wheeled around and kicked the poor helpless boy square in the back with both feet. The sickening thud of the shod hooves made me shiver as I watched the body of the youngster being flung face first into the barbed wire fence. We raced to his rescue as he struggled for breath, still dangling from the fence with a bewildered, frantic look on his freckled face. He did recover quickly but probably wears the horseshoe-shaped brand on his back to this day. Needless to say, Brownie never got ridden after that day and we figured out many devious ways to remove the pony herd without getting in his way.

On this particular day, we had successfully extracted all of the other ponies from the barbed wire fenced pasture and were heading up the hill toward the house when we heard the retired race horse begin his screaming rampage. He raced back and forth, screaming and bucking across the field in his rage. I watched with horror as he approached the north fence line at a full sprint. Now foaming with exertion, his glistening, sweat-drenched-body slammed into the barbed wire fence with a sickening screech. The loud squeak of the barbed wire being wrenched from the fence posts, along with a sharp snapping noise as several wooden fence posts were sheared off at the ground, rang through the air as the big proud-cut gelding was launched through the air upside down, landing on his back with a resonating thud. The once proud herd master, now lay still for an instant, then struggling for breath, attempted to rise from the ground that had interrupted his fall. Kicking like a newborn, he finally wobbled to his feet, bleeding profusely from the deep gash in his chest that had been inflicted by the harsh barbed wire upon impact with the sagging fence. He shook himself, then immediately continued his screaming rampage across the fields of the adjoining pasture. "Dang knot head!" I muttered with disgust as I rushed toward the house to enlist my father into the fray. The pony herd soon lost their psychotic leader to the glue factory, and life returned to normal among the scrappy herd of misfit ponies.

My hunting partner and I recently fired a new recruit named Geronimo, from our pack string who had similar tendencies for stupidity and self destruction, like Brownie the thoroughbred. He even looks alot like Brownie. The goofy bugger went into one of those psychotic fits and rolled himself down the mountain end-over-end, on our last pack trip. Maybe he is the reincarnated version of my sister's dumb horse. I don't think he'll end up at the glue factory, but I know for sure that he won't be returning to the mountains with us next year!

Cow Pies and Lady Fingers

Times have changed since I was a kid, in regards to the discipline of children. Back in those days we could take a well deserved beating that might be considered abuse in today's society. I'm sure I deserved the flogging that I received in exchange for the antics described in this story, but I assure you that the fun was well worth the pain and suffering!

We lived in the old Babcock house that we had rented for a short period of time in order to get closer to town as we found more suitable housing. What seemed like a mansion to me as a small boy, really was just an old two story home that was surrounded by stately pine trees and jungles of lilac bushes, giving us lots of hiding places and fort building opportunities. The old dilapidated woodshed at the rear of the home served its intended purpose along with becoming a cozy milking parlor for the family cow. The property seemed bigger then, but must have been only a couple of acres. Just enough pasture to sustain the one cow that had become part of the family and provided the much needed dairy products to the household. The fenced yard contained ample room for a play space but we oftentimes ventured into the back pasture to expand our horizons.

One such day we had left the gate to the back yard open, which allowed the cow to wander onto the lush green lawn for a change of pace. In this case the grass really was greener on the other side of the fence and Bossy spent several hours gorging on it's tender goodness. Much to our delight she had left behind some huge circular piles of manure, which we quickly used to our advantage as a play toy. Somehow we had acquired several packs of contraband Lady Finger firecrackers which were not allowed in our household. The messy explosions that were created by placing the tiny fire crackers gingerly down into the fresh cow pies, were awesome! The displaced manure would fly in all directions, leaving a giant crater in each sloppy pile. It became a contest to see who's pyrotechnic's could fling the most smelly poop the highest on the worn green asphalt siding of the neglected old homestead.

The afternoon became evening as we lost track of time, engrossed in this quality fun! We continued our contest around the perimeter of the house, following the green trail of cow patties like Dorothy on the yellow brick road. The mini-sticks of dynamite finally ran out and we were forced to return to a less attractive past time. With the twisted perception of a young bored country boy, I had decided that this was the highlight of the week and that we were going to have to smuggle some more of the tiny explosives into the house. We moved onto other less appealing activities, and quickly forgot about the rank mess that we had left behind, not thinking of the consequences of our actions.

My father returned home earlier than normal that day and somehow discovered the new coating of smelly cow dung which now had dried and stuck to the backside of the house, like stucco on a Mexican hacienda. My trip to the woodshed that day was almost as memorable as the Lady Fingers and cow pies,.... but not quite!

Bug Bomb

This story title should not be confused with 'bag balm' that sticky substance with the unique strong smell that is used to salve the chapped teats of the family cow, and well, . . . many human ailments of a similar nature. Nor should this title be misconstrued for the type of bug killer that is more like a fogger, killing from a safe distance. Maybe the title should have read, "Mosquito repellant Bomb," but that didn't sound as good quite frankly, and wouldn't have gotten this much attention just on the explanation.

It all started one day when the ragtag group of Boy Scouts dragged their sorry behinds into the lush green meadow of the high lake's campground. I had long since moved away from the little country town of Halfway, but had returned to the area and to Pine Lakes for the last leg of a fifty-mile trip with my own group of Scouts. We had been camping at the high altitude lake for about a day and a half, with no interruption or competition from other visitors, so when the group of tired young misfits came up over the rise, they created quite a stir in the once-quiet basin. We watched from our campsite across the emerald blue lake, as the small band marched into the clearing at the opposite edge of the lake and dropped their heavy burdens to the ground. Even from the long distance across the glistening waters of the cold clear lake, I had recognized the form and voice of my long time friend, Craig. Since we hadn't collaborated on this surprise meeting, and had not seen each other for quite some time, I began to make immediate plans to hike around the lake to renew our acquaintance and talk about old times.

I relayed to my young Scouts, the news that this new group had arrived on the other side of the lake, and that I would be making the short trip around the beautiful lake to visit the newcomers. Only one of the young men decided to accompany me in the jaunt, since it was nearly evening and they had already expended most of their energy earlier in the day and had no connection with the strangers. We arrived on the hill above the somber group of tired boys, just as the sun had disappeared from the early evening sky and immediately realized that the group hadn't noticed our approach. Todd and I crouched quickly down in the group of small alpine fir trees to avoid detection, whispering excitedly to each other a plan to surprise and scare the wits out of the local group of boys and their unsuspecting leader.

As we lay prone in the brushy hideout, like a couple of Indian scouts, we planned our attack. We would lay in wait until the darkness had fully enveloped us and we could sneak unseen across the open meadow below us. We would then jump from the shadows, screaming bloody murder, hoping to give a good fright to the unaware and preoccupied bunch of boys.

As the darkness fell around us, we noticed that the once-somber-group had perked up a bit and had built a roaring fire that had warmed their spirits. As we crawled on our hands and knees to shorten the distance between us, we noticed that their circle of tiny pup tents had been slowly erected close to the brightly burning fire.

We could hear the conversation turn a bit rowdy as the boys began to play around the fire, teasing and playing with youthful vigor. We watched from our perch at the edge of the steep embankment overlooking the active campers, who were still totally unaware of the eyes in the dark that gazed upon them, waiting to pounce. All of the sudden, one of the gangly teens, snatched a small bundle from his pack and announced to his group of friends that he would return in a moment. We retreated several yards backwards at the announcement, crouching even lower to the ground to avoid detection.

The heavy breathing came closer and closer to our hideout, as the youth staggered up the steep hill to take care of some serious business. Satisfied that he was out of eyesight of the other members of his party, and visibly uneasy with the spookiness of the surrounding darkness, he dropped his worn trousers and squatted to make his smelly contribution to the world. Since we were within just a few short feet of the sorry pilgrim, we could hear every grunt and sound he made. I was tempted to reach out and grab the poor youngster, but restrained myself in order to wait for a more opportune moment to frighten the whole lot of them together. The hilarious predicament became more than we could stand, as the gross noises continued next to us. I held my breath and put my hand tightly to my mouth, shaking violently from the uncontrollable laughter that had over come me and noticed my younger companion doing the same. We finally breathed a sigh of relief, still trembling with amusement, as the unsuspecting youth fastened his belt buckle and trotted quickly back down the hill.

"Whew! That was close!" I exclaimed, still laughing uncontrollably. "The poor bugger wouldn't have survived if we had grabbed him in the midst of doing his duty!" Todd giggled. We snorted and stamped with glee, tickled that we had gone unnoticed, but wondering if we should have given the lone hiker the scare of his short life. We raised up to our hands and knees, giving a wide berth to the new bathroom facilities, and crawled to our original vantage point overlooking the activities of the unorganized camp.

The unruly bunch had lost interest in their previous antics and had begun to play in their brightly burning fire like a bunch of frenzied pyro-maniacs. Unbeknownst to us, one of the rascals had placed a partially used can of bug spray into the glowing coals to see if it would ignite. At the exact moment that we had chosen to raise to our feet and commence our attack, a huge explosion shattered the night air, shooting a bright multicolored flame in all directions. We continued our rush down the hill, screaming bloody murder, in our attempts to scare the unsuspecting group of new Boy Scouts, but our loud rampage went totally unnoticed. The shooting flames of exploding Mosquito repellant had sprayed several of the nylon tents with the burning liquid and the scrambling pyro-maniacs had turned suddenly into fire fighters. We scampered into the fiasco with vigor, still hoping to get some mileage out of our carefully planned siege, though still mostly ignored by the scrambling little terrorists.

We watched with horror as one of the tents burned to the ground in a matter of seconds and left a smoldering mass of melted nylon and scattered equipment. Finally noticing our presence in the aftermath of the bug bomb, my adult friend recognized my familiar face in the still flickering light of the smoldering tent and strode over to greet me heartily. We laughed together as we slapped each other on the back and wondered how we had chanced to meet like this in the middle of the wilderness. He shook his head at the sorry mess around us, muttering some excuse about the antics of his uncontrollable band of rowdies and stomped out the last flickering remnant of the burned out tent.

We had both been part of a similar group of boys, years before, so this incident didn't surprise us much. We chatted excitedly about old times, ignoring the milling group of teenagers. The group of misfits regrouped and ran off toward the lake, oblivious to the damage they had just caused, shifting their attention to their new game of hide-and-go-seek. We laughed together about the "bug bomb" and reminisced about the good ole days of our youth.

Buttermilk and Bologna Sandwiches

Young boys are an impressionable lot, always looking to their mentors for direction. Most of us wouldn't admit it as teenagers, but as aging adults, it is easy to see that we have become the spitting image of our parents. As a very young boy, I had thought of my father as a Superman of sorts. "He must be the smartest and strongest man in the world!" I thought. He would bulge up his biceps while making the comment, "This one's made of iron and this one's made of steel, if the right one don't getcha, then the left one will!" I would watch everything he did, careful not to miss any of the details.

One of my favorite activities was to travel along with him when we did the local milk route. We would travel around Pine Valley and then Eagle Valley in the wee hours of the morning, collecting the ten gallon milk cans from each barn's crude coolers. Some dairies would have many cans of the chilled milk and others would consistently have just a few. After collecting the heavy milk cans, and sliding them onto the double decker truck, we would drive for several hours to the nearest creamery in Payette, Idaho to drop our load and return for the next day's haul. The invention of the bulk tanks made this method antiquated, but we continued this business until most of the smaller dairies either went out of business or switched to the bulk tanks.

On these long trips, which were wearisome for my hard-working father, we would have lots of time to talk and tease and listen to the radio. The staple for our lunch seemed to be a bologna sandwich, washed down with a tangy, smooth swig of fresh buttermilk. "Aaaahh, nothing better than buttermilk with a bologna sandwich!" my dad would say, wiping the thick moo-stash from his upper lip. Since my dad seemed to cherish the delicacy, I soon developed a taste for the tangy cultured milk, not realizing until later in life that it was really just rotten, clotty milk, and the sandwich consisted of ground up beef, pig lips and eyes and snouts, slathered with a little mayo and corralled by a couple of slices of bread. The scant cheap meal, seemed more like a banquet to me because I was convinced that this was the fare of the smart and strong people of the world. "My dad would know all about that!" I mused thoughtfully, as we bounced down the graveled county roads in the darkness of the early morning.

The day we climbed out of the crashed truck, in the middle of the night, while returning home from one of these long milk hauling trips was the first time I realized that my dad must not have been made of steel. He yelled our names in the darkness, frantically trying to assess the condition of the three children that had accompanied him on this trip, with blood streaming from the long gash in his forehead. All accounted for, we clambered sleepily out of the overturned truck, wondering what had happened while we slept. At two o'clock in the morning the road was abandoned accept for our small family huddled in the cold moonlight looking at the overturned milk truck.

Many years have passed since those long, tiring, but cherished, days on the road. I still get a hankering every once in a while for a cold bologna sandwich and a tall carton of tangy buttermilk. My young boys watch with disgust as I wash down the beef by-products with the cold clotty buttermilk and say, "It don't git no better than this boys! Cold buttermilk and a bologna sandwich!" They think I'm teasing, but I really am serious.

The Spring Box

My breath came in short controlled bursts, mostly because I was nervous, but also because I thought by controlling the volume of my wheezing breath, it would be quieter, which allowed me to listen closer to the night noises around me. The night sounds seemed to come alive as I inched my way up the dirt road on the blackest of nights. The dark clouds muted any dim light that might have been provided by the evening starlight on a clear night, making it seem more eery than normal. The flashlight that clanked in my coat pocket had been forbidden by my father, but hadn't given much light anyway, before going completely dead. I had called for my faithful dog, Kip, but had been disappointed when he didn't come. "Don't come back in the house until you have written your name on the lid of the spring box," said my stern father with a sincere scowl. "You do it without a flashlight too!" he exclaimed as I skulked out the back door of the daylight basement, consumed with fear and trepidation.

His sharp words rang in my ear as I forced my heavy legs to continue my tiptoe up the hill. "Who, Who!" an owl screeched, piercing the darkness and making me jump. "Dang, I wish Kip could be here with me!" I worried to myself. Until my eyes adjusted to the almost-total-darkness, I had to walk stooped over a bit in order to feel my way along the berm of the old logging trail. It seemed like hours of frightful sneaking, before I reached the old barbed wire fence at the property line and entered the dark canopy of trees at the edge of the National Forest Boundary. "Only a couple hundred more yards, and I'm there!" I coaxed myself, trembling in fear. I fumbled around in my pocket to feel for the short wood pencil that I had brought along for the inscription just to make sure it was still there, and grasped it tightly to be sure it remained there until the dreadful mission was completed. I didn't want to have to do that trip in the dark again!.

My imagination began to run wild, as I neared the ravine and began wading through the waist-high brush toward the dark hump that must be the spring box. I followed the gurgling noise until my hands finally caressed the wood lid and I sighed with relief. I pressed the stubby lead of the number two pencil into the plywood surface, careful to leave no doubt that my presence had been documented. The pencil lead had no more than left the course surface when I turned quickly to begin the scary trip back down the hill. The suspense was just about more than I could take, so I began a swift trot toward the lights of the house at the bottom of the long hill. The thought of something getting me from behind had been heightened now that I was going the other way and my back would be facing the scary woods.

My father had continually warned me never to use his tools without replacing them to their original spot in his tool belt, but I had not heeded the multiple warnings and he decided that my punishment would be to make me walk up the hill in the dark to the spring box. I hadn't really given the punishment much thought until this day when I had forgotten and left a hammer laying in the dirt. My trek to the spring box seemed further this time than it had ever seemed before.

The spring box was nothing more than a four-foot perforated culvert stuck in the ground on end, with a plywood top cut to fit and hinged on one side. About ten or twelve feet down, the clear, icy water rushed into the holes from one side with such force, that it would jet clear to the other side of the culvert before falling with a roar. It was piped down the hill over a ½ mile, arriving at the house with such force that the system didn't require the usual pressure tank. The spring box had been a destination point for us during many of our Sunday afternoon hikes and play excursions, since it was always a shady spot, located in a secluded draw above the road under a tall canopy of evergreens. It was always fun just to lift the lid and watch the water squirt with force into the deep culvert. The ancient water-right had been used for years, but the spring head itself had recently been updated and improved by the hard work and ingenuity of my father.

I returned to the spring box last year during a family reunion to that old homestead. I looked for any evidence of my writing without finding anything. Though completely faded out because of the years of exposure, the lid had once been inscribed with my signature.

As I continued my trot down the road, I came to the property line and wriggled through the barbed wire gate at the fence line. My heart about leaped out of my chest when I heard a huffing noise and a wild animal come pouncing out of the bushes toward me. "AaaaaghhhhheeeeeeEEEEE," I squawked in total fear and panic. If I had been able to see to run fast, I would have broken the school record for the hundred-yard dash. The animal leaped up and smothered me with slobbery dog kisses. "Kip!" I yelped with relief. "Where have you been?" I scolded playfully. I started to run toward the house with the lights far below as my beacon and with the dog now alongside to guard me from my unseen enemies. I shuddered with relief and quickened my pace even more. When I reached the house, I went straight for my bedroom and slid beneath the covers without even taking my clothes off. "Whew! What a relief! The night time trip to the spring box wouldn't soon be forgotten.

Brandon's First Bull

The scratchy sound of the radio could be heard above my heavy breathing, and I picked it up to respond. "Come again," I said. "I'm in position," came the swift reply. "Roger that! I'm heading through, so be ready!" I responded. We had planned this hunt with a lot of care and didn't want to botch it up. It would be important to know exactly where everyone was. "How bout it Stan? You got a copy?" I questioned into the little black microphone on the headset. "Copy that Jim. I'm on my stand and ready to go!" "Okay! Fasten your seat belts boys! Here we go!" I said with excitement in my voice, eager for the hunt. The last several years of hunting here had taught us, that when spooked even a little bit, the elk in this upper basin would run down an established escape route to avoid the hunting pressure. We had positioned Stan and Brandon in strategic places along the well worn trail. This plan had worked on several occasions, bringing meat to the table each time, so we were confident that it would work again.

This was Brandon's first real elk hunt with a bow so we had allowed him to sit in my favorite spot in order to give him the best opportunity possible. He had already missed several elk and had left un-found arrows laying all over the country side (that may be a bit of an exaggeration). This was the day that he was ready to turn his fortunes around, and as he sat shivering in the cold morning air, his mind was preparing for the quick action that was to follow. His breath came in short gulps as he prepared his compound bow for action. When he heard me signal that the drive had begun, he shivered again, this time not because of the cold, but because of the excitement.

The zig zag path took me over hills and meadows and through thick stands of dark timber, searching carefully for our prey. I had hoped to get close enough to get a shot before the elk spooked and went stampeding down the familiar path toward the ambush, but as luck would have it, they winded me long before I was close enough. Thumpity, thump, went the thundering clatter of elk hooves as they jumped and ran as if they knew exactly where they were supposed to go. "Here they come!" I shouted breathlessly into the tiny microphone. "Get ready! Here they come!" I repeated in earnest. There was no reply from the other end which I expected, since they would have to be quiet as they lay in wait for the big ambush.

It seemed like an eternity until I finally heard my son's trembling voice over the radio. "I got a hit!" came the scratchy message. "I think I hit one too!" said the other, older voice. "Yes!" I thought to myself with satisfaction and with a big grin on my whiskered face. We had been at it for several long hard days, and it was good to finally have the success we'd been looking for. We had seen several elk hanging out in this high basin, and the timing had worked out perfectly for this particular ambush. "What did you hit?" I asked over the short wave radio. "It's a bull!" came his satisfied reply. "Just sit tight until I get to you!" I counseled the first-timer. "I'll be there in a couple of minutes and then we'll see if we can find some blood."

His grin was stretched from ear to ear, as I approached the small clearing where he stood patiently waiting. "What happened?" I questioned enthusiastically. "Well, the cow came through the clearing first and stopped and then I saw the bull out of the corner of my eye and switched my attention to him. He stopped momentarily, lowering his antlers to push the cow out of his way, and that's when I drilled him." said the sweating teenager, who now looked more like a man than a boy. "Do you know where you hit him?" I asked with concern, knowing that it could be a long day if the hit wasn't just in the right spot. "The arrow went all the way through and hit him low, behind the shoulder." the man continued to explain with excitement in his voice. "Here's some blood." I said, hopeful that we would find the animal quickly.

It was as he said, and we found the massive bull laying piled up in the bushes just a few hundred feet from the site of the ambush. "There he is dad!" spoke the excited hunter, not sure exactly how to react or what to do next. This was his very first archery kill, and it was a dandy! "Give us a big yippeeee!" I encouraged him. "Yippee." he said reluctantly. "Come on you can do better than that!" I scolded in fun. A loud "YIPPEEEEEEE and YEEHAWWW," could be heard from down the trail. Stan had heard the commentary on the voice activated radio, and had given Brandon a lesson on how to begin the celebration. Grandpa acknowledged that he too had been in on the hunt, from his perch across the deep canyon, with binoculars and radio in hand. "Way to go Brandon!" he congratulated.

I grabbed the big bull by the thick antler, pulling his head upright out of the thick brush, and exclaimed with awe, "Wow! Look at the size of that monster!" That turned out to be a little foreshadowing of the rest of the day, since it took a great deal of effort to get the nearly eight hundred pounds of meat to the locker. Brandon started the gutting process while I went to help saddle the horses for the long pack to the trail head. Since the days had been warm, our practice for taking care of the meat properly was to get it skinned and quartered and hauled to town as quickly as possible, so that we could get it into cold storage as soon as possible. We toiled throughout the day until we accomplished the grueling task, riding the ten miles to the trail head and arriving at the little grocery store's meat locker well after dark.

The twelve hours of labor had drained us, so we plopped down on the soft seats at the local bar and grill to take a much needed rest and refreshment. We ate the two large pizzas in silence, pausing only to wash it down with large gulps of cold root beer. Finally satisfied, we sat back in our comfortable chairs and recounted the grand events of the day. "Way to go Brandon!" we both congratulated the newcomer to our camp. "This is what it's all about!" I said with pleasure at having been a part of my son's first elk and first archery kill. "What a bull!" acknowledged my long time hunting partner. "It took three horses!" he continued to brag. "That rack sure looked cool riding down the trail on the back of Dally Donk!" I said, referring to the spotted mule we have used for years. We nodded at each other's commentary, tickled at our good fortune as Brandon just sat in his chair and smiled. His first big bull! What a great day!

Choc-aholic

She lay unconscious, sprawled across the front seat of the parked Suburban, like a drunken bum passed out with his half empty bottle of Annie Green Springs wine laying next to his limp hand. The bottle of Hershey's syrup lay on its side next to her, open and dribbling a delicious stream of dark liquid across the velour seat of the car. The tale-tell marks of her addiction were apparent as the sticky chocolate fluid oozed out of the corner of her half-open mouth. The smeared marks across the back of her hand were evidence that she had attempted to wipe her face to hide the fact that she had been sucking on the bottle of sweet thick liquid, addicted to it's comforting goodness.

The vision of an inebriated drunkard passed out on a park bench, invaded my imagination as I surveyed the hilarious scene from the passenger side window. "Hey! What are you doing?" I barked in a loud voice. "Are you some kind of a choc-aholic?" I teased. She awoke and quickly jerked herself into a semi-upright position, muttering something about being sleepy. "What have you been up to?" I continued to pry. "I can tell what you've been doing,…. and I have finally caught you in the act!" I said with a pleased grin. "What are you talking about?" she sputtered groggily, obviously annoyed that I had prematurely interrupted her after-work nap. I showed her the gooey mess on the seat and relayed to her my mental image of the drunk comatose vagrant. We laughed heartily as I slipped into the back seat to avoid the spilt syrup.

She had been waiting for me in the parking lot of the local grocery store with the windows rolled down on the sultry day and had fallen fast asleep next to the open bottle of chocolate syrup that one of our sweet children had evidently abandoned on the car seat. The long day at her job as a dental assistant had left her exhausted and she had quickly succumbed to the fatigue as she sat in the warm waning rays of the evening sun waiting for me to emerge from the store. She drove home as I continued to playfully harass her about her addiction, suggesting that she really should seek professional help.

My dear wife has formed a tried-and-tested theory that chocolate is a diet food and has helped her to lose unwanted pounds on many occasions. Now I can't say that I don't believe her since she is very convincing and generally shares her tasty treats with me. I have been able to swoon and seduce her into an amorous mood multiple times with the help of the soothing drug of chocolate. One red rose and a large Hershey chocolate bar usually convince my sweet heart to overlook a multitude of sins. I have in fact, formed a viable theory of my own, which has something to do with the phenomenon that chocolate can make a woman blind to fact that their lover is a portly, middle-aged-bald-man with fungus toes, and makes them see us as hunky Chippendale types with irresistible sex appeal. My tendency to enable my dear choc-aholic wife has served me well through the years.

I reminded her of this mutually beneficial addiction the other day, shortly after she had gotten into a car accident while traveling home from a church pie social. Having driven separate cars to the event, I had been ahead of the accident and had been summoned back by her phone call. As I approached the scene of the accident, I asked the sheriff in charge if there was any evidence that my wife's chocolate addiction may have played a part in the accident and informed him that she had just consumed a healthy portion of a chocolate pie at the church social. His slight grin signified his acknowledgment of my untimely joke as he sternly assured me that there was no evidence of her driving under the influence of chocolate and the accident had been the fault of the other driver. I guess they don't have a breath-a-lizer test for that yet. I sighed with relief to find that she was okay, and leaned over to give my choc-aholic a big squeeze.

Cliff Jumping

The fear of falling is inborn in even the smallest of human beings, and takes some doing to overcome this natural inhibition in order to participate in some of the more extreme outdoor sports of our day. A simple trip to the country or to the lake cabin used to be the recreational choice of most outdoors men of years past, but it seems as though in our visual and violent society, we have resorted to more extreme passions to get our thrills. Though I have never tried sky diving or bungee jumping, I have resorted to the fine art of cliff jumping to soothe my passion for adventure.

I say that with tongue-in-cheek for two reasons. First of all, I hate heights. Jumping from dizzying heights into the hard and usually frigid waters below, scares me. Not only that but the thoughts of being down that deep in the water where the scarey monsters could brush up against you, gives me the willys. But I do it, simply because it does scare me and I hate being scared of anything. Secondly, it has never been a fine art with me. It's more like dropping a retarded cow off the cliff, instead of the graceful swan-like dives of professional cliff jumpers. The huge splashes are usually followed by the gee-haws and giggles of the onlookers, who generally gather like a flock of vultures to a road kill, to see if the old hairy fat guy will survive the fall.

Our favorite cliff jumping spot has been a place in the Oxbow Reservoir on the Snake River, where the old railroad tunnel was covered up by the backed-up waters of the new dam. Jumping from the rock face above the old tunnel entrance became our best location because it not only had a variety of heights for the differing comfort levels of jumpers, but also assured us that the water was plenty deep enough for safety sake. On hot summer days you would find the cliffs littered with would-be jumpers, who stood fidgeting in their struggle to overcome that basic fear of falling. For some, the addiction to that adrenaline rush that occurs in the horrible first moments of the fall, is their prime motivation for jumping, but for this old fat guy, those shivers of horror get harder to overcome each and every time.

The uncomfortable side affects, like water enemas and the fat lips and bruises and the sharp sting of water being forced up my sinuses, I can take with a grain of salt, but that sinking feeling, that sensation of falling just gets worse each time. I have jumped from the high bridges spanning the cold waters of the Kettle River in Washington, from the sheer cliffs of the Imnaha River's famous Blue Hole, into the warm stagnate waters of the Snake River and various ponds and lakes, from rock outcroppings and log jams and into the warm waters of the Fire Hole on Yellowstone's Madison River, and all sorts of stupid places, but I still never get used to it. Several times I have jumped in the dark of night, just to see if the awful sensation would subside if I couldn't see where I was going, but to no avail. It was a failed experiment. I did find out that without seeing the landing spot, you could swallow more water than normal and have your eyelids peeled back and scrubbed real good.

Now that I'm old, I enjoy watching the psychology at these favorite gathering places. The tanned and buffed teenage boys will strut their stuff at the cliffs edge, while keeping a furtive eye on the bikini clad babes that they have brought along to witness their heroics. That motivation went away a long time ago for me! The fatter, whiter, and more timid jumpers like myself, are normally situated further back from the edge where it's safer. Some of these nerds are wrapped in a towel for security, like Linus on Charley Brown with his stupid blanket. While sitting there gathering up enough courage to actually do such a stupid thing, these groupies are usually degraded and verbally abused by the snide comments of the more active jumpers. "Hey do you think that fat old white guy is really going to do it? Let me get my umbrella before that guy makes his big splash". Or "Whoa dude! Let me put on my sunglasses so that white hairy guy doesn't totally blind me!" These are some of the mean comments that I have endured in these later years. None-the-less, I keep on jumping. Mind you, with a lot less frequency than when I was the tanned and buff teenager, but I do it on occasion just to prove that I can still overcome that basic fear.

"OOHHHHH SHOOT!" you can hear me mutter as my feet leave the rock ledge. "AAAAAWWWWWWWW", then KERSPLASH! The droplets from the huge splash are still falling as my sputtering head emerges from the deep and I say, "YEE HAAWWW! It don't git no better than that boys!" "YEEE HAAAWWWW!" I rub the stinging sore spots under my arm pits as my words echo off the canyon walls.

Bat in the House

There is nothing quite as repulsive to me as the nasty little rats with wings that hang upside down in dark places. It's no wonder that they only come out at night. They have a face only a mother could love, a mother bat that is. I have been to places like dark caves where there are multitudes of the tiny freaks of nature, without really worrying much about it, but when they invade the homeland, I become a raving lunatic. The night a fluttering bat invaded our city home after a Fourth of July fireworks display had sent it scurrying for cover, was an example of what I'm talking about. Passing motorists must have thought we had created some sort of new midnight dance, equipped with tennis rackets and bed sheets, as they gawked through our windows while driving by, and saw us waving and yelling and carrying on with hands waving wildly above our heads.

"There's a bat in the house!" my startled wife screeched with horror. "Get it Jim! Get it out of here!" I woke with a start to realize that it had happened again. There was a bat inside our new country home! The high cathedral ceilings made it difficult to get to the creepy little vampire with any weapon I had previously used. Contrary to popular belief, a bat has a hard time detecting the stretched wire of a tennis racket, which I had used to dispose of the undesirable creatures before. But this time the flittering black demon, remained totally out of my reach, which drove me insane. The thoughts of sleeping with the bat in the house gave me the creeps, but after chasing the evasive critter back and forth while standing on the top step of the ladder, I became exasperated and decided to get some sleep. We closed the bedroom door and plugged the crack at the floor with a blanket and finally dozed off to sleep.

"Uuuuuaaaaaaagh!" I yelled with a shiver running down my spine. I had forgotten the bat was still in the house and had been surprised as it flitted about my head the next morning. "Gosh danged filthy vermin!" I swore, reminded of my annoyance with the species of rodents. After several sleepless nights we began to relax a bit and forgot about the pesky critter that was hiding somewhere above our heads in the crack of the big log beams that ran the full length of the rustic home. It bothered me considerably that the bat might still be in the house, though there was no evidence of it for several days.

The blood curdling screams of my wife rang through the house as I realized that our pest had become visible again. I knew that there would be no peace in the house until I had solved this uniquely difficult problem. The door to our bedroom slammed shut as I cornered the beast and sealed off all the possible escape routes. "Bring me a sheet and hold the four corners!" I said forcefully, as I barked orders to the other squeamish occupants of the home. "Now hold it above the bed and pull it tight so that when it falls you can catch it before it hits my bed." I instructed the reluctant helpers. I aimed the .22 rifle at the skulking dark shadow in the crack of the log and pulled the trigger. The tiny pellets of bird shot, did the trick, killing the vermin where it sat huddled, without doing any real damage to the finished sheet rock ceiling. The icky carcass convulsed and slowing dropped from it's hiding place and onto the waiting sheet. The helpers cringed at the repulsive dying creature and nearly missed breaking it's fall from the tall ceiling above. They reminded me of the goofy clowns waiting for Dumbo to jump from his tall platform, while moving about frantically with the safety net.

The bat in the house made my wife question my bravery for the first time. It's amazing that such a tiny creature can have such a chilling affect on a grown man. None-the-less, the next time it happens, I'm getting the shotgun!

Bears up a Tree

There are generally two kinds of city people, those who are deathly afraid of bears thinking that they will get torn from limb to limb and eaten, or those who don't have much fear of the furry creatures, thinking of them as the roly-poly Smokey-the-Bear creatures or something out of a Disney animation that is cute and harmless. The latter, is the type that generally get into trouble with the bruins while feeding them or photographing them in the state parks where they are unnaturally congregated. Both types of thinking are born out of ignorance and propaganda, not having any basis in reality. Don't get me wrong, I have seen some very cute fuzzy bears through the years, but most black bears, whether small or large can be very dangerous under the right circumstances and are to be respected immensely, though they generally are reclusive, keeping to themselves if at all possible. Black bears rarely attack humans even when provoked, but in most documented attack cases it has been proven that they will eat a human if they attack at all. This is a combination of stories about some of my contacts with the fascinating creatures.

One hunting season I had decided to shoot a bear using the somewhat controversial method of baiting. I had placed a tree stand in a strategic spot on the back of my property and had been baiting this particular bear for quite some time. I had a lot of fun with him! In addition to the normal bait which consisted mostly of meat and fruit scraps from the local grocery store, I had been placing marshmallows all in a row to entice the bear and to see what extremes he would go to in order to consume the fluffy white treats.

Several days in a row, I had crawled up a tree to place my sweets out of reach of the hungry prowler. He had always figured out a way to get to the treats regardless of how high or how well I hid them.

The time came to try to catch the unsuspecting prey at the bait, so I climbed into my tree stand early in the day. The wait was almost more than I could bear (no pun intended), since the wait dragged on for many hours. Late in the afternoon, I decided that I'd had enough and climbed down from the tall tree stand. I walked quietly to the house to rest from my sitting and to get a snack. You'd think that it wouldn't be hard to just sit, but it is extremely difficult to remain motionless for that many hours at a time. Anyone with any real hunting experience can relate to that. I decided to crawl back into the stand for the last hour of daylight, just in case the wary bear would still come in daylight hours. Sure enough, at about ten minutes before legal shooting hours were over, the sound of the panting bear reached my alert ears. He came to the bait sight at a full run, panting with exertion like he'd come a great distance to be at this spot. It reminded me of my teenage sons as they slide into their places at the dinner table, just in time. Always present, but always a bit late.

I watched with fascination as the medium-sized-chocolate-colored-bear sat down and politely picked through the bucket of goodies. After he had sampled everything in the bucket at least once, he started sniffing around for dessert. After following the trail of marshmallows I had laid out, he went back and sat down on his haunches to finish what was left in the bait bucket. That's when I nailed him. The bullet from the .300 Savage found it's mark and he rolled around the brush in his death groan.

Satisfied that he had indeed expired, I began to lower my weapon out of the tree stand with the muzzle facing downward. My plan was to lower the gun and carefully lay it at the base of the tree and then climb down to retrieve it. My plan backfired when the string broke and the gun fell to the ground, sticking in the soft duff and pine needles like a monument to my stupidity. I cautiously climbed to the ground, all the while keeping a fixed eye on the unmoving carcass. Having taken many species of animals before, I was fully aware that the beast could spring back to life at any moment. I quickly grabbed the gun and tapped the muzzle to dislodge the debris that had plugged it solid. "This is not good!" I thought as the bear convulsed again with a loud groan. Being certain that the gun was now operable, I dispatched the writhing bear with a shot to the head.

My friend Rob had been baiting for years and had yet to collect his prize. I had been giving him a hard time about his inadequacy as a hunter and kindly explained that he should hire a better hunting guide. I offered to take him to a spot where I'd seen some bear sign, in an effort to tease him further, not realizing that he would actually take me up on the sarcastic offer. We arrived at the logging job where I had been seeing the bear tracks in the dust each day and started up the timbered draw to look around. He had left his rifle in the truck, so I suggested that he would need it since I was the hunting guide today. He laughed, but took my advice and we strolled up the draw with rifle in hand. As we were standing there talking about where he could set up a stand, I heard the scratching sound of a bear climbing up a tree. Rob thought I was crazy when I suggested that there was a bear climbing up a tree less than a hundred yards away. When he glanced the direction I was pointing, his mouth dropped open in surprise as the scrappy bear clambered up the tree to see what all the fuss was about. After choosing a good shooting point, he touched off the shot, only to see that the dying bear had latched onto the lowest branch of the tree as it died and stayed there, stuck in the tall fir tree. We scratched our heads trying to figure out how we would retrieve the dead bear from it's perch over sixty feet in the air. There wasn't a branch on the fat tree trunk below the bear, so climbing the tree was just out of the question. We finally called my friend who was a tree trimmer and had him climb the tree with his climbing gear and tip the dead bear out of the tall tree.

Several years later, I was reminded of this incident when I was hunting for elk and spotted a black bear busily digging into an ant infested stump. The unsuspecting bruin was only about twenty yards away which normally would have been an easy shot for me, but my arrow went high just as the bear looked up and darted for cover. I was grateful for the miss, since it turned out that the bear was a nursing mother. The spooked sow ran up the hill and stopped to look back at the ghost who had scared her. I wondered what the smart little bear was up to since they usually run away never to be seen again. I walked over to the tree were my arrow had stuck to attempt to retrieve it. After struggling for several seconds in my efforts to dislodge the expensive broadhead tipped arrow, I heard that familiar scratching noise again and realized that the sound was coming from the tree right next to me. I looked up and was surprised to see three tiny cubs scrambling down the skinny tree. I could have reached out and touched the little guys they were so close! The patient and nervous young sow, waited until each of her offspring had filed past her to turn tail and run. I pulled the arrow from the tree and sighed with relief at my fortunate miss. "Poor little guys wouldn't have made it without their mother!" I thought. "It's a good thing I missed! I wonder if their guardian angel tipped that arrow?" I chuckled at my good fortune at my narrow miss and wondered what the bears up the tree had been thinking as I walked around underneath them. I wish Rob would have been there to see that!

Mcbride Ditch

"**H**elp Mommy!" screamed the terrified girl who was clinging desperately to the foot of the toddler. The strong suction of the rushing water was pulling the young child from her grasp and toward the whirlpool at the large culvert. I waded through the waist-deep water, struggling to grab hold of my young sibling who had teetered into the water face down. I finally caught hold of the big toe of the youngster and held on for dear life. "Mommy!" we screamed in unison as we braced ourselves against the swift current of the creek.

We had traveled up the mountain to the McBride Ditch, which looked more like a medium sized creek, even though it had been man-made, to carry the precious water from the snow capped peaks of the high country, to the dry hillsides of Eagle Valley for irrigation. The green grass of the meadow had been cropped close to the ground by the lazy but wary cows that inhabited this summer range, making the meadow near the creek bank look like a manicured lawn except for the random piles of sun-dried cow dung. We had brought along a blanket to sit on and a picnic lunch to snack on. The cold waters of the ditch had become more inviting as the early-afternoon-sun beat down on us.

My mother had found a comfortable spot in the shade to lay the soft blanket and had settled in for a short nap while we splashed around in the water for a while. My baby brother, while not really the adventuresome type, had strayed from my mother's side and stood curiously looking at the fun we were having in the water. The water wasn't really deep enough for an adult to swim, but offered plenty of fun and adventure for us kids. We turned over rocks searching for periwinkles and splashed around, enjoying the cooling effect of the fresh, clean water.

The toddler had waddled over to the edge of the bank, which dropped off sharply into the deep part of the creek, having been cut into and washed away by the rushing waters. He stumbled off the steep bank anxious to join in on the fun. We watched with horror as the small boy disappeared under the water and began floating down the stream, face down. My sister Kathy and I, had slogged through the current of the waist-deep water to rescue the poor drowning tyke and now clung desperately to the submersed, diapered toddler.

Our frantic screams quickly roused our napping mother and she raced to the rescue. As she sprinted across the grass to the side of the stream, she could see that our desperate cries for help were for real and she lunged into the stream to pull her small son from the water. The child sputtered and began to cry as she scooped the soggy-bottomed-boy into her arms, safe from the looming danger of the big culvert. She clasped him tightly to her bosom as she waded to the grassy bank and collapsed with relief. The four young children, who kept her running ragged most of the time, gathered around her in a silent group hug. The ride home was unusually quiet that day, as we pondered the events of the day. The McBride Ditch will always be a place of great memories for me, since it was one of our favorite fishing spots, but I'll never forget that fateful day and the childhood memory of the rescue of the little soggy-bottomed-boy.

Bigfoot Visits Scout Camp

S ometimes if you believe in an idea hard enough, it can come true, or can seem like it is true at the time. Sometimes things are not exactly what they appear to be. Such is the case of the time that Bigfoot visited my brothers Boy Scout campout.

The campout had been planned several months in advance, to be sure that all things would be in order for the young troop of Scouts, which consisted mostly of inexperienced twelve-year old boys. The place was Woodward Meadow which had been a favorite spot of groups in the past. Eldon had been serving as the Scout Advisor for enough time to gain an intimate knowledge of what made these boys tick. He had asked me to prepare a surprise for the boys in the form of an appearance of the legendary Bigfoot.

My friend Mark, had acquired a black, furry gorilla suit that he enthusiastically consented to let me use. The full-body-suit came complete with a head that could reasonably pass for Bigfoot if the circumstances were right. The night arrived for my performance, so I loaded my disguise into the little Ford Pinto and headed for the meadow only a 15 minute drive away. Since I wasn't sure exactly where their rowdy camp would be located, I slowed my car to a crawl and edged ahead along the forest road until I caught a glimpse of the campfire reflecting off the dark trees in front of me. I quickly shut off the engine, hoping that I had not been detected and quietly slipped into the furry suit and mask. I soon realized that my vision would be minimal, since I would not have the benefit of a light, nor would the small eye holes offer much of a window to see my prey. The handicap slowed me only momentarily since my eyes soon became accustomed to the darkness and I learned how to tip my head just right in order to see from the eye holes. I crept into place for the ambush and sat down to wait for the exact right moment to initiate the green outdoors men.

What I did not realize, was that earlier in the day, the young men had pitched their tents some distance from the main fire, but had moved them closer as the dark pressed in, because they had been teasing each other about seeing Bigfoot and had become somewhat spooked already. This unknown advantage quickly manifested itself as the big scare unfolded and I saw that their pre-conditioned minds quickly responded to the intended stimulus.

As I lay in wait to formulate my plan of attach, I could tell by the tone of their fireside chatter that they had no clue that I was there. I rose and began to rake a big stick against the brush and made a loud grunting sound. Their delayed reaction gave me time to move in a bit closer to adjust for the distance and to come closer to their fire. I continued my noisy rampage until the unnatural ruckus became apparent to the majority of boys. "What is that?" "Shhhhh…., be quiet, there's something up there making noise!," I could hear someone stammer. Their devious leader, now sure that the game was on, made sure that even the Doubting Thomas among them would be convinced, by making a big deal out of counting the boys to be sure they were all there and stating, "Everyone get in here close! There is something out there and we need to make sure we are all accounted for!" I took the cue and began my grunting rampage in earnest.

One of the junior leaders, who had not been let in on the gag, decided that he would show the boys what a brave protector he could be, and started moving cautiously toward me with mace in one hand and his foot long mag-light in the other. He moved up to the side of the car that I was hiding behind and had decided that he would simply shine his light and expose the hoax. What he hadn't counted on was that I had pasted some reflective tape to the eye lids of the mask so that when the light shined, it gave the appearance of glowing eyeballs.

My deception worked and he began a stumbling, backward retreat that quickly inflamed the vivid imaginations of the now terrified green horns. As he continued his quick retreat, wildly spraying his economy sized mace can like a scared puppy peeing uncontrollably on the carpet, I followed his frenzied departure closely, which heightened his realization that he had made a huge miscalculation and that he might just become dinner for this enraged wild beast. Since, my sight was severely limited, I stumbled forward in a crouched stance, all the while making the most horrible guttural grunting noises that I could muster between my slips of laughter. Through the tiny peep holes, I could make out the scurrying forms of the little scared scouts frantically stumbling through the campfire to make a desperate escape from the Bigfoot demon that had become more than a shadow. Sparks and ashes flew everywhere as the clatter of flying pots and pans added to the confusion and din of the moment. Their short lives passed before their eyes as they prepared for their certain doom.

In an instant, one terrified observer had realized that the furry creature had a zipper, which brought a dogpile of relieved boys, ending the whole charade. Filled with emotional relief, the mob began a nervous chatter of confusion as each boy began to share their version of what they had just experienced. One boy confessed that his life had literally passed before his eyes, since he had dreamed just a night before that he was going to die. Another had wet his pants, but none offered to ridicule since they had not fared much better. Several boys had to spend the next couple of nights in their parents bed until their nightmares departed. One of the adult advisers admitted that he had thought it was real, even though he had been told ahead of time that it would be happening. All in all, it had been a successful scare to say the least. All present in the camp that night would forever have a story to tell, about the night that Bigfoot visited their campfire.

First Buck

The first buck is always a memorable experience for a hunter, since it is usually preceded by much anxiety, enhanced by many previous failures. I was reminded of this recently as I accompanied my young 13 year old boy, Nathan, on a horseback hunt where he shot his first buck. He had shot several does in the previous years but had missed his share and scared off quite a few too. He had anxiously awaited this year because he had decided to wait for a chance at a buck, rather than to settle for a fat doe. After crippling the young forked horn and after a long chase that seemed to last forever, he finally ended the life of the buck with a shot to the head. Even though he had a long walk home in the pouring rain, and took awhile to warm up and recover from his exertion, he immediately began to spread the good news among his family and friends. Great memories had been created! Such was the experience with my first buck. I can remember it like it was yesterday!

Having missed my mark on many prior opportunities, I had begun to wonder if I would ever be able to kill a deer. My Grandpa Pope would always say, "there's a lot of room around them!", in an attempt to make me feel better for being such a miserable failure at my most sought after goal. My friend and neighbor had killed his first buck the year before with a quick brush shot that had miraculously found it's mark, even though he hadn't really aimed. Since he had really played it up, bragging that his errant shot had been so perfectly and purposely placed, I had become rather annoyed.

This motivated me to top his meager accomplishment with something bigger and better.

The first day of the season finally arrived after much anxious waiting and preparation. I had cleaned and polished the old bolt action military style 30-06 that belonged to my father, over and over again, until I nearly wore it out, scheming and stewing over my plans for the approaching opener. We lived on eighty acres bordering the National Forest lands where we would hunt, so it was natural to start our hike from the house. We would travel up the creek and then up the mountain toward Bear Wallow. Our destination was no more than a big mud flat in a sizable clearing, since the seasonal pond water had all but dried up by this time of the year. We carefully scoured the woodlands along our chosen route, hopeful that we would find an unsuspecting buck that would end my long dry streak. As a fourteen-year-old boy, I had become accustom to the ribbing and teasing of my dad and uncles, who found it somehow amusing that I could not hit the broadside of a barn with the old rifle. The ravages of buck fever had taken it's toll on me through the years, squelching any ability I had to point and hold the gun in the right direction on each of my previous opportunities. I had gained quite a reputation for missing the deer, all the while insisting that I was just training them to escape so that they could grow larger antlers.

I slowly crept along the dry grassy ridge that surrounded the small valley called Bear Wallow. My brother had accompanied me but was now nowhere to be seen as I continued my slow sneak through the sparse timber. As my eyes strained toward the clearing, attentively scanning the available cover for any sign of my prey, I suddenly caught sight of a slight movement behind me to my left. "Had I walked right past a deer without me seeing it?" I asked myself disgustingly. Sure enough! The next movement revealed the flicker of a deer's tail behind a small bush. My heart immediately began it's trademark "thumpity, thumpity, thump", as I struggled to maintain some sort of composure in my battle against 'the fever.' By the time I finally realized that this unsuspecting deer actually had antlers, I was completely debilitated by the disease that had caused me so much grief. With a determined grip on the well used rifle, I quickly sat down and settled into a stance that would allow me to hold the rifle still, since my shaking hands might otherwise betray me once again. Gasping for breath, I rested the heavy weapon on my knee and took aim. Wincing like a school boy receiving his first tetanus shot, I closed my eyes and yanked the trigger. The small forked-horn dropped immediately to the ground and began a frantic stumble down the hill towards me without the use of his hind legs that had now been rendered useless. A large mature buck with a huge rack, now made his presence known as he too began to flee the commotion. The sight of the monster buck and the desperate attempts of the smaller buck to escape it's unseen enemy, had only fueled the flame of my un-checked case of buck fever and I rose to my feet shaking like a leaf in a hurricane. The gun weaved back and forth as I aimed to take another shot in my frantic attempt to stop the buck from running away. "Dang it!" I swore to myself as the second shot missed it's intended target. The sharp kick and loud report of the gun went unnoticed as the third round found it's mark, anniallating the front end of the fleeing animal, bringing it to a halt as it collapsed in a heap just twenty yards from where I was standing. I stood gawking at the record book buck trotting across the hillside above me, totally frozen, stunned and numbed by the intense adrenaline surge that had just coursed through my body. "Wow!" I thought out loud. By the time I gained enough composure to realize that my brother could tag the other buck, the elusive monarch had disappeared into the thick brush of the northern slope that we had just waded through.

I strode quickly to my small antlered prize that now lay dead, attached my tag to it's spindly antler and breathed a big sigh of relief. The long awaited quest for that first buck had come to an end! Having never gutted a deer by myself, I began the tedious process of hacking and stabbing until the gruesome project was completed and then headed for home to get the old jeep that would haul my trophy home. A wide grin soon replaced my grim, anxious look, as I began to polish the story that I would tell over and over again. "Hit him on the run!" I thought with pride. "My first buck!" My smile widened further and my step became quicker as I plodded towards home.

Crusty Old Mountain Men

One of my favorite things to do is reenact the dress habits and recite the lingo of the earliest of pioneers in this country, the mountain men. I kid around with my wife, that her influence with Deity, is the only reason I was assigned to come to earth in this time in history rather than in the 1800's as a mountain man with her as my squaw. We laugh about it and she thinks it's a funny thought, but wouldn't have wanted the tough life and the hardships that went with it. I'm a little more serious about it than she thinks I should be sometimes, but she has humored me through the years as I have outfitted myself with authentic mountain man garb, and attended many mountain man rendezvous.

Part of the yearly ritual, in getting ready for the rendezvous, is to watch my favorite movie, Jeremiah Johnson, which stars the actor Robert Redford in the lead role. The movie is about the real man who was so tough that he ended up with the historic reputation and the title of 'Liver Eat'in Johnson,' reputedly eating the livers of the natives that he killed, in defiance of the fact that they had murdered and mutilated his Indian wife and adopted child. Having seen this movie over and over again, it is no wonder that I have been able to memorize the entire dialogue word for word. The fact that my friend John has also accomplished this same feat, has almost convinced my wife that I've not yet progressed to the mania or fetish stage of obsession but that I'm just plain weird. Sometimes I have to admit that I get a little carried away, and the antics of this story may illustrate that point in her favor.

John and I had traveled to the Chewack River drainage of the Pasayten Wilderness with some other friends for several days of camping to participate in the early September high buck hunt. After four hard days of hunting in the intermittent rain, without even seeing a deer to shoot at, we packed our soggy belongings and started the long haul back to the trail head. Being damp and dirty, with the start of a rough looking beard, we were beginning to feel sort of like crusty mountain men, so it is little wonder that we started to slip into the imagined role of our former day heros.

It might have been the fumes from our odiferous filthy clothing that got us started recanting portions of the dialogue from the Jeremiah Johnson movie, or maybe just the overall atmosphere of the horse ride with the beauty of the fast running river and the high mountain air. Whatever it was, the emergence of the mountain man in us was close to the surface and started to spill out as we rode single-file down the muddy trail.

As we traversed around the mountain side towards the Chewach Driveway, which had been our entry point and had been a traditional sheep roundup area in this summer range, we began a contest-of-sorts, to see who could recite the movie dialogue correctly. It was there that we gave each other the nick names that we call each other still to this day. I was dubbed Jeremiah and John was to be Del Jue "with an E" as it says in the movie. "When I told my ma and pap I was headed fer the Rocky Mountains, they acted like they was gut shot! I told em that the Rocky Mountains was the marrow of the world, and by gosh, I was right!" spouted Del as we rode along. "The Andes is foothills and the Alps is fer children ta play on!" continued Del. We took turns spewing forth this memorized dialogue for several miles down the trail until we got to the part that is yelled by Del Jue, "I got the fastest horse, the ugliest dog and the prettiest woman,...I can out shoot, out wrestle and throw down any man or beast this side of the Mississippi!...By gosh, I'm a mountain man, and a mountain man I'll die!"

The exchange had reached it's cretendo just as we happened upon a pair of grinning hikers. We sheepishly admitted that it was us, that had been making all that racket, as they revealed that they had heard us coming for about a half a mile. Moving quickly onward, we giggled like a couple of caught school boys, as we rounded the corner out of sight of the amused pedestrians. "They must have thought we were crazy!" we lamented.

"Nahhhh,… they thought we were just a couple of crusty old mountain men!" we wishfully thought to ourselves.

Since then, John and I have become separated by new jobs and great distances. From our now-long-distance locations, we talk about that day every once in a while, then from the slothful security of our office chairs, we fondly bid each other goodbye in mountain man lingo. "Keep yer powder dry, pilgrim!". "Watch yer top knot!" "Ya,.. watch yorn!" "Keep yer nose ta the wind and yer eye on the skyline!" The phones click simultaneously, as we reluctantly resume our modern hectic lives.

Keep Off The Grass

My dad has always been the kind of guy that has been very serious about life, always with his nose to the grindstone. While I wouldn't say that I have never heard him laugh or have a sense of humor, I also wouldn't describe him as a jovial person. He has always known what he wanted and worked like a dog to get it accomplished and while in that mode never really took much of a break. As a kid, I would never have played a practical joke on him for fear that it would not be appreciated. As an adult, I have continually prodded him to slow down and to stop and smell the roses and in the process have kidded him about some of his unconventional relaxation methods. While some people head for the security of their motor home or to warm sandy beaches to relax their aging bones, my dad seemed intent on taking up a hobby that is very labor intensive.

Sometime after the last of my younger siblings left home, my dad decided to begin a part-time career as a mule skinner. Initially, he obtained several gentle burros from a friend, along with all of the pack saddles and tack that would allow him to travel to the mountains with me on our annual pilgrimage to the high country. While I was pleased about his intentions to spend time with me, my unrelenting chidings about his new hobby as a green-horn-packer, could have been a bit discouraging to someone with lessor intensity. His sorry looking remuda of donkeys became his trademark in the local parades, all outfitted in their pack gear with yards signs positioned on the sides of the saddle panniers to promote our newly founded Real Estate office. The gangly beasts would either go too fast down the parade route, dragging my frustrated father up the road, or they would balk at some benign roadside object while he tugged and encouraged the sluggards in a fashion more charateristic of the breed. He soon discovered the reason why the dopey, floppy eared beasts of burden have been called "asses" throughout the centuries. But the stubborn disposition of his precious new darlings, didn't seem to dampen his enthusiasm for his new endeavor.

His curious neighbors paid particular attention to his growing menagary of Long Ears, gawking with strained necks to inventory any new arrivals as they drove slowly by. His donkey pasture at the corner location would always warrant a passing glance even after the newness of this neighborhood petting zoo had wained. My mild disdain for the critters continually motivated me to playfully tease my father about his new charges and caused me to constantly slander the oblivious hay burners.

One day while in the local hardware store, while perusing through the yard sign section in search of a "house for rent" sign, my eye caught sight of a black metal sign with flourescent orange letters. It read, "KEEP OFF THE GRASS!" My devious mind immediately recognized, that by carefully covering the "G" and the "R" with black electrical tape, the sign could be used to pester and tease my sober father about his shaggy farm animals. I gleefully chuckled to myself, pleased at my genious, as I plucked the previously idle sign from it's regular location on the metal shelf. I wiped the dust from it's surface and giggled with anticipation as I covered the "GR" with my hand and imagined it hanging from the fence at my dad's roadside donkey pasture.

My wide grin could not be stifled as I looked both ways before installing the hilarious message on the woven wire of the fence. "That will really get Dad's goat!" I exclaimed, still chuckling to myself. Satisfied that the coast was clear, I quickly fastened the new proclamation to the fence and stood back to admire my handiwork. "That really ought to get his goat, especially if the always alert neighbors see it before he can take it down." I continued to myself.

"KEEP OFF THE ASS" showed up, bright and shiny, like a pimple on prom night. My anxious musings continued as I drove away from the scene of the crime like an excited little kid on April Fool's day. I waited anxiously for some kind of a reaction which never came. The sign hung there for the next couple of months, then disappeared without a trace or the anticipated fanfare. Other than a slight smile acknowledging the genius of the prank, my dad never said much, but the neighbors sure got a kick out of it!

Dad Goes Airborne

"Any day in the high country is better than the best day at home," I have often been heard to say. There have been many times that this theory has been tested to the limit with great success. This story is one of those times.

My dad had been given a set of donkeys from a well intentioned friend and had decided to bring them along as pack animals on a trip to Crater Lake in the Eagle Cap Wilderness. The rest of our party was there to hunt deer and elk, but dad was there to enjoy a couple of days of rest and relaxation and would return to the trailhead sooner than us. From the very beginning it seemed as though rest and relaxation would elude him.

We arrived at the Summit Point trail head bright and early with expectations of having a great day. Dad and my cousin Cam packed up the two sway-backed burros and headed up the trail an hour or so before the main pack string, in order to get a head start, since we anticipated that they would be considerably slower than the rest.

It wasn't long until the bright clear morning turned into a huge hail storm that nearly blew us off the mountain. The pebble sized hail quickly covered the ground until it was as white as though it were winter. As the pack animals squirmed and fidgeted under the stinging blows of the icy down pour, I thought about Dad and his pair of lowland hay burners and wondered if they were weathering the storm as poorly as we.

We finished our task of loading the beasts of burden and headed north towards Little Eagle Meadows and beyond. The horses lined up and went up the trail at a fast pace, so it was little surprise when we passed the sluggish Jetta and Jeanie at about the halfway point. We finished the 10 mile jaunt in record time and spent the next several hours setting up camp and getting comfortable. After several hours, Cam sauntered into camp minus Dad and the two hay burners. He informed us that the reluctant pack animals had run out of gas and requested that we return to finish what they had started.

When we reached the small meadow which they had picked as their finish line, Dad explained that he would leave the quitters there on a picket line and would come back for them later. Well, there never was a later because they were so stove up for the next several days, that we just ended up leaving them there.

When his chosen departure date arrived, Dad left to saddle up his charges and we were to arrive later with his gear. He was in the process of taking the hobbles off when we arrived with a clamor. The silly asses that had a short time before been barely able to wiggle, all-of-the-sudden came to life and started bounding through the woods, like a stampede of ghetto roaches when the lights come on. We wanted to help but it was like watching a slow motion scene in a movie where you are merely a spectator with no power to change the scene. As the faster of the two jackasses sprinted across the small opening in the timber, the byte of the rope caught Dad around the ankles with such force that it lifted him high in the air like a world class acrobat on a dismount from the parallel bars, flipping him end over end until he stuck a landing that was more characteristic of a wide eyed bug splatting on the windshield of a moving car. The other donkey headed down the trail, but was soon intercepted by one of our party.

What seems to the outsider, like a chaotic misguided undertaking, had really just been another classic adventure destined to become fodder for easily amused authors like myself. So you see, the worst disaster in the high country can still be better than the best day at the office!

Boo!

Don was the kind of friend that was like a little puppy, he just liked you no matter what. We had worked together at the local grocery store which is where we first became acquainted and soon became fast friends. Even though he was many years my junior, we had a lot in common and started doing things together after work. He had convinced me to take up archery and had sold me his old compound bow with some junk arrows to get started with. We began to shoot with a local archery club a couple of times a month. By September I had become rather proficient with the used bow and shot a little buck on my first night out. My new friend was a little jealous since he had been the one to get me started, yet he had never killed anything with his bow. The next fall came around and I convinced Don that he could sit in my tree stand in order to break his dry streak. The season opener rolled around and the chunky grocer clambered into the tree and waited for his big opportunity. My suggestion that he did not shoot the first deer that came under his stand went unheeded, and he bagged a young yearling doe that night. It was small, but it was his first kill and he was ready to move onto bigger and better things.

The late season opened without fanfare, since we couldn't get off work to go hunting on that first day, but we soon made plans to head for my favorite elk hunting spot. Since he had this first kill under his belt, Don was raring to go. We arrived at the parking spot in the darkness of the early morning and sat like a couple of excited children waiting to open presents on Christmas morning. Our spirits were not dampened in the least by the howling wind and blowing snow. There was already over a foot of new snow on the ground and we had seen a lot of elk tracks on our drive in. Daylight finally came and I did my best to explain to the inexperienced greenhorn, the direction he must head and the path that he would be taking in order to have the best chance at an elk. I carefully explained to him which trail to take and how to get back to the truck. On the drive up, I had been bragging to him about my fantastic sneaking ability, in sort of a mocking way, hoping that he would catch onto the fact that I was joking with him. Like an attentive little puppy, he had watched and listened with intense interest, soaking up all of my lies like a damp sponge on a bathroom floor. I didn't have the heart to tell him I had been yanking his chain, so I began to devise a plan to show him that it was at least partially true.

The hike to the top of the mountain was long and cold, since the snow was deep and the wind continued to blow with gusto. The visibility had been very poor all morning so I had been unable to spot where Don was supposed to show up on the hillside above me. I sat near my favorite stump, waiting and hoping that he would arrive at his scheduled destination, because I was too worn out to go looking for any sorry lost pilgrims. All of the sudden, the fog and blizzard subsided momentarily, and I spotted his bundled figure, bent over to protect himself against the bitter wind, moving at a quick pace down the mountain road toward me. I quickly moved up the road and jumped off to the side to lie in wait for the big scare. The snow began to fall again, which soon completely covered my tracks in the fluffy white stuff.

He trudged down the trail like an old work horse, plodding along in the traces with his head down, hoping that the work would soon be over. He continued on past me, oblivious to the fact that I had fallen in step behind him, mimicking every step. I followed his every move for a minute or so, until I realized that he still had no idea that I was behind him. I continued to follow him, waiting for just the right moment. I had thought that I should yell really load or make a growling animal noise or something, but then it dawned on me what I should do. I simply reached out and gently grabbed his shoulder. The scare was more than his body could handle and he let out a little girlish squeal, dropping to the snow in a quivering heap of nerves. He had been totally lost, frantic to return to somewhere that he recognized and never even thought that I was within a hundred miles of his location. "Gotcha!" I exclaimed with glee that my plan had worked out. "Told you that I could sneak up on you without you hearing me!" I bragged with increasing vigor. He lay there in the snow near tears, relieved that he wasn't lost anymore, but still recovering physically and mentally from his near heart attack and emotional melt down. The burly archer had been reduced to a quivering mass of jelly, totally and completely overcome by the scare.

He mumbled something about me being a big jerk, as he slowly regained his composure and we headed down the trail together. "Boo!" I teased, as we headed for the warmth of the truck. "Gotcha! Watch out for the bogy man!" He shook his head in disgust, wondering if I had really snuck up on him or if he had just happened by at the right time. A smile replaced his bewildered look as I continued to gently tease. "Boo!"

Goats in Elk Camp

Nahhhhhhhhh!!!!! The piercing cry shattered the wilderness silence and brought all within earshot to full attention. Naahhhhhhhh! Naaahhhhhhhh! The sounds continued and became almost immediately annoying.

Dally Donk the appaloosa mule, had been tethered to a small tree when the interuption brought him to an instant state of sheer terror. The small herd of pack goats continued into the established elk camp and had the attention of all present. As the goats drew near to the tree where Donk was tethered, the pychotic half-horse lost his remaining composure and bolted for safety. These strange monsters must be mule slayers! As Donk headed for cover, the tree that had been his home for the past week was ripped from the ground, roots and all, and became just another monster following his every jump and scamper like a shadow on a bright day. Donk has a knack for making normal situations stressful and this was no exception. It appeared that unless interrupted, his new found energy would carry him into the next county. The alert on-duty wrangler immediately collected him as we all rolled with laughter at his wide eyed antics. The other pack animals looked on with interest but lacked the enthusiasm of the spotted one.

Naahhhhhhhh! Naahhhhhhhh! Naaaaahhhhhh! The annoying cadence continued. My brother Kim and his son Kimball had arrived with their furry entorage in grand style. After the usual backslapping and kidding, the attention quickly shifted to the subject of Donk's new found nightmare, the pack goats. This was their first trip to the mountains and their nervousness of the new surroundings expressed itself in that irritating cadence. Naaahhhh! Naaaaaaahhhhhhh! Kim had become their new daddy and each time he moved out of sight, the troubled young ones cries would increase in volume and intensity.

By the following evening the situation had not improved for the poor little creatures and they continued to express their feelings verbally. I had began to mimic the pitiful cries and became quite adept at it. Armed with my new found talent, I began to tease my young nephew about his irritating goat kids. Seemingly unaffected by my constant ribbing, his young poker face gave only slight indications that I was making any headway to getting a rise out of him. In an effort to turn it up a notch, I picked up my bow and knocked a hunting arrow, giving every indication that I was about to kill one of the obnoxious goats.

As I came to full draw and sighted in on the center goat, he seemed to take an immediate interest in what I was about to do. He came over and anxiously asked, " Uncle Jim, do you think you can kill that one over there instead? Because the one in the middle is mine!"

I laughed as I slipped the compound bow safely back into it's case. The goats somehow had instantly become less annoying and my relentless teasing came to a halt. Maybe Donk could get used to them too!

Buck Feathers

I t is amazing sometimes how the human brain can be fooled and be down right deceived by our eyeballs. I suppose that is why we have such a fascination with magicians and illusions. This story is about a time when Mother Nature played a grand illusion on me.

John and I had packed into the Pasayten Wilderness on the east side of Washington's Cascade Mountains near the Canadian Border. After several days of hunting out of our established base camp, we had decided to take the horses out farther from our camp to check out a new location. This was the first big trip for my three-year-old gelding named Rerun, so I was being careful since much of this was a totally new experience for him. We trotted out of camp at daybreak, trying to control our hyperactive mounts who had been standing around camp for several days and now wanted to go. I let him have his head for a minute to see what he would do. The trail was narrow and muddy, but that didn't seem to be a hindrance to the big Appaloosa. His footing was sure and his gait was easy, as we cantered down the trail headed for our new hunting spot. As we rounded a corner in the trail, I spotted a large blue grouse standing in the middle of the trail directly in front of us. "Whoa!" I hissed. The obedient horse skidded to an immediate stop as I slid the open sighted 30-06 out of the rifle scabbard and stepped out of the saddle. I dropped the reins, knelt down and shot the plump grouse in the head. I had never shot around this horse before and was uncertain as to what his reaction would be, but besides a slight flinch at the instant of the muzzle blast, he didn't seem to be bothered by it. We gutted the grouse and continued down the trail toward our goal.

We crested the small hill and started looking for a place to park the horses near the ridge that we had decided to hunt that morning. I tied the big horse to a tree and turned around to see what John was up to. He had spotted what he thought was another grouse and was pointing it out to me when he said, "It's a big blue grouse drumming." Since we both had grouse on the brain because of our previous experience, we both stood and saw the same thing. The big grouse was standing on a large granite boulder as big as a car and was really strutting his stuff. "Drumming" is when the male grouse struts around while rapidly beating his wings, which generally makes a drumming sound, attracting the attention of the female grouse. "Shoot him!" I whispered. "It's your turn!" He knelt for a second to take a rest, but stopped suddenly when the fat grouse turned sideways and immediately turned into a young spike mule deer. The illusion instantly melted away as our eyes began to see the real picture. The deer had been standing down the hill with its body concealed by the large rock, with only it's head being visible. It's long floppy ears had been wagging back and forth giving the illusion of the grouse drumming. Two experienced woodsmen stood spell bound, as our mouths dropped open and our eyes got as big as saucers. We both looked at the little buck, then at each other, then back at the deer. The burst of nervous laughter that followed revealed our total surprise and embarrassment at having been so deceived. "Could both of us have seen the same illusion at the exact same time?" I asked sheepishly. "When you said grouse,...that's what I saw!" I admitted with a grin. "I could have sworn....." "Wow, what if I had shot that grouse!" John exclaimed. We giggled, relieved that we had seen reality, but still confused at what we had seen. "That buck had feathers!" John chuckled heartily, still shaking his head in disbelief. "Buck feathers!" The dumb little buck walked away while the two puzzled mountain men looked on in awe.

Fainting Spells

The Scout Olympics had been a great success but the time had come to pack it all up and leave for home. We had camped up Cusick Creek for several days with a large group of Boy Scouts who had been busy passing off merit badges like the Pioneering merit badge and others. There had been competitive games and events like the obstacle course and the John Colter Race. The young men were worn out from all the great fun and adventure we had been having and were ready to go home. What they didn't know was that the day was far from over.

Our Scout Committee had carefully set up a staged car accident that we would have to pass by on our way down the graveled road to the highway. The wrecked pickup looked like it had run off the road on a steep incline and plowed into a tree. The victims were scattered out like a real accident with fake blood and compound fractures and glass sticking out of wounds. We had gone to great lengths to make it look as real as possible. One of the victims looked like they had gone through the windshield and was lying on the hood of the truck, blue and unconscious. There were beer cans strewn around in the vehicle and on the ground, to look as if they had been drinking. We had even placed a smoke bomb under the hood to give the appearance that the motor was still smoking. The lookout radioed to the actors that we were almost there and to get ready.

I pretended to drive by, but slammed on the brakes when one of the Scouts said, "Hey, it looks like there was an accident!" I pulled over and began my acting job. "Get out and go see if you can help!" I encouraged with concern in my voice. "It looks like some of them need first aid really badly!" I said, with fake concern. The happy carefree faces of the boys turned to horror, as they piled out and cautiously approached the accident scene. I pulled over and stopped the suburban while the other vehicles pulled up behind me and they all piled out. It was quite a scene, with several boys helping each pretend victim, totally convinced that this was a real accident. It was at least fifteen minutes before one of the more skeptical boys realized that the smoke was coming from a smoke bomb and spread the news that it must be fake. We quickly interrupted him and informed them that the whole setup had been fake, in order to test them on their first aid skills in a realistic setting. We even had on-staff medics hiding in the woods to critique their performance so we could debrief them and show them how they could have done better. As we gathered around the nurses to discuss the accident, I noticed that one of the boys was looking a bit white and peaked. He sat down and immediately passed out, from the trauma caused by witnessing the accident. Even though he now knew it was only fake, his mind and body were still convinced and he had been overcome with the emotion.

We gathered up the boys and headed for home, finally finished with the Scout Olympics. I asked the older boys who were riding with me if they would like to stop for a pizza or something and that I was buying, but they declined, stating that they didn't really feel like it. When do Boy Scouts ever decline free food? They had really been affected by the fake accident, even though they hadn't all fainted like Matt.

The next Olympics were held in a different location the following year up Chewelah Creek. We had been through some intense first aid training in order to pass off the boys on the merit badge requirements. I had been wandering amoungst the groups of boys who were practicing their skills, interviewing them to pass them off on the test part of the merit badge. I was sitting in a small group of boys asking questions about what to do in case of severe bleeding and shock, when Matt cut his finger severely while whittling on a stick. We broke out the first aid kit and had the boys bandage the wound so they could have some real live practice. All of the sudden the queasy victim started to turn white and fainted dead away just like he had done a year ago at the same event. "Well, treat him for shock!" I said to the panicked boys. I laughed as the memory of his previous fainting came back to my mind. "Matt just gets queasy and has fainting spells when he sees blood," I said, giggling at the hilarious scene. The phony first aid session had turned real once again.

Buck Fever

"**B**uck Fever Hotline!" the voice stated matter-of-factly, on the other line. "Hhhh, Hhhh, Hhhelp me please!" I pleaded breathlessly, with mock soberness. "I n-n-need ta t-t-t-talk to someone now! Aaaaaa, I have a real problem" I continued mockingly. My brother laughed on the other end of the long distance line as he acknowledged me. His tendency to become rather spell bound and consumed by the ravages of Buck Fever has become rather legendary in our yearly hunting camp and has caused him a great deal of ribbing from me. Hence, he usually beats me to the punch when he recognizes my number on his caller ID and starts the mocking on his own.

It all started when as a young boy he accompanied me on a short day hunt to one of my usual whitetail 'honey-holes' that had produced many times before. He was many years my junior and had never been able to go with me before, so he was excited to tag along even though he was too young to hunt legally. In an attempt to make him feel part of the hunt, I had given him my .22 long rifle to hold, with the instructions to shoot the deer in the head if he saw one. Never in a million years did I expect that he would actually see something!

We started up the hill following an established logging trail in order to avoid the thick brush that had a strangle-hold on this particular patch of woods. While almost impossible to navigate through, the thick brush offered seclusion and sanctuary to many forms of wildlife, which was the reason that many big bucks inhabited this hideout. We sneaked along the old roadway with anticipation and with hope born of the memory of previously successful encounters with these elusive critters at this location. Many times a brief glimpse of a white tail waving goodbye through the thick brush as an alert deer had successfully eluded me, was the only visible evidence of their presence, but with persistence I had occasionally caught the unsuspecting prey in a mistake and had put venison on the table. Being an astute student of the whitetail deer's many predictable habits, had taught me how to increase my chances at this intense game of life and death, and so when a group of deer jumped across the road in front of us, our anticipation heightened and the game was on.

I quietly hissed orders to my younger, eager sibling and explained that I would be going back the way we came and that he must sit quietly and await my return. My intention was to intercept the deer as they circled around behind us, which was their habit. His clear blue eyes widened as the gangly youngster nodded that he understood and I continued to explain that if he saw a big buck that he could use the .22 rifle to shoot the deer in the head. "Don't bother to shoot it unless you can hit it right in the eye!" I explained, doubtful that he would even see anything and sure that the old rimfire Remington was not capable of downing anything as large as a deer, unless the shot was placed properly. Convinced that the deer would soon emerge back where we had just come from, I was posting Eldon on stand just so that he wouldn't make any noise while I did my sneak. He scratched at the ground nervously with the worn tip of his hand-me-down boots, thrust his cold hands deep into the pockets of his over-sized wool pants and leaned against the old gray snag that was to be his stand for the next nerve racking 20 minutes. "Don't move a muscle!" I strongly advised. "If you see a big buck, just shoot him in the eye," I reminded him, confident that he wouldn't see anything but an occasional squirrel or chipmunk. His thin freckled face peered after me from under his jauntily placed stocking cap, as I disappeared down the faint old skid trail to where the action awaited me. My last glance in his direction revealed the scrawny, excited boy huddled next to the decayed stub-of-a-tree, his frozen breath slowing rising, illuminated by the golden rays of sunlight above his bundled head. Even though he wasn't old enough to have a hunting license, he was thoroughly convinced that since I had let him carry a gun, this was the real thing, and he was a full fledged hunter. He had always been interested in hunting and I could tell by his tense enthusiasm that his emotions were very near the surface and he was fighting to contain it inside himself.

When I returned to his location a short time later, I immediately discerned by the disturbed look on his ruddy little face, that something had happened to bring an eruption of pent-up emotion to the surface. As I approached his trembling frame, he began to cry and then had a total emotional melt-down. It took several minutes to calm him down enough for me to interpret from his babblings, that a very large whitetail buck had walked out into the small clearing in front of him, stopped to look around, and then had slowing walked away. He had been so flustered in his anxious efforts to fix his sights on the big brown eye of the monarch, that he had forgotten to take the gun off safety. The big deer, oblivious to his presence, had calmly walked off while he frantically tugged at the fixed trigger of his inadequate weapon.

"Why are you crying?" I sympathetically asked as I put a hand on his shoulder to give some moral support. "Let me feel your forehead." I asked in a sober voice. "Yep!" "You have it bad!" I announced affirmatively. "What? What do I have?" he sniffled, as he continued to release a flood of emotion. "Ya got Buck Fever!" I blurted assuredly, as I continued to explain the symptoms of the condition he was now suffering. "It may be the first time… ,,but it sure won't be the last!" I offered with some degree of assurance. "Nothing to be ashamed of,…though you will learn to control it better as time goes on!" I explained tenderly as I continued to console the disturbed youngster. His sobs of relief began to subside as he wiped his wet eyes and we walked slowly down the hill towards the truck.

Years have passed since then, but the debilitating affects of this un-explainable phenomenon have continued to plague this now-grown-man. As he would attest to readily, many times since that day, he has battled this seemingly unshakable malady. The evidence of his lingering ailment has been revealed to me several times in recent years as we have vigorously pursued the elusive elk at the height of the September rut, when he has had many close encounters with the magnificent creatures. Through the crackle of the intermittent radio signal, his tense voice could be heard, as he communicated his location to us on a recent hunt. "Hhhhhhh, Hhhhhhh, haaaaaagh,……there's a big bull standing bbbbbroadside,…….(crackle, crackle)". His tense stuttering voice continued breathlessly, "Stan (one of our hunting partners with an available tag), can I shoot him? He, he he's ssstanding right next to me!" A wide smile stretched across my bearded face, as I said out loud to myself from my distant location, "he's still got it! Ha! He's still got the Fever!"

"Buck Fever Hotline!" I announce as I recognize his number on my caller ID. "How can we help you today?" I mockingly query. "HHHHHHghhhh, hhhhhhhelp me! I n-n-n-n-need to talk to someone now!" he playfully sputters. We laugh as usual and begin our long distance conversation where we left off the last time we talked.

My New Cowboy Hat

The hat caught my eye as I passed by the clothing department at The General Store on my way to the fishing department. I hadn't planned on purchasing a hat, let alone even look at one. It had been on my mind for awhile though, that if I found just the right look in a hat that I would buy it. Maybe this secret desire was why my round-about-detour to the sporting goods, had steered me the long way around through the clothing department. Being a cowboy has not really been on my list of things to do, though I do consider myself a horseman.

The wide brimmed hat seemed to draw me near and as I picked it up to examine it carefully, it seemed even more attractive. "Nice looking hat! But probably won't fit," I thought to myself. It's thin leather band seemed to give it just the right finishing touch. I slipped it onto my ever-so-slightly-balding-head and was pleasantly surprised to find that it was a perfect match. "Huh,...$50 bucks! Too much. Awe, but it sure is what I've been looking for!" I reasoned. I strode over to take a look in the full length mirror. "Dang! That's a good looking hat! Sure is a handsome fella too!", I kidded myself. Continuing through the store, I picked up several other items, then proceeded through the checkout stand.

The talkative middle aged cashier seemed to be preoccupied with her personal life as she related that she was to be spending the evening with her aged father who was celebrating a birthday. I smiled impatiently as she slowly picked through the items in my basket. "Do you want to wear the hat out of the store, or do you want it in the bag?" she queried. Still a little uncomfortable with the idea of wearing a cowboy hat, I declined and asked her to bag it up.

Before leaving the parking lot, I dug through the bag, retrieved the handsome hat and perched it on top of my head. "Maybe I'll wear it home in the truck to get used to it." I thought, still uneasy with my new look. It sort of bugged me that it bothered me to wear it, since it really was a neat hat! I guess the only thing that I can compare it to, is when you get a brand new hair style and you are coming out in public for the first time. Maybe it is the fear of what someone will think, and not wanting to draw attention to one's self. I pulled up to the stop light. "Huh. That guy sitting next to me didn't seem to pay too much attention. Maybe it will be ok." I mused.

The hat sat perched on the rack at home for several weeks, until I finally found a suitable day for it's debut out into the public eye. It had to be just the right event, or it would have seemed like I was too eager to show it off. Maybe if I wore it to the rodeo, it would blend in, and I could pretend that I had been wearing it for awhile. "Or would I look like a dorky want-to-be?" I worried.

My seventeen-year old daughter Shauneen, giggled as I plopped it onto my head, on the way to the home town event. "Why are you laughing?" I asked shamefully. "Don't you like my hat?" "It's just that you never wear that kind of a hat!" she snickered. "I think it's an awesome hat!" I countered, with only a slight hint of doubt. We traveled the short distance to the local rodeo grounds in silence, as I periodically checked the rear view mirror in order to sneak a reassuring look at myself. The car doors slammed shut and we sauntered down the warm sidewalk, which was still radiating the warmth that it had absorbed during the blistering afternoon sun. We chattered excitedly as we neared the entrance to the main event.

I was to participate in the Businessman's Calf Tie, a contest designed mainly for the amusement of the rowdy audience, while they waited for the bulls to be loaded for the second round of the rough stock event. I noticed as we walked along that I was attracting quite a bit of attention. Each carload of cowboys that motored by, seemed to pay particular attention to me. "Must be the cool hat!" I thought with satisfaction. It was just then that it dawned on me, that the little girl walking closely behind me had suddenly blossomed into a full blown woman! My little girl, who was dressed in her Fair Queen sash, to be announced as royalty at the opening ceremony of the rodeo, was now it seemed, attracting a great deal of attention from the male gender, as we strode by. The realization was sort of a double whammy. My cool hat was not what was attracting the attention after all! But worse yet, I was suddenly confronted with the stark reality that my baby had grown up!

The revelation unexpectedly saddened me, as I thought back to the childhood memories I had of this vivacious girl. "She's all grown up. Can't blame the boys for looking I guess." I soberly pouted. Her beautiful, freckled face flushed slightly as I told her what I had just figured out. We had a good laugh together as I tipped my cool hat to the gorgeous women who was the reigning Fair Queen and said, " Guess they weren't admiring the new cowboy hat after all!"

Cowboys and Indians

"Yip, yip, yeeeeeee!" yelled the freckled faced, white Indian. He sat teetering on the fat, short pony, grasping a thick handful of the mane in one hand and the leather reins in the other. The chubby pony trotted reluctantly up the hill, until the ground leveled out and he broke into a choppy gallop. The Cowboy was following quickly behind on the painted horse, hot on the heels of the shorter pony, racing to catch up in order to capture or kill the marauding pretend red man.

My brothers and I had begun a game of Cowboys and Indians that consisted of pretend battles from the backs of our proud mounts. The magnificent horses we were riding really were the only one's that we could catch out of our sorry menagerie of misfit ponies. My father had collected the herd of free equines from various previous owners who had gladly pawned the sorry looking critters off on him, with the condition that they not be returned if they didn't turn out. We had ridden them enough to figure out all of their little quirks and bad habits, along with their good qualities which were few and far between. Since we didn't have the money to purchase enough saddles or tack for the whole lot of them, we took turns with the available bridles and the one bareback pad that had a cinch and floppy stirrups.

At first it didn't seem like much fun, but it did teach us how to stick to the back of a horse. The round, plump ponies where more difficult to ride since their gait was short and choppy and they were almost too round to grasp firmly with both feet. Balance was important, along with a tight squeeze of the knees and a firm wrap of the matted mane around one's hand. We rode the hills until we became bored with the same old scenery and then began looking for games with more excitement.

The small clearing above the house was our preferred destination since our forts were located in the sprawling weeping willow tree that grew among the island of thick brush at the edge of our designated battle ground. We would start at the barn, and ride bent-for-heck up the hill, kicking and prodding our lazy mounts until they finally broke stride and galloped across the rough ground in the meadow. Yelling and screaming to add authenticity to the pageantry, we would ride bouncing up and down on the sweaty backs of the pudgy ponies, up the hill and through the meadow, while trying to dislodge each other from the backs of our ponies. The winner would be the one that remained seated, declaring victory with a loud "Whoopeee!" Sometimes the Indians won and sometimes the Cowboys won.

Since I was the oldest boy (our sisters rarely participated in this rough game), it was unusual for me to become unseated and lose the battle. Luckily, it wasn't very far to the ground for any of the participants to fall and there never were any serious injuries. My mother might have killed us if she had known we were playing so rough. She still thinks we were all little angels! What she doesn't know won't hurt her!

The clatter of unshod hooves thundered up the dirt road toward the grassy meadow, as we began a new round of the Cowboy and Indian game. The fat ponies waddled up the hill and sprinted across the field like a bunch of obese fathers at the Cub Scouts' father-son Olympics. Grunting and sweating, they would pound across the open ground of the meadow, continuing their run until the rider was unseated and they would skid to a quick stop, drop their heads and munch on the grass until the games began all over again.

"Yippee yippeee!" yelled the grass stained Indians as they clung desperately to the back of their ponies like a monkey in some three-ringed-circus. "Yeeee Hawwwww!" yells the Cowboy in hot pursuit.

Mice in the Culvert

For some reason, the follies and so called pleasures of youth have a much different appeal years later, than they do at the time of happening. For instance, pulling the wings off of a grasshopper, getting your younger brother to eat a worm, catching a seagull on a fishing pole, blowing up a frog with a fire cracker, spearing crappie with a blowgun, or squishing a fresh cow pie between your toes. Such is this story. Though interesting, the following described event, may not be as gut-bustingly funny as the day it happened.

We had been bailing hay on the first cutting in July when it began to rain, stopping our progress. It rained, and rained and rained until the hay turned black and was basically unusable. The moldy bales sat in the field for many days until we were faced with the task of removing them from the field to accommodate additional cuttings. As we started this task, we were delighted to find that under each bale was a nest of mice, which by careful planning could be caught and placed in a bucket for our later entertainment. It wasn't long until we had completely filled a plastic 5 gallon bucket almost to overflowing with live mice. Not sure what to do with them once we had them, we pondered the situation until we came up with a solution. We rushed to the culvert with gleeful anticipation of the fun we would have!

The small stream came through our yard and gurgled down through a culvert, emerging on the other end, into a large pool. Perfect! One of us had the duty of dumping the load of squashed field mice into the gurgling end of the culvert, and then raced to the other end to help with the final destruction. As the bobbing mice emerged at the other end, total mayhem ensued as the easily amused farm boys bombed the swimming critters with rocks in a desperate attempt to discourage any from escaping this crude death. With the greatest event of the week, or month for that matter, over, we sat on the banks of the stream and laughed till our sides hurt. The slight twinge of regret for being an accomplice to this nasty deed, would only truly be appreciated later in our life.

Posey Valley

T he old two story ranch house sat among the large shade trees overlooking the green expanse of the beautiful, hidden valley. Posey Valley was home to my Aunt Bev and Uncle Darold who were the parents of two rambunchous boys and a sweet blond headed girl. Randy, the cousin closest to my age, was one of the rowdy boys, and was my tour guide to the secluded valley. The ditch that ran high across the hill above the sprawling Eastern Oregon ranch, carried the cold, clear water from the melting snow of the high Wallowa Mountains, and kept the little valley lush and green all summer long, even though the surrounding hills were nothing but sage brush and dry range grass.

I spent many of the long lazy summer days in the company of my favorite cousin, as we ran wild through the tall grass fields and climbed the steep hill behind the house to play in the cooling waters of the irrigation ditch. One of our favorite games was to gather a handful of rocks, and lay down in the middle of a field somewhere to ambush the curious range cows that grazed lazily on the lush grass. They would see us disappear and with curiosity getting the best of them, would soon come looking for us. Careful to avoid the large wet piles of fresh manure, we lay in the muggy shade of the tall grass, brushing away the flies and waiting quietly, as the big dumb beasts sought us out. "Wait! Not yet!" my barefooted cousin would hiss. He wasn't really barefoot, but the holey tennis shoes were only hanging there for decoration, since he had worn them ragged as we trounced around the country side.

The dark faces of the Angus cows or the white faces of the red colored Herefords, would appear, as they cautiously stalked us. With heads down and wet noses sniffing the ground, they would lumber up to within inches of us and stop to stare at the two dirty, sun-burned boys huddled in the grass. We would then leap to our feet and throw the hand picked rocks at the hard foreheads of the stupid bovines. They would run just a few steps away and turn back to look at who had just pelted them, shaking their slobbery noses at us with annoyance. Since they always came back for more, we assumed that their thick skulls were thicker than their tiny brains.

The large gray barn stood down the hill from the house near the road, and was another favorite spot to play. We would spend hours and hours, carefully re-stacking the heavy bales of grass hay, until we were satisfied that our cool fort was finished. The neat fort would have yards of hidden tunnels and escape routes, one of which lead to the thick rope swing that dangled from the sturdy rafters above. We would pretend that we had to escape some invading enemy and scamper down the dusty tunnels to our escape hatch. Then swinging from the frayed manila rope, we would land at the floor level of the musty barn in a big, soft pile of loose hay. To this day, anytime I walk into a barn and smell the hay and the manure and the pigeon poop, my memory returns to those good old days in the huge old barn.

One day, while attempting to fashion a stick seat for the rope swing, my freckled cousin nearly chopped off his big toe with the dull hatchet we had been using. Our attempts to shorten the thick tree limb to fit our purposes, came to a temporary halt, while we doctored the hanging portion of his bloodied toe. Since his old tattered low-top tennis shoes were not much protection to his tough calloused feet, he was used to the cuts and scrapes that made him famous. He was always picking at some scab that adored his battered body, since he was accident prone and never stopped long enough to think before he leaped. We tore a long strip of soiled cotton cloth from the tail of his tee shirt and wrapped it around the injured toe. I had barely completed tying the square knot on the makeshift bandage, when he grabbed the hatchet to complete our project.

I have lots of other great memories of that place. The damp musty basement of the old house was always an adventure in itself. The old tattered bear rug that had been throw there, was always something I looked forward to seeing even though it scared me a bit. The old rear porch of the house would be adorned with the drying, salted pelts of the squirrels that my older cousins had slaughtered. The day that the big sorrel horse, Blaze, fell into the old cess pool was an event that I vividly recall, even though I was too young to remember most of the details. The stench of the raw sewage permeated the air as the young gelding thrashed around while being pulled from the mucky mess by the old blue station wagon and a long rope. I remember my uncle hosing the horse down, while laughing in his usual carefree way.

Whenever I smell freshly cut hay or sneeze from the pollen of tall timothy grass, or walk into an old rickety barn, I remember those wonderful days spent running wild in the beautiful Posey Valley and think, "Awe, the good ole days! Where have they gone?"

A Fish Story

"The fish was this big," says the fisherman while holding his outstretched hands as if to measure some imaginary fish. "But he got away!" says the bragger. This is a big fish story, but is not about the one that got away! I really did have a tape measure and witnesses.

The setting was the beautiful Crater Lake, situated high in the Eagle Cap Wilderness Area of Eastern Oregon. The small troop of Boy Scouts had toiled all day up the gradual incline of the Cliff River Trail and had arrived at the north end of the emerald blue lake late in the afternoon. The group was outfitted with small pup tents, which they began to assemble upon arrival at the long awaited destination. Each boy had partnered up with another, making short work of the tedious task which they were now getting adept at, having already camped at other locations for the several days prior. "I can handle the rest," said my tent partner. So I assembled my well used pack rod that doubled as a fly rod or spin rod. "I'm going to go dip a fly," said I, with pole in hand and creel draped over my shoulder.

I looked out over the familiar scenery, took a deep breath of the fresh mountain air, and began picking my way down toward the water's edge. The water was smooth, like glass, as I peeled yards of fly line out of the old automatic Perrine reel and began to flip it toward one of the ripples that had recently disturbed the surface, indicating that a fish had just risen to feed. The new Spruce fly, fat from the coiled peacock feather wrapping, looked enticing as it lay floating on the top of the clear water. I could see the fish coming from deep below the surface, oblivious to everything else as it honed in on the new delicacy that sat at the surface. The flashy brook trout grabbed the imitation bait and turned toward the bottom, as I gave the limber pole a yank to set the hook deep into it's large mouth. Fish at this elevation typically grow very large gills and hence, have very big heads in proportion to the rest of their body. I measured the slimy fish with the marks on my faded green creel and slid it into the opening. "Ten inches! Not bad for a start!" I exclaimed, knowing that I had been watched by several of my younger companions. I hadn't been a Scout leader for long, but had come to realize early on, that these vulnerable young men certainly paid attention to the example of their leaders. I moved on around the lake a few yards to try another cast.

I could feel the eyes upon me now, as I raised the tip of the old South Bend fly rod and began the casting all over again. The fly rolled out to the end of the tapered leader and plopped softly into the ripple that had just formed from the turbulence of another rising fish. I quickly raised the tip of the pole in response to the hungry fish, and exclaimed, "Got another one! Yeehaaww! It don't git no better than this boys!" It took a little longer to land the plump fish this time, and I grunted with satisfaction as it slid through the narrow opening of the smelly creel. "Thirteen inches. Not bad for the second fish!" I gloated. I moved on around the lake to a sandy beach on the west side of the lake. I had been watching the ripples on this side from my previous location, and it seemed like there had been a lot of activity here. Dusk began to fall as the evening sun disappeared behind the mountains some 60 miles to the west. "One or two more casts will be all we're gonna git tonight," I thought to myself, as I began stripping the green line out of the blue and silver reel.

Pleased with the length of the cast and with the soft presentation of the hand-tied fly, I grinned and waited in suspense for the fish to turn toward the fake bait. The couple of seconds seemed like a long time compared to the previous two catches, so I tugged gently at the fly to make it more enticing. "It is getting a bit dark.....". The words in my head trailed off abruptly as the water boiled where the fly once lay. I yanked the pack rod toward the dimming sky and found a lot of resistance. "Holy cow! It's a pig!" I stammered to myself. "Yeeeeeeeeehawwwwww!!!!" could be heard echoing across the lake. I could see the flicker of the camp fire as my pole bent nearly in two. "Don't horse it," I coached myself, like my grandpa used to tell me. I peeled out more line as the massive brookie fought for his life and headed for deeper waters. "Holy cow!" I swore again, as I tightened my grip on the cork handle of the pole. The crowd of boys had begun to gather behind me, as the trusting entourage caught up to me. "He's huge!" exclaimed Todd, who had been an avid fisherman since he was weaned. (He later would become my brother-in-law, marrying my wife's younger sister) The florescent orange and white underbelly of the monster fish, flashed in the fading light as he broke the surface of the water, wildly splashing in a vain attempt to loosen the hook that was sunk deep into his upper jaw. Five or ten minutes passed by, in what seemed like an eternity, until the flashy-submarine-of-a-fish began to tire. The yards of line had been retrieved and the big fish neared the shallows of the sandy shore. With one last tug in his final run for freedom, the big fish gave up and I pulled it to shore.

We stood admiring the beautiful colors of the native fish, wondering how it could grow so big, up so high. Normally the fish at this altitude didn't grow this big. The fat fish was amazingly deep and thick, measuring eighteen and a half inches in length. Since this was not one of those corny fishing shows where they ooh and ahh and pet the fish and then throw it back, I thumped the old fish on the head and started toward camp and the fry pan. When I gutted the monster fish, I found that he had recently swallowed a ten-inch fish that was still intact in his stomach. The unfortunate one must have not even seen the large predator coming, since other than being bleached white by the stomach acids, had not a mark on it. He must have swallowed it in one big gulp!

We cut it into several large chunks and slapped it into the sizzling frying pan. The fish ended up as a filling dinner not only for me and the five hungry Scouts, but also for the black bear that visited the camp later in the night to slick up the remains that lay on the rock next to our campfire. That was a BIG FISH!

Panther Eckstein

"Who would name a kid Panther?" I thought, as I glanced over the roster of the opposing football team. "What a dumb name!" I chuckled, as my eyes continued to scan the data from the long roster. "Holy Cow! The kid must be a real blimp! The list says he weighs more than three hundred pounds!" I said out loud for my team mates to hear, hoping that I would be able to push the pudgy guy around the field all night. We had arrived in the small logging town of Elgin, known for it's rugged athletes and tough atmosphere. I had gotten hold of the team roster from the program that had been printed for the evening's football game. This was to be our first game under lights, since most of our Friday games were played in the late afternoon. Only a few of our competitors had lights on their fields, since most schools in our scattered league were not able to afford such luxuries. Most of the fields were used for events other than football and were bumpy, with less than ideal conditions for good footing.

I had not turned out for football until my junior year in high school, but had learned quickly and had progressed to the ranks of first string Varsity in a matter of days. I didn't know much about the actual workings of the rough game, but I had learned to hit hard and found that I liked it a lot. I was anxious for the game to start, since we were undefeated and would soon clash with the undefeated Huskies. "Who would want to have a stupid dog for a mascot?" I had said earlier in the day, as we passed the time on the three-hour bus ride to the Eastern Oregon town. "I think Spartan is a much better name for a team!" I had pronounced with importance. Our neat new red Spartan jerseys showed up brightly under the gleaming lights of the field.

This was to be the big showdown and would be our first real test, to see if we had what it took to progress onto the State tournament. We had blown by most of our previous contenders with ease, but had prepared carefully for this game, knowing that we would have our hands full. I paced nervously along the sidelines waiting for the announcer to say my name so I could run onto the field with the rest of my teammates. I played right tackle on offense and defense and had mastered my position without really knowing the finer workings of the rest of the game. All I knew is that I had to block out the big fat guy that I had seen on the roster.

"At left tackle for the offense,… Panther Eckstein!" announced the loud speaker. My jaw about dropped to the ground as I saw what I had imagined to be a slow, pudgy fat guy. Instead, out walked the tallest and strongest looking three-hundred pound giant that I had ever seen! His bulging biceps must have been as big around as my thighs and his neck was as big around as my waist. He was huge! My heart sank, as I realized that the monster Panther would be playing heads on against me.

The kick-off commenced and in my usual fashion, I wove through the charging line of opposing players and smashed the running ball carrier into the soft turf with a loud grunt. I had a goal of getting the tackle on each kickoff and had been successful on most outings. The next play brought me head on with Panther Eckstein, who began to school me on some of the finer techniques of a lineman. I soon realized that it was going to be a very long evening on the football field. The first series ended in a punt and we switched over to offense. The play was a run up my hole, which required me to standup the opposing player and push them inside as the running back blasted through the widening hole.

The cadence of the quarterback brought us all to life as the ball was snapped and the action began. I exploded off the line and ran into the brick wall that had the stupid name. His massive muscular body absorbed the shock of my hit, as he reached out with his thick arm and clothes- lined the rushing running back. "Uuuughhh!" grunted the short stout running back, as his Adams' apple absorbed the shock of the smashing arm. His feet left the ground and he dropped in a heap at the line-of-scrimmage. This play was to be the foreshadowing of a very long night for me. Normally I and the guard would totally dominate the opposing defense, causing the coach to call a lot of the plays on our side of the line, but tonight would be different. The giant Panther tossed me around like a rag doll all game long, offering me few chances to rest. I could only handle the blitzing lineman by chop-blocking the knees of the monster gorilla, on most of the passing plays. I would like to see the video of that game if there were such a thing. I imagine that it must have looked something like a huge African lion, shaking a gazelle around until it practically went to pieces.

The mother of the goliath must have named the rascal only after struggling to deliver such a huge baby boy. His name couldn't have been more fitting! He was all over me like a Mack truck! I'm not sure what college he played at after his high school career was completed, but he could have played most anywhere. "Another tackle by Panther Eckstein!" yelled the announcer. "Sure wish that guy would shut up!" I grumbled to myself, buried under a pile of crumpled players. "Maybe his name could have been Moose, or Train or even locomotive." It was going to be a long night!

Green Horn

"**W**here is my bow?" asked the puzzled hunter. "I laid it right next to this tree on the other side of the tethered horse." He continued to search the ground and began to mutter with frustration. "You dang knot-headed green horn!" I stated, while shaking my head in disbelief. "The horse has trampled it into the ground!" I added with disgust at his dilemma. "She better not be cut up from your broad heads!" I cautioned him, concerned for the safety of my trusted mountain horse who stood stock-still as I examined her carefully.

The beautiful black and white mare was one of several horses we had ridden out of our elk hunting camp that day. We had left them tied to the trees there, as we went into the timbered basin on foot, hunting for elk that afternoon. I had killed a cow elk a short distance from there and had begun the butchering process while my brother Eldon had returned to the horses to retrieve several of them to pack the heavy elk carcass back to camp. He had left a couple of the horses there and had laid his bow next to the tree, thinking that it would be safe. The fussy horse, anxious for the return of her departed corral mates, had pranced around the perimeter of her rope until she had become entangled in the strings of the compound bow. She had stomped it into pieces around her until it lay scattered in all directions, leaving no resemblance to the fancy weapon that had been laid there.

My disappointed brother began gathering up the pieces of his broken bow, realizing that his hunting trip might have come to an abrupt end because of his ignorance. "You should have known that the horse could reach it!" I scolded him. "Dang Green Horn anyway!" I continued to berate the sober rookie. The ride back to camp was a quiet one, interrupted only by the occasional cough of a horse, or the clank of a horse shoe on the granite rocks. It was dark by the time we rode into camp, exhausted from the day of hunting and butchering. After caring for the hungry horses and gulping down a couple of cans of lukewarm Western Family chili, we crawled into our bedrolls for the night, anxious for the much needed bed rest.

The next morning was spent lazily lounging around camp, recuperating from the previous days work, giving us a chance to catch up on some of the backed-up camp chores, like washing clothes and mending equipment. Eldon seemed intent in his futile efforts to reconstruct his damaged bow, bent over it like a careful craftsman, with his roll of sticky duct tape and baling wire. His somber mood indicated his concern that the weapon might be reduced to something more primitive than he had expected. He slaved over the puzzling project most of the day, periodically testing the bow to see how it was shooting. He finally announced that his patch work was completed, holding the cobbled-up bow for all to see. I grinned with amusement and grunted my approval of the pieced-together-contraption. "Dang Green Horn!" I exclaimed again, teasing the novice about his inadequacies as a horseman and hunter.

That next Christmas, a package arrived at his house via the U.S. Postal Service, wrapped with bright green wrapping paper and with the attached note stating, "Don't open until Christmas!" It contained an assortment of items that could be used to patch things together, including a new roll of duct tape, super glue, epoxy, etc., along with a set of tiny forked-horn deer antlers that had been attached to a board and spray-painted a bright green color. "The Green Horn Award," was printed carefully at the bottom of the crude board.

The phone rang early Christmas morning with the grinning Green Horn attached to the other end. We laughed together, happy to hear each other's voice, acknowledging the appropriateness of the carefully-thought-out gift. We talked again of our great adventure together and made plans for the upcoming season, hopeful that it would go better for him the next time. I reluctantly hung up the phone, anxious for the next time I could see this younger sibling that I was partial to because of his enthusiasm for the outdoors like me. This last hunting season did go a little better for him, even though he didn't fill his tags again. I watched as he lifted his half-burned hunting cap from the drying rack near the campfire, laughing as he lifted the smoldering hat to his balding head. "Dang Green Horn!" I muttered with an affectionate grin, wondering how soon it would be before he would be able to shed that label.

Hero Worship

When I was a young lad, my prim and proper Sunday school teacher would warn us about things like the evil of idle worship. "There are many things that people worship other than the God of the universe," she would preach. "Some worship false gods, and some worship objects like fancy cars, boats, money, or even people such as rock stars or movie actors," she continued seriously. Most of the time the wrinkled grey-haired spinster had a difficult time controlling the small group of vigorous pre-teen boys, but I sat riveted to every word she said. Having been to her quaint country home several times, I had seen the old worn photos of her in the prime of life and had developed a great deal of awe and respect for this fine god-fearing woman. She had told me many stories of her younger life and on one particular visit showed me photos of a giant sturgeon she had caught in the perilous waters of Hells Canyon's Snake River. The photo showed the head of the monster fish sitting on the seat of the buckboard wagon and it's tail dragging the ground. I had heard a lot of unsubstantiated fish stories before and had turned into something of a skeptic, so when I saw the actual proof of her story, my suspicions vanished and I developed an immediate trust for everything she said.

As I sat in the tiny classroom of the small country church that had once been a school house, my eyes were glued to the respectable old lady as I absorbed every word. "Anyone that could catch a fish that big, had to be a very cool person," I reasoned. I cherished those years, learning a lot from my seasoned friend, and was saddened at her passing a few years later.

Through the years I have recalled her teachings many times and had the opportunity to show my unshakeable trust in her, by following the wisdom of her words.

Like my great Sunday school teacher, many trusted people have developed a sort of "hero" status to me, maybe not quite to the idle-worship-stature, but almost. I was reminded of this concept the other day as I was preparing my horses for a local parade, dressed in my authentic mountain man garb. My young freckled nephew, Isaac who has always paid particular attention to his somewhat eccentric uncle, blurted out "Uncle Jim has the tallest horse in the county!" The matter-of-fact statement by the bright five year old, brought a smile to my face as I realized that he had elevated me and my big Appaloosa, Rerun, to somewhat of a hero status. My sister often recites stories of his playtime escapades, which often include something about him being a mountain man and having a horse named Rerun. This type of healthy hero worship is something quite different from the hysteria of screaming fans at a rock concert, or the phenomenon of elevating people to "star" status, who pretend to be someone else for a living. Real people doing real things whom we come to trust and respect for their greatness in performing the every day simple things of life, are the true heros, yet often are ignored by most of the general public.

When I returned home from a mission to New York for my church, as a strapping young 21 year old, several of my little brothers would follow me around like little friendly puppy dogs, watching intently every move that I made. Evidently the wonders of my travels in the world, had impressed the gawky little fledglings enough that they had placed me in their 'heros hall of fame,' without me really being aware that I had done anything truly extraordinary. The youngest of the group, Stephen, an intelligent fellow who later would see the error of his idle worshiping ways, watched with interest one day as I struggled to clear my stuffy allergy-laden nostril from it's dried mass of mucous. A short time later, his earnest, concerned little boy voice piped up, "Jimmy, I didn't know that missionewy's picked thew bouggews!" I rubbed his dirty little crew- cut head, as I explained with amusement, that I was just a normal guy and that I was sorry to have let him down. "I'll have to be careful what I do around here!" I mused to myself. "The little bugger thinks I'm some sort of a hero, or something!"

Late in my life I have realized that lots of heros have affected my life. Some are no longer living and some are just starting their sojourn here on this earth. My Grandpa Pope, whom I miss immensely, was one of those idols to me. It became rather evident to me one day as I was struggling to control an unruly young colt that had trampled my foot in the process of maneuvering away from some benign object that had suddenly turned into a monster. As the sharp pain shot up my leg, I blurted out an expletive, characteristic of words I had heard my grandfather say when he was frustrated with someone or something. "Son-of-a-b_____!" he would blurt out. The instant the irreverent profanity slipped from my lips, my mind was flooded with warm, fond memories of my deceased hero. Oddly as it may seem, those words have become a term of endearment to me rather than a profanity because it reminds me so much of Grandpa. Don't get me wrong, I don't condone it and don't normally cuss, but occasionally an event occurs that causes me a temporary loss of linguistic control, usually related to my interaction with a dumb beast of burden. Each and every time I slip, my thoughts are drawn back in time and the tender thoughts of Grandpa inundate my mind.

Heros come in all shapes and sizes with no regard to age or social esteem. Dad's and Mom's are always prime candidates along with some that are a little less obvious. One of my newest heros is my little redheaded mountain man wanna-be nephew. He doesn't know it because he is caught up in his own form of worship. I guess it's sort of mutual adoration. Every time I hear him make some profoundly hilarious statement, I am awed at his brilliance and wonder why I can't be more like him!

Hornet in The Window

The old '47 Chevy flatbed puttered down the narrow paved road toward The Dump, a destination that had become one of my favorites, since it allowed me to get out of other less desirable work at our family owned country grocery store. The duty of taking the garbage to the town dump had fallen on me simply because I could drive and no one else wanted the smelly job. Since it allowed me an escape from my normal dull routine, I looked forward to the twice-a-week trip to the dump. I continued down the old highway, which had been abandoned in favor of a new route. Now serving as the only road to the dump, it continued on to where it ended in the Brownlee Reservoir at what we called "The Sag." With the creation of the Brownlee Dam on the Snake River, the back waters of this new reservoir had covered several miles of the old highway route from Halfway to Baker City, but this portion of the road remained open.

The high racks of the old flatbed rattled with each bump in the road as I turned off the pavement onto the short stretch of graveled road that led to the dump site. The heat of the day seemed only to enhance the odors that rose from the huge mounds of trash, as I backed the green truck up to the man-made bank and shut off the steaming six cylinder engine. I walked along the bank, peering into the mounds of debris searching for treasures that may have been dumped with the trash. I don't know why I looked, because I never really found anything of value, but was constantly amazed at what you can find out about people when you look at their trash. I returned to the truck and began the tedious job of emptying the piles of garbage bags and flattened cardboard boxes over the steep bank. Beads of sweat rolled down my face as I replaced the makeshift tailgate and climbed back into the cab of the worn out old truck. I soon realized that leaving the window down had been a bad idea! The cab was full of swarming black flies, attracted to the cab by the smell of my half-eaten lunch. The engine revved as I ground the gears into low and released the clutch. I quickly accelerated and shifted until I reached fourth gear which would allow me to travel back down the road at a pretty good clip. I opened all of the windows in order to blow all of the nasty flies out of the cab. After several hundred yards, the flies seemed to have vanished, but I continued my accellerated rate of speed down the road.

It wasn't long before I realized that though the flies had been successfully flushed from the cab, a hornet had escaped the turbulence and was buzzing around angrily inside the windshield. Not realizing that I should slow down or stop before removing the agitated insect from my window, I began to swat vigorously at the yellow and black menace. While reaching as far to my right as I could, I swatted at the hornet, desperately hoping that it, like the flies, would be sucked out the window in the turbulence of wind. I mashed the gas pedal to the floor, encouraging the old Chevrolet one-ton to move faster down the road in order to create a better wind tunnel in the cab. The hornet seemed to miraculously avoid the force of the wind that now raged through the dusty truck cab as it now began to buzz around on the drivers side window. I made a fist and gave the feisty little bugger a whack. I now realized, with horror, that in the heat of the moment, the distraction had allowed me to deviate from my desired course and the rusty truck was heading down the bank and into the barrow pit. My head nearly hit the ceiling as I bounced along in the weed choked ditch for several hundred yards. With all the coolness of an off-road race driver, I guided the truck back up onto the pavement and continued down the road lickety-split! "That was fun!" I chuckled to myself with the innocence of youth. "Better not leave the windows down again!" I counseled myself, never thinking to slow down even a little bit. I pulled into the back lot of the little store and backed up to the loading dock. "Another fun trip to the dump!" I thought as the weary engine sputtered to a stop and I slid to the ground. "Sure wish this old baby had air conditioning!"

Mouse Hunt

Remember the old cartoon with Elmer Fudd as the rabbit hunter? "Kill the wabbit! Kill the wabbit!" he would chant. His every hour consumed with the obsession to kill the poor rabbit. I can sort of relate to the goofy inept hunter. When I was approximately sixteen years old, we were given the commission by our father to annihilate the droves of mice that had infested our new home and I had become rather obsessed with killing the gray vermin. My father had recently built a new home on eighty acres of woodlands and for some reason that first winter, the mice had found a way in and had become not only a nuisance, but a real health problem.

Since my bedroom was in the far corner of the finished basement, every time I went upstairs I had to walk the full length of the basement, passing through the family room and up the stairs. Almost every time I turned the lights on, coming or going from my room, I would spot one or two of the nasty little critters scurrying across the floor toward their hiding places. The problem had not been resolved as quickly as my father had anticipated, so he raised the bounty to two dollars a piece. With the prospect of making a lot of money, I became not only obsessed with the project, but rather good at it, devising many clever traps that made the venture very lucrative for a young boy.

The common mouse trap with the little-wire-snappy-thing, soon became a thing of the past as we invented faster and more creative methods. One day, after discovering a mouse stuck in a half empty bowl of burnt honey left over from one of my sisters failed baking projects, I realized that the method could be improved upon by using a larger bowl with an increased volume of the sticky solution. Cooking the honey would make it more tacky than normal honey, especially when it was chilled by the evening air. I would leave the shallow bowl on the shelf in the garage overnight and would awaken early just to check out the results of my latest trap. It was like Christmas every day, with all of the suspense, but a rather different present. Some days, the gooey trap would ensnare several mice at a time. I would bop the frantic fur balls on the head and then scoop them into the burning barrel with a stick.

I used the proceeds from my trapping venture, to purchase several different kinds of store-bought traps with the sticky stuff that seemed to be more high tech than my messier version. I also tried the small live traps that appealed to the more kind hearted trapper, but none of these store-bought traps could compete with the sloppy, honey bowl method. Another method we perfected, was to grab a pair of dirty jeans by the pant legs, wrapping them around your hand and then twisting the legs to make a contraption that worked sort of like a long fly swatter. I would sneak to the basement with my denim weapon in hand, turn on the lights and try to whack the scurrying beasts before they escaped. Whack! Whack! "Got another one!" I announced. It was common for me to kill at least one a day using my fly swatter method.

After earning several hundred dollars, the earnings began to be fewer, since the population of mice had nearly become extinct. I persisted, much like Elmer Fudd chasing Bugs Bunny, becoming more obsessed than ever. It seemed as though I now did twice the work, for half the pay, but I continued to assassinate the smelly buggers like a paid mob hit man. My father's wallet had taken such a hit, that he soon discontinued the bounty, much to my dismay. It was many months before we saw any evidence of a mouse in the house, since the species had nearly gone the way of the Dodo bird. The mouse hunt had been a complete success.

I Hate Cats

Iff you are a cat lover this may be offensive to you, since this article makes no attempt to be politically correct, and is the very biased opinion of the author. If you are still reading then I assume that you are either interested in the topic as a sympathizer or you are curious as to why someone as cultured as me could be so adverse to the cuddly little fur balls that have graced your life. My negative experience with the feline creatures through the years has convinced me, that in the beginning of time when Adam was booted out of the garden of Eden and God cursed the earth with thistles and thorns to torment man, he must have also created hornets, squash, stupid drivers and cats (see Genesis 3:18). Of course I could be wrong, but that would take all the fun out of this story.

It all started when I was a young boy and had been introduced to the task of milking the family cow. For an eight-year old boy this chore was often overwhelming and the cause of most of the frustration and anxiety I experienced at that age. The normal carefree days of early youth were interrupted twice a day as my sister and I tediously stripped the fat, rich milk from the gentle jersey cow named Bossy. We actually became rather good at the milking portion of the activity, but our youthful inexperience often caused us grief and left us far short of the normal daily portion of the rich white liquid that was a necessary staple for our large family.

We innocently tempted the mangy, runny-eyed barn cats that frequented the premises, by squirting them with milk to see who could win the contest for distance. This seemingly harmless activity soon conditioned the devious carnivores into believing that they were owed a free breakfast and dinner at our expense. The clank of the stainless steel bucket was enough to bring them scurrying for the chow line. We would have to maintain a constant vigil in order to keep the persistent little beggars from dunking their disgusting heads into the foamy warm liquid while we weren't looking. This caused us to discard many buckets of milk that had been contaminated, much to my dismay and frustration.

I could hardly stand the sight of the flea-infested cats, let alone stomach the thoughts of drinking my favorite liquid that had been subjected to such a revolting violation. I became rather good at drop-kicking cats through the door of the barn and did it with such frequency that I could have gone to the Olympics if it had been allowed as an event. One day the unusually thirsty cats had tried my patience to the limit and had successfully avoided the toe of my manure speckled boot. After turning my back to the cow for an instant to scatter the gathering pride of domestic miniature lions, I discovered a scraggly kitten totally submersed in my half-full bucket of warm milk.

That was it! It was as if I had instantly gone from a strong dislike, but tolerant acceptance of the critters, to a frenzied, hate filled tantrum that was intended to send the whole lot of them into extinction. In a swift motion I snatched the gangly juvenile by the tail, which was the only part of the cat that was not hidden in the foamy froth, swung the squalling wet mass around my head like an Olympic hammer thrower, eventually slamming it into the weathered wall of the milk parlor. Somehow it escaped to live another day, but not because of lack of trying on my part. Years later, after returning to my parents home for a brief stay, I was given the opportunity for revenge on the species. My mother had gone to visit my older sister to help with a newborn baby, and my father who was on his way out the door to work, simply stated, "oh,… and if some of these darn cats where to mysteriously disappear around here, it wouldn't hurt my feelings. The .22 is in my closet." This was all I needed for encouragement to unleash my festering vengeance against a population of cats that had exploded out of control. "Too many bleeding hearts around here!" I thought to myself. "Someone has to take charge here." The pungent odor of cat urine in the carport and wood shed had become too strong to tolerate for my father, but he didn't have the time or the stomach for the task of thinning out the filthy creatures. My thirst for vengeance would have ample opportunity to be slaked as the once over populated cats came near to qualifying as an endangered species in that household. In those days the Humane Society had not yet taken their current stance nor begun their campaign for pet population control, so it was up to the land owners to accomplish this task.

Since then, my overwhelming hatred for cats has dwindled somewhat, but has not totally been extinguished. Our family cat periodically pretends to be a football after presumptuously rubbing up against my leg and finding itself airborne. Whenever I see a squashed cat on the road, a slight smile creeps onto my face as I ponder yet another small victory over one of the thistles of earth life. "A little victory bell rings in Heaven every time a cat dies!" I have been heard to say. The other day, after spotting the badly decomposed body of one of these flattened felines in the ditch, I noticed the "like new" flea collar still around the shrunken neck of the pitiful remains, and thought to myself, "what a waste of a perfectly good flea collar!"

Mice In The Well

Being an avid hiker and camper has been a real passion for me through the years and has brought me in contact with many who profess a knowledge of the outdoors. For example, one of the most talked about subjects when planning a Boy Scout 50-miler, has always been about making sure that the boys filter the water. "Giardia, will really make you sick!" says a serious adult, who has never been in the mountains long enough to grow a three day shadow, but somehow is an expert on wilderness survival. "Make sure you filter all of your water! It may look good and taste sweet, but it is just full of contaminants!", the expert commentator continues. While I agree in principle with the idea that one must be careful, I have been somewhat callused when it comes to drinking water, since I have stuck my head in many a frog pond to slake a voracious thirst during these outings to various parts of wilderness. Other than an occasional extra trip to the outhouse, I have never suffered any ill side affects from this politically incorrect practice. This story is about a time that pushed the limits of my usually strong constitution and made me think twice about the water that I consume.

The lanky horseshoer sauntered into my real estate office one day and asked if I would represent him in the sale of his small farmhouse in Williams Valley, since he was considering a move to Texas, which he claimed would be more profitable for his horseshoing business. I enthusiastically agreed to the job and went to work on the marketing plan. Several months later, after consummating a deal for the sale of his quaint 2 story farm house, I was handed a copy of the water samples, which indicated that his well was high in coliform bacteria and that we would have to address that situation. My call to the pump company was discouraging to say the least. The experienced contractor assured me that this was quite possibly the worst water sample he had ever seen in his many years of well sampling. He agreed to make an attempt to purge the well of it's very apparent impurities, which is something he had done many times successfully, but didn't realize at the time what he was in for.

The shallow country well had been drilled sometime in the early 50's, replacing the old hand dug well of earlier years, but upon completion the well had never been properly sealed. The rusty screen fastened with baling wire had deteriorated to a point that had allowed whole generations of kamikaze mice to be lured by the smell of the water, into taking the 60 foot plunge to the dark icy waters below. The filthy vermin had evidently continued this lemming like behavior, for several years during the ownership of the young bachelor cowboy. The normally hardy Water Sampler, began to feel queezy, as he continued to explain what he had encountered. "When we discovered that mice had entered the well, we began the tedious process of sucking them out with the pump setup that I had previously used for similar jobs." He was barely able to control the gagging sensation, as he continued to expound the gruesome details of this tale. "We extracted two full buckets of mice carcasses and hair, that were in varying degrees of decomposition," he said, as he turned to suppress another retching spasm.

Long story short, he explained that he was able to properly purge the water well from all debris and contamination, seal it properly and run a final sample through the lab that proved that his unpleasant task had been successful. After completing the sale and visiting for the last time with the departing farrier, I listened with reluctance as he gleefully announced that his severe rash of about a 3 year duration had completely gone away immediately after the well had been cleansed. I shudder to think about this story again, but the mice in the well have at least made me think twice before dunking my hot dusty head into that remote mountain water hole.

John's Buck

Remember the biology lesson from high school about natural selection? Well, in short, it is the process that nature has concocted to eliminate the weak. In other words, survival of the fittest. I have seen dumb people fall victim to this terrestrial principle, as well as animals. My wife kept hounding me for years to finish the railing on our front deck so little kids would not fall through, but I kept stalling and would say, "If a kid is dumb enough to fall off then he's probably too dumb to survive very long in life anyway. Good old survival of the fittest," I would be heard to say.

My scrappy little 3 year old nephew constantly tests this law but remains unscathed. He leads a totally charmed life. Relatives have been heard to say, "if that kid lives to be 10 it will be a miracle." He continually tempts the law of natural selection and is continually spared the consequence. He has no fear which may be the reason that he can survive so well. He's like the little kid in the movie 'Babies Day Out,' who constantly escapes injury as he crawls around in a big city while being chased by bad guys.

This story is not about little kids, but is about a young mule deer buck that had a death wish. It is interesting how some creatures have that strong will to live and others do not. Some have all the luck and some have none. I have observed big old monarch bucks, that had such a will to live that they could run hundreds of yards with no heart after being fatally hit with a bullet, and conversely have seen small inexperienced bucks lay down immediately to die having suffered only a minor leg injury, succumbing quickly to the hunters will.

It all started when my friend John and I had decided to stay for an extra day after packing out from an extended trip into the mountains. He still had a deer tag and we thought that we could possibly find one of those bucks that would be too dumb to survive very long. We camped along the rushing creek in the old mining town of Cornucopia, which is somewhat of a ghost town. Once a gold rush boom town that was a thriving city with hotel, stores, and homes, now only a few dilapidated buildings remain as evidence of it's prior glory. We had gained permission from UNC., a mining company that still holds property there, to park on their property for a few days. After taking a short horseback ride that evening with no success, we laid our sleeping bags out on a tarp to settle in for the night. Our plans were to rise early and do the same little horse hunt as the night before and then head for home.

My forty-year old bladder woke me early but the chill of the morning kept me from venturing out of my warm sleeping bag. John rolled over and said, "Palmer, you awake?" "Ya. Just not up yet," I returned. At the same instant we both caught a glimpse of a little mule deer buck that had ventured directly into our camp. I said to John, "well,… will you look at that! See the little suicide note tied to his antlers?" I turned to see if John had heard me, but he had already slipped his shoes on and was heading for his bow that was sitting on the truck seat. "Can't find my release!" hissed John. "Guess I'll just have to use fingers." As I struggled to tie my boots, I heard the thwack of his bow and the "dang it! I missed!" come from the other side of the truck. "He just slowly trotted down the road." said John, "I think I'll go after him." "Awe, he's gone now," I whined. "We'd be better off to saddle the horses and go for our ride."

A few short minutes later, we were heading down the road, which was once a bustling city street. Out of the bushes popped the same little buck with the same note still tied to his antlers. "Kill me!" it stated. "I'm just too dumb to survive!" Now hopefully you are not as gullible as my wife, in thinking that the note was real! John quickly baled off the jogging Pinto, handed me the reins, and headed off to intercept the dumb little buck. Thwack, went the bow again. The buck stood still for a second and then put his head down and started eating again. Thwack! "Are you out of arrows yet?" I jested. Thwack, came the sound again, instantly followed by a loud,

WHACK! "I hit that old building!" yelled John. "Dumb beggar is still standing here!" Thwack, and finally, the thud of an arrow penetrating flesh. "Got him!" yelled John with a chuckle. "Dumb thing just stood there and let me shoot him!" "It's a good thing I hit him cause I'm out of arrows." "I'll have to go dig that one out of the side of that old building."

I've read stories of native Indians thanking the Great Spirit for game that they believed had been miraculously sent to them by the higher power. Not that I don't believe that God can help us out in a pinch, but I just can't help but think that this time, the young dead buck, just had a bout with the law of natural selection. We gutted and skinned John's little forked horn, loaded the gear and horses and started for home! It had been a good trip. Three dumb forked-horn bucks had fallen victim to the law of the fittest.

Dog on the Faucet

The telephone kept ringing as I scrambled from the shower trying to pick it up before the other party hung up. I fumbled to get the slippery phone to my wet ear, dropping it several times before I heard my wife's frantic voice on the other end of the line. "Come to the neighbors quickly! The dog is stuck on a hose faucet! Come quickly!" The phone clicked and I scrambled to dry off and throw some clothes on really quick. My imagination ran wild as I thought of what the frantic message had meant. I jumped into the car with my feet crammed halfway into my shoes and drove the half mile to the neighbor's house, unsure of what I would find.

My wife was used to walking several miles early in each morning, up and down the private road from our home each day and had been taking the young German Shepherd with her for an added sense of security. As I pulled up and skidded to a stop at the neighbor's house, I heard the frantic yelps of the young female dog before I could see her. My wife was struggling to hold the wriggling dog in a position that would make her more comfortable, but was obviously having a hard time controlling the panicked dog.

She had darted from my wife's side in hot pursuit of the neighbor's cat, which had scampered in a circle attempting to avoid the jaws of the relentless attacking dog. The cat had jumped quickly up the bank of a retaining wall where a stand pipe with a faucet and hose bib were located. The pipe stuck out of the ground several feet in the air and had impaled the airborne dog as she leaped up the steep bank after the cat. The impact had broken the skin on the inside of the big dog's thigh, driving the entire hose bib and faucet deep into the big muscle of her rear leg. The gaping wound was no less than ten inches across and exposed a great deal of innards. The struggling dog had spun around several times in her vain attempts to free herself from the painful metal lance that had brought her chase to an abrupt halt.

I grasped the dog with both arms and attempted to lift her high enough to pull her free, but realized in an instant that it would be much more complicated than that. I reached my hand deep inside the gaping bloody wound in an effort to evaluate how I could free her. The thick thigh muscle had separated enough to allow the water spigot through. Then the muscle had become wrapped tightly around the faucet handle when the poor impaled critter had spun around the pipe stand. The muscle had contracted tightly to make matters worse and I struggled to work the tight strands of muscles loose enough to pull them back over the faucet handle, but to no avail. "Go get me a sharp knife!" I gasped with exertion. "I don't know what else to do! I'm going to have to cut the muscle to get her off!" I said with exasperation.

My mind raced to think of any other possible alternative, but time was running out as the dog began to go into shock from loss of blood and the extreme trauma. I held the whimpering dog tightly in my arms to keep her from moving and to offer some sort of comfort to the suffering beast. The knife arrived, but certainly had never seen the sharpening stone, at least not recently. But I was grateful for something, anything that would work. I asked my wife to relieve me from holding the large dog momentarily, since I would need both hands to accomplish the nasty operation. I grasped the knife in one hand, running my pointing finger along the back of the knife for optimum control and reached into the wound with the other, to locate the strands of muscle that had become so tightly wound around the faucet.

"Aughhhhh, uuuggg!" I grunted with disgust at the graphic nature of the crude operation that I was forced to perform. The muscles contracted with pain, each time I touched them, as I continued probing around in the ghastly hole. Finally the offending strands of muscle were isolated under my finger and I began to saw the muscle in half with the dull butcher knife. "Ooooohhhhhh!" I continued to lament at the intense pain the dog was suffering, indicated by her whining, but mostly by the tense contractions of the muscle that were now partially wrapped around my imbedded hand. Finally the muscle was cut and I delicately unwrapped it from the round handle of the hose bib. We hoisted the dog together and she dropped to the ground, free from her crude crucifixion.

I wrapped the trembling dog in my arms and quickly strode to the car. "I don't think she is going to make it!" I said quietly. "She is already in deep shock and has lost a lot of blood!" I continued to prepare my wife for the inevitable outcome of this tragedy. "Wow, what a freak accident!" I thought out loud. I have seen a lot of animals die in my life time, some caused by my hunting excursions and some accidental, but I have never been able to stomach suffering on any level, and this was no exception. "I'll have to put her down quickly, so she doesn't suffer any more." I said with sadness. I had actually become quite attached to the beautiful half-breed, which was unusual since I rarely got attached to any of the guard dogs that my wife had brought home. My hunting dogs had always received the bulk of my affection and attention.

"She'll never even make it to the vet." I lamented. I was a little grumpy because I was always the one to have to do the dirty work at our house. Whenever an animal needed to be put out of their misery, I was always the one people called upon to take care of the task that they had no stomach for. It wasn't that I was so callous or indifferent to these lives, but rather I felt a great respect for animals and could not stand to see them suffer. This had come to wear on me and I wiped a tear away as I looked down into the pitiful brown eyes of the suffering dog. "Sorry!" I whispered as I gently touched the muzzle of the rifle to the soft forehead of the family pet. She slipped quickly away as the report of the gun signaled the end of her intense suffering. I wiped a tear as I returned the gun to its place behind the bedroom door, careful to conceal my tender feelings for the dog that I had never wanted. It would be awhile before I came across another accident as freak as this one. I would have to be more careful not to become attached to them the next time.

Lemonade Stand

The brothers gathered their camping gear into neat little piles on the living room floor, excited to be heading for the mountains with their scout troop. I had long since moved out of the house since I was married with young children, but was visiting for Sunday dinner and had become amused by the enthusiasm of my younger brothers. We had grown up in the remote area near the Eagle Cap Wilderness Area in Eastern Oregon's Wallowa Mountains (and now lived near Spokane WA), so they were excited to guide their new troop to this wilderness wonderland of high snow capped peaks for the summer's fifty mile hike. They had begged me to come along, but I had insisted that my work schedule would not allow me to take the time off. What they didn't know was, that I had secretly planned to ambush them somewhere along their long trek.

"So, where are you going to go exactly?" I had quizzed them, trying to assess what their intended route would be. They had recited their itinary in detail as I nodded with approval at their explanation. "That should be a very fun trip over some really neat country!" I explained confidently. "Now you know that when you cross over the backside of Hawkins Pass, there is a lemonade stand there?" I teased. "Right!" my brother Marc retorted. "Jimmy, you are so full of it!" he continued to scold. "No really! It's been there for years and is maintained by the Forest Service." I fibbed. The four young teenagers didn't really believe me, but the seed of doubt was planted and I had accomplished my goal.

The day came for the trip and we waved goodbye to the departing caravan of anxious Boy Scouts and leaders. It would be a long drive to the starting point on the south side of the wilderness where they would begin their adventure. Little did they know that they would get a big surprise about mid-week. My wife and I planned to leave several days later and would travel from the opposite side of the mountain range in order to beat them to the appointed ambush site. I mixed the strong yellow lemonade in the gallon jug and loaded it into my heavy pack.

We arrived at Wallowa Lake at the exact time we had planned and started our trudge up the long winding trail. We traveled at a quick pace, motivated by the anticipation of their surprised looks when they came over the tall peak and saw the lemonade stand in the very spot that I had indicated. The trail was long and hard and we began to realize that we may have over estimated our endurance level. After several long breaks we had become rejuvenated enough to continue the marathon up the trail.

I could see the bobbing dark figures as the first group of weary travelers peaked the top of Hawkins Pass far up the mountain from our location. I realized that I would never make it to the top as I had planned without being seen, so I ran up the trail a ways and placed the jug on the side of the trail. I quickly scribbled, "Free Lemonade"on the side of the plastic jug, then hustled back down the mountain to lie in wait. I barely made it to our hiding spot, when the frazzled group arrived at the makeshift lemonade stand.

We lay hidden in the group of short alpine spruce trees, giggling with excitement at our brilliant plan. The puzzled look on my brother's sweaty face was a sight to behold. He had been the first to arrive, traveling well ahead of the slower hikers and now stood looking around, bewildered at the sight of the lemonade. He had remembered my comments, but now had become a believer. He started back down the trail, shaking his head, wondering who could have placed the jug in that remote location. As he approached our hideout, we jumped from our cover to surprise him. He stood for a moment, totally freaked out that we could be in that place, far from nowhere. He recovered quickly from being startled and decided to enhance the experience for the younger of the four siblings on the trip, by running the lemonade jug further up the long switch backs before they saw who had placed it there. The prank was a complete success. The surprised but extremely weary travelers could not comprehend why someone would go to such extremes just to play a practical joke at their expense. Now when

I make some bizarre claim, they pay attention, wondering if I'm joking or telling the truth. "There's a secret tunnel through the mountain that could save you about a day's hike if you can find the entrance," I tease. "Maybe it could be true! You never know!" I can tell by the look on their faces, that the lemonade stand has kept them wondering.

I Do It All The Time!

Most of the time our lives are pretty normal and even mundane, which is probably why we like the TV programs that show just the highlights. It is non-stop action showing only the best performances. It doesn't happen very often, but when one of these highlight performances happens to me, it usually ends up as one of my stories that is told over and over again until it is sufficiently polished. On occasion, I am lucky enough to have someone else witness one of these unusual events, and in that case my standard reply to their "great job!", or "what a great shot!", is to just declare in a matter-of-fact voice, "I do it all the time!" If I'm extremely lucky, the person witnessing the event would be a new friend or a greenhorn that would then spread the story around giving it extra life. This usually works pretty well until one of my regular hunting partners gets wind of the story and puts a prospective on the story that generally lowers my hero status a couple of notches.

One day I was in the company of a couple of young men who were both hunters, but because they were currently serving a religious mission for their church, were unable to hunt and in-fact were bound by the rules of their mission not to hold or discharge a firearm. I mentioned that I was going to go for an evening road hunt for grouse that evening which happened to be their day off. They excitedly requested that they be allowed to tag along just for the ride and for the change of pace, which I heartily agreed to.

The time came to leave and I loaded my faithful Brittany into the bed of the pickup and we all climbed in and headed for the woods. Evening hunts for grouse along established roadbeds, have been a favorite pastime for me since it allows me to get out of the house for brief hunts when there isn't time to do a real hunt. As we bumped slowly along the old logging roads looking for even a glimpse of a grouse, I continued to recite my favorite hunting stories, giving my passengers a non-stop highlight version of a lifetime of hunting. The young impressionable green horns seemed to take it all in, not realizing that hunting is usually tedious and only occasionally sprinkled with highlights. As we rounded the next bend in the rough roadway, a grouse raced for the safety of cover and we skidded to a stop. Little did I know that what was to happen next would be one of those highlight performances that I had been telling them about. It would come with impeccable timing and would serve to solidify in these young minds that everything I had been telling them must be true.

I quickly slid a shell into my reliable old Remington 12 gauge, and called for my dog Shasta to "git the bird." The experienced Brittany was already out of the truck and had instantly located the now-hidden-bird. It was our practice to point and flush these spooky birds in order to get a shot on the fly rather than to shot them on the ground, and this was to be no exception. The excited hunting dog immediately locked up in a classic stiff point. Her trembling stub of a tail was the only indication of her waivering restraint, which allowed me to approach the bird before it flew. The elusive ruffed grouse exploded from the roadside cover (which can give even the most seasoned hunter a mild heart attack if you don't know it's coming), rising high enough to clear the embankment, then sailed like a bullet for the cover of a bushy cedar tree. Without thinking and in one fluid motion, I quickly raised the shotgun to my shoulder, pulling the trigger just as the grouse reached the cover that it sought so desperately. The grouse dropped to the ground with a thud along with a couple of the green branches that were to be it's new hiding place. The well trained dog which had never taken her eyes off the prey, raced quickly on cue, to retrieve the tasty mountain poultry, then dropped it at my feet as if to say, "Let's go get another one!"

My enthralled companions who had watched the whole event with intent interest, were just barely stepping out of the truck when they exclaimed in unison, "Wow! That was a great shot and a great point and retrieve!" "Ya, know." was my practiced reply. "I do it all the time!"

You see, it is important to sound thoroughly convincing, even at the risk of sounding a bit cocky if you are going to convince people that you are for real. If you hunt often enough, you are bound to accumulate enough highlights during the course of your life to assure that "all the time" is only a slight embellishment of the truth.

Another such event occurred while on a horse back trip to the Salmo Wilderness in northeastern Washington. I and several green horn companions had packed into the Leola Creek area and had taken a short day trip along Crowell Ridge looking for an acceptable mulie buck. My new friend Scott had tagged along with no expectations other than having a good time and seeing some new country. As we traveled up the worn mountain trail which led out of the thick timber into the high alpine meadows and craggy peaks towards Crowell Ridge, I spotted a large blue grouse about twenty yards ahead, perched innocently in a clump of grass at the edge of the winding path. Quickly baling off my steady mount, I slid the peep-sighted .300 Savage out of the rifle scabbard and dropped to one knee. "Watch this!" I said, hopeful that this would be a 'highlight' moment. "You're not going to shoot it with that gun are you?" Scott said doubtfully. "You'll blow it to bits!" he exclaimed confidently. "Nah, I'll just shoot it in the neck and slit it's throat!" I said with an air of cockiness. "Really?" he asked, knowing that I must really be putting him on. "Watch." I said again, as I steadied the worn rifle on my raised knee and squeezed off a shot. "Got him!" he exclaimed. "But is there anything left?" he continued skeptically. I walked over to the plump dum-dum bird which was still flopping around, picked it up by it's furry legs and returned to my companions. "Check it out!" I said with glee. "You really did slit it's throat, didn't you?" Scott exclaimed with disbelief. "I do it all the time!" I announced confidently, all the while wondering how long it would be before the next 'highlight moment' came along.

Skunk in the Backseat

The phone clicked as I set it down and went back to sit down at the family dinner table. "Who was it?" asked my mother. "It was the neighbor, she wants me to come over sometime and trap some of the skunks that are living under her barn," I explained soberly. I had gained somewhat of a reputation in the neighborhood because of my trapping skills. I had already eliminated several skunks for the neighbor to the south and the news must have spread fast. There had been a large family of skunks living in the area and they had taken up residence under Mrs. Barnhart's old barn. "I'll go over there tomorrow after practice," I mumbled with a mouth full of food. I wiped my chin with the back of my hand as I thoughtfully planned a strategy.

Several days later the skunk family had been eliminated with a combination of traps and the old, .22 slug-in-the-eyeball trick. I would wait till dark, then shine the light under the back edge of the barn. When the shiny little beady eyes would show up in the dark, I would shoot them with the .22 rifle. The disadvantage of that strategy was that it was difficult, if not impossible, to retrieve the dead carcass, which meant that the poor little old lady would have to grin and bear it until the carcass had decomposed enough not to smell anymore. One of the skunks, a large one, had fallen for my bait and trap method, and now lay in the bushes dead. My job was done here.

The next day was the homecoming dance and I was without a date, since I had broken up with my girlfriend the day before. "I won't go out with anyone for a long time!" she sobbed in reply to my comment that she would find someone really fast. "It's just that I'm not interested in going with just one girl," I tried to explain. "You are a very beautiful girl, but I'm not ready for anything this steady!" I continued to stick my foot in my mouth. She walked away down the long sidewalk toward her home, wringing her slender soft hands and crying the whole way. "Boy, what a dummy I am," I sighed as I watched her cute figure walk away for the last time. "Nah, I'm better off this way!" I assured myself. "She would have gotten me into trouble for sure."

The evening of the dance approached and I made a trip by the school just for kicks to see whose car's were there and who was actually at the dance. Normally I was quite a social bug, but for some reason, I didn't have the stomach for it this time. I walked into the dance and saw my x-girl friend sitting there cuddled up next to my worst enemy. She was already looking very cozy there in his arms, but really played it up when she saw me walk through the door of the gym. "Sure, she won't go out with anyone for a long time!" I thought angrily. "She is just rubbing it in and trying to get even with me!" The long haired, redheaded jerk who was a year younger than I in school now thought that he really had hit the jackpot. She was getting even with me and he had an instant honey, that seemed to really like him. I ducked out the door with clenched fist and jaw, thinking about revenge, even though I had been the cause of the soap-opera-like exchange of hurt feelings. I jumped into the passenger side of the Chevy pickup and said to the driver, "Let's get out of here!"

We peeled out of the graveled student parking lot, leaving a cloud of dust behind. "Hey, isn't that his car?" I blurted out. "I have a great idea!" We drove away to the skunk graveyard to collect our latest victim. Mark, the driver, was the grandson of the little lady next door and had been hanging around with me since I had been placed in charge of the skunk extermination duties. "It's still frozen solid!" he exclaimed as he tapped the freshly killed carcass with the shovel. It had lain there in the grass overnight where we had left it and had frozen in the chill of the fall evening. We giggled with glee at our horribly devious plot. "He would never know who did it," we reasoned together. "It doesn't even smell bad," I thought. "Too bad we couldn't make it spray!" I laughed.

The parking lot was empty since the dance was now in full swing, as we pulled back into the dimly lit lot and stopped behind the jerk's polished car. "Hey! The back door is open!" I whispered loudly. "Hold it open and I'll huck it in!" I scooped the black and white pole cat onto the shovel and balanced it there while I shuttled over to the open door. I dropped the half-frozen skunk carcass directly in the middle of the plush back seat. "Guess that will teach the S.O.B.!" I muttered under my breath without even a twinge of remorse. "Hurry before someone sees us!" I hissed to the giggling driver. I looked out the rear window of the half-ton pickup to make sure no one saw us drive away. "Yessssss! We actually did it!" I yelled with glee, while rubbing my hands together.

The jerk pulled up along side me the next night in the parking lot of my family's grocery store, accusing me of the atrocity, while tapping the baseball bat that sat in the gun rack of his friend's pickup. "What skunk?" I said mockingly. I walked over to the truck window and grabbed the under-class-men by the collar of his red lettermen's jacket, pulling him nearly out of the open window. "You'd better use that bat, if you want to have half a chance!" I hissed, as I shoved him back inside the window. "Where is your fancy car?" I asked mockingly. "You say someone put a skunk in the backseat?" "What a mean thing to do!" I said sincerely as I climbed back into my car and drove away. I don't know if I ever saw the jerk again, or my old girl friend for that matter. It has been years later and I do feel a bit of guilt, for putting that skunk on his nice back seat,... but not really!

Sleep Walk

The leaded glass in the front door of the big two story house rattled as I opened the door and walked inside. "Oh, it's just you!" exclaimed my dad, who had been hiding behind the door with a baseball bat. "What are you doing outside at 2 a.m. in your underwear?" he asked with a puzzled grin. "Guess I was sleep walking again!" I whispered sheepishly as I looked at the floor and hurried off to bed.

This wasn't the first time I had been caught sleep walking, but one of the most embarrassing. Evidently, I had walked out of the house and down the street until I had reached the street corner and woke up. There I stood under the street light, all alone in nothing but my whitey tighties. It was kind of like some of the dreams I'd had, only it was the real thing! (I wish I could act out the one in which I can flap my arms and fly!) When the full realization of what had happened hit me between the eyes, I raced as fast as my tender bare feet would carry me, the full block down the street to my house. My dad had heard the door rattling as I struggled to get back in and had hid behind the door to ambush the burglar.

That story happened when I was a young man of tender age, but it certainly wouldn't be the last time I would have adventures in my sleep! After I had been married for ten years or so and was the father of several children, my wife and I had decided to move out of the town we lived in to get out onto the twenty-three acre parcel of land we had owned for several years. We had purchased a modest single wide mobile home, in which we would live until the home we were building could be completed.

Our bedroom was on the end of the long home and was situated towards the driveway and the garden space.

One night, I awoke with a start and realized that I had been dreaming and had not only been sleep walking, but was having an interactive dream and sleep walk with my dear wife. I stood at the built-in dresser by the now shattered window, with blood dripping down my arms, trembling from the exertion of what had just happened and listening to the deer snort at me from the shadows of the corn patch just outside. The crisp night air had awakened me completely and had cleared my head. I sat down on the bed next to my groggy wife to figure out what in the heck had just transpired.

We finally put the pieces of the puzzle together and then had a long laugh together. She had been dreaming that a man was trying to get into the house and that he was peering into the bedroom window that was now mostly missing. In her dream and sleep walking mode, she had sat up and yelled to me that "there is a man looking in the window!" I had heard her in my sleep and had approached the window with the vision of a man standing there. I had punched the man in the face with both hands, shattering the window, and the dream. I then had stood there shaking until I had snapped back to consciousness. "What a nightmare!" she said, as we cuddled together and laughed, embarrassed that we were both so weird.

Several of our children have had bouts with the same malady, much to our amusement. The other night one of our children who had fallen asleep on the couch while watching television, awoke with a start and began to babble in a sleep walking stupor. We looked at each other and laughed. "Sleep walk!" we both chime in, as we look at each other with a knowing grin. "They must take after your side of the family!"

Beulah Goes To Hell

"She's a young one, but going to be a good one!" said Bishop Deakins, the pastor of our local congregation. As I eyed the lanky four-year old mule over the pole fence, my mind was focused on the fact that the asking price was only four-hundred dollars for this fine figure of a half-ass. "I just don't have the time to invest in her and it wouldn't be fair for me to keep her," repeated the Bishop. "Sold!" said I, and shook hands to consummate the deal. Several days later, while backing up the horse trailer to the corral, I saw in the rear-view mirror the struggling clergyman attempting to lead the reluctant half-breed towards the trailer. After multiple attempts to get the stubborn beast to enter the confines of the trailer, all four feet and head and tail were finally loaded, so I slammed the door, emptied my wallet and headed for home.

The ensuing months went by fast as the time was spent trying to outwit this halter-shy escape artist. The next foreshadowing of impending trouble was the full day spent trying to put the pack saddle on Beulah the mule, as the trusted clergy had dubbed her. She was as allergic to that pad and saddle as I was to squash and cooked carrots. The next couple of months gave me hope as Beulah progressed under saddle and became a moderately good pack animal. Several trips to the wilderness had finally convinced me that the Bishop might be right about this spoiled daughter of a thoroughbred. The day finally came for a long anticipated hunting trip to the mountains of Eastern Oregon. Beulah had progressed to the point that I felt she could make the trip in fine style.

After the long journey to the trail head, we loaded the animals and headed up the Kettle Creek Trail. The repetitive switch-backs of this hot, dusty trail began to wear on human and beast alike, since we had packed more than was originally planned. Instead of riding, I was forced to walk and pack my riding horse. Somewhere near the top of the mountain, Beulah decided that she had enough. She went on a strike as stubborn as the local teachers union and would not budge. The only way to get her to move was to load all of the stuff on another animal and proceed with her in tow.

After ten days of leisure, it came time to load up and head for the truck. Beulah was the first to be loaded and waited patiently while we loaded the camp supplies and elk quarters on the other pack animals. Beulah and I started out down the trail in the lead and traveled down the trail several hundred yards when the first explosion happened. By the time the dust settled I realized that my arm was still in it's socket, but that the pack and it's contents had been bucked off and trampled on by this devil-of-a-mule. I snubbed her up to a fir tree and began the process of picking up the gear and the pieces of the pack saddle to piece back together.

To make a long story shorter, this process happened again, and again, and again, each time I stayed calm and tried everything short of exorcism to calm this troubled beast. The last attempt at loading my now tattered belongings ended with a still defiant, loco mule and a bloodied, torn and furious owner. I said to my brother Joel, who had stayed behind to watch the rodeo, "go to the truck and bring back my horses and the .44 Magnum." I settled in for the long wait on the remnants of my sleeping pad and figured that by the time he returned, the mule would be ready to at least go to the truck empty. I untied her to see if she would travel to the trailer to be with the other horses. Nothing doing! She was not going to leave that mountain!

When the wearied messenger had returned with my previous wishes, and after attempting another loading of the packs, I decided that Beulah would not be returning to the heavenly pastures of home. With one slightly off-centered, forty-four-caliber sized hole in her forehead, I sent Beulah the mule to hell. Her bones have been a landmark in the trail to our elk camp ever since. We never forget to tip our hats to Beulah as we ride by on less stubborn critters than she. My hope is to never see Beulah again, though there are some that think I might!

Long Walk Home

Earth life is filled with a variety of experiences, seemingly designed by Deity to give us happiness and joy, along with the tests and fiery trials that stretch us to the limit of our endurance. Some days are black like a descending thunder storm, making us wonder and think about the realities of life and yearn for the sunshine. This grim story is about one of those days. While cemented in my memory, it is an event that one would rather forget than remember. With the passage of time, some of the hurt has faded and it has become a story worth telling, if only for the historical value.

The horses and riders jogged down the road away from the confines of the truck and trailer, excited for the adventures of the day. The crisp fall air smelled of decaying leaves, revealing that the change of seasons was well on it's way, with summer giving way to fall, yet still keeping old man winter at bay. The sound of clattery hoofs soon settled into a rhythmic cadence, interrupted only by the occasional chatter of the alert hunters who had ventured here to this 'no motorized vehicle zone,' to get away from the usual heavy weekend rush, that would happen in the more accessible locations.

Denny was the more experienced of the trio, which is really just a nice way of saying that he was the old guy. I and my full-grown son (that means he's bigger than I), Brandon, had decided to accompany him for a day of horseback riding, under the guise of looking for elk and doing a little deer hunting from horseback. Even though I didn't have a rifle tag for deer, I carried my trusty 30-06 Browning in the rifle scabbard, just in case a bear or cougar would dare to make an appearance. I carried tags for both, knowing that the chance of seeing one was slim, but glad that it gave me the excuse to pack a weapon.

The day remained rather gloomy, which later would prove to be the foreshadowing of the day's events. The air had been chilly that morning, but we soon peeled our outer jackets as the day progressed and the temperature rose to a more comfortable level. After stopping for a brief break to stretch our saddle weary legs, we continued our search for any sign of the elusive animals we would be hunting later in the season. Our travels led us to the timbered ridge between Boyer Mountain and Nelson Peak and then onward to the top of Nelson where we paused again for lunch to enjoy the panoramic view from our mountain top perch. After conversing about a possible route off the mountain, we had decided to drop abruptly off the top of the peak to the south, traversing cross-country until we reached the logging road far below us. That decision would later come back to haunt us.

The going was tough as we progressed down the steep incline over the deadfall caused by the aftermath of a recent logging operation. We struggled to pick our way through the tangled mess, while becoming more apprehensive about the path we had chosen. We breathed a sigh of relief when we finally reached the road, knowing that the hard part was over and we had been lucky to have escaped without incident. Our confidence was short lived however, as we soon departed the main road again, looking for a more direct route to a road that we knew would return us to our original point of beginning, and began to encounter conditions similar to the hillside above us. As we continued to pick our way through the slash piles and logging debris, we soon gained sight of the road which had been our goal when we left the top of the mountain. Encouraged by our progress, we prodded our sure-footed mounts onward toward the landing below.

After taking the lead to navigate across a small water course that bubbled intermittently down the now gentle slope, I soon realized that I might have made a mistake in plotting this particular course. As my big gelding stubbled across the marshy terrain of the small spring, which was made even more treacherous by the scattered logging slash, he suddenly sank to his belly in the muck, frantically lounging until he could obtain solid footing on the other side of the slight seepage. "Watch yourself!" I warned sternly, as I turned in the saddle to look back at my companions and realized that it was too late for Denny. He had already started across and had become entangled in the mess of mud and sticks. His normally sure-footed horse had turned back for the other side while floundering to free himself from the slimy bog. He strained for the other side and lost his balance, rolling to his side on top of his now unseated rider. The big horse struggled to regain his footing, flopping back and forth violently, which gave Denny the opportunity to dislodge his pinned leg and roll to safety. I looked on with helpless horror as the incident unfolded, convinced that neither would escape without injury. I stepped off my horse to assess the damage and was relieved to see that both horse and rider had returned to their feet and appeared to be okay. "We're all right!" assured the burly cowboy, who had escaped many prior close calls without permanent injury. The muddy horse shook himself as the pedestrian cowboy gathered the reins and began leading the horse in a safer direction than I had chosen.

Satisfied that my partner was okay, I turned, with reins in hand and picked my way on foot through the tangle of broken limbs down the hill toward the log landing on the road below. After reaching the landing, I checked the horse over to assure that he had escaped the bog without injury. The urgent call from the hill above jerked me to attention as I struggled to understand the words from the hill above. "Jim, I have a problem! My horse is bleeding really badly!" yelled Denny with urgency. Thinking that he had been cut or scraped by a stick during the prior incident in the mud hole, I hollered for him to bring the injured horse to the log landing so that we could examine him to assess his condition. "He's hurt real bad!" came the frantic response. The tough outdoorsman appeared visibly rattled as they slid down the embankment onto the level road bed. Brandon followed quickly indicating his assessment of the grim situation. "His guts are coming out!" cried Denny with a helpless tone. I dropped the reins of my horse and rushed to help my disturbed companion.

The horse had escaped the incident at the bog totally unscathed, but on the short trip down the hill afterwards had stepped on a long, stout stick which had then flipped up into his groin, startling him. As he lounged forward in fright, the stick had impaled him and portions of his guts had immediately dropped out of the gaping hole. Our panic-stricken faces mirrored the antics of the frightened quarter horse, as he tossed his head and groaned in pain. Blood continued to pour from the sickening wound as we struggled to decide how we could save the poor critter from this awful fate. What seemed like eternity, must have been only a couple of minutes, as the tragic episode unfolded.

Denny quickly unfastened and removed the saddle, hoping to relief the pressure of the cinch, while I struggled to control the distraught animal by clinging tightly to the halter. The hanging mess slapped his blood drenched legs, as the wormlike grey intestines dropped closer to the ground with each frantic movement. "Maybe we can stuff the guts back in the hole, cram a coat there, and fasten a cinch to hold it all in place until we can get a trailer in here to haul him out," I said with hopefulness. Denny gagged as he attempted the messy chore, quickly realizing that it was not only a smelly job, but a futile effort and that the large critter was bleeding to death from a severed artery. Moaning with helpless disbelief that this was really happening, we both concluded that there was only one alternative. "He's got to be put down now!" I blurted. "He's in a lot of pain and we need to put him out of his misery!" I continued in my efforts to convince the shocked cowboy, who already knew what needed to be done. "I can't do it!" he sputtered, shaking his head with disbelief that this was happening. His quivering voice betrayed his toughness, as we watched the poor beast stagger to a standstill with feet splayed outward to steady himself. The horse moaned and lowered his head, resigned to his fate as I walked to my bewildered mount and removed the rifle from the well-oiled scabbard. Denny patted the old rodeo horse on the neck, as if to say goodbye to an old friend, and turned away. He cringed slightly as the loud report of the large caliber rifle signified the end to the animals suffering. The large animal dropped lifelessly to the ground and laid still.

We stood with heads down in total silence for several minutes, stunned by the graphic and tragic death of this magnificent animal. "It was a freak accident," I said, breaking the long silence. "It couldn't have been helped!" I continued in my efforts to console my still-stunned partner. He nodded in agreement, then shook his head sideways, still in total disbelief at the misfortune that had happened so quickly. In just a matter of minutes this fine specimen had gone from a living, vibrant animal to the disemboweled carcass sprawled across the dirt road.

We loaded the saddle and bridle on top of the saddle of one of the other horses and started walking the six miles back toward the truck in total, stunned silence. Denny held back a little, reluctantly emotional, as he plodded along behind us with his head down. It would be a long walk home.

Raisins For Lunch

My good friend Alan, is truly a good sport and is game for about any outdoor activity even if it puts him a little out of his normal comfort zone. He loves to hunt, but his experience prior to this story had been limited to activities somewhere near the four-wheeler or the truck. This particular year several of us had decided to make an extended horse pack trip into an area of wilderness that none of us had ventured to before. Alan was excited to go! It had been years since he had been on a horse and years since he had been that deep in any woods.

Our friendship was still in the beginning stages which allowed me to periodically pull the wool over his eyes, since he hadn't quite learned yet, that there was a prank around every corner when he was with me. His naive, trusting personality hadn't developed a thick enough skin yet to be fully protected from my shenanigans, and so, I had been laying the early ground work for a delightful prank, weeks before I actually sprang the trap.

I had been telling him how good of a tracker I had become and that in fact, I was about as good as anyone had ever been at that game. Every time the subject came up in the weeks prior to this big hunting trip, I would mention some fact about tracking that would keep him thinking about it for several days. I had told him that I could tell how old deer droppings were by plopping them into my mouth and tasting them. He didn't really seem to believe that one, but I could tell by his doubtful countenance that he really wasn't sure if I was joking or not.

The day came for the trip and we traveled several hours from home and packed deep into the Pasayten Wilderness. After a few days of non-productive hunting, I had been able to plan my method of attack fairly easily since Alan's method of hunting from the safety of camp had allowed me to pinpoint his movements for most of the day. That day, I made a short loop in a half-hearted hunt, and then uncharacteristically found my way back into camp before the lunch hour. As I had suspected, Alan had beat me back to camp and was in the process of hobbling a horse. I decided that I should see how alert he was to his environment and began a short sneak to hone my stalking skills.

After a careful stalk, I was able to observe some of his personal skills (like nose picking) that I had not previously had the pleasure of observing. Finally, tired of the boring antics of my prey, I sprang from my hiding place hollering like a banshee, which I learned may not be such a good idea when you are that far from a defibbulator and a heart surgeon. After his recovery from his slight heart attack, I chronicled my activities of that morning, all the while making a big deal out of the different ages of droppings that I had observed and of course had tasted in order to be sure exactly when the deer had passed by. With a hint of resentment for my previous scare, he emphatically protested the validity of my statements as he said, "Oh, bull Palmer! You are so full of it!" "You are always feeding me such baloney!"he snorted! I quickly countered with, "I'll show you!"

As I walked a short distance from him to a place that I had previously discovered deer pellets, I secretly emptied most of the contents of a bag of scrumptious Raisinettes (chocolate covered raisins) into my cupped hand and bent as if to pick up what convincingly appeared to be real deer droppings. As I held the hand full of pretend deer droppings for him to plainly see, his once doubtful, almost irritated look, began to change to the sober face of a reluctant convert. "See... watch this! These look like they are few days old, but one must check to be sure!" His eyes grew wider as my hand raised to my mouth and my lips enveloped the shiny little fake turds. "No! No,...you didn't really..." he stared wide eyed with disbelief. Like a freckled faced grade school jester sucumbing to a lunch room dare, I opened my mouth wide to reveal the dark chocolate mess, that he now assumed, was used deer feed. "Oh my gosh! I can't believe you really..." He shook his head with disbelief like he had just seen his first pair of girls underwear. "You see, by chewing them properly, you can tell what the age is, almost down to the hour," I soberly added. "You don't have to swallow of course…" I muttered as I turned and feigned spitting, to hide the fact that I was valiantly struggling to control my sobs of laughter. "Palmer, I never would have believed it, if I had not seen it! I thought you were just yanking my chain this whole time!" he exclaimed with a sense of relief, convinced that I really must be a stand up guy after all. I waited to come clean for just the right moment.

We puttered around camp for the rest of the afternoon, and periodically he would mutter something like, "I can't believe you really did it! You really are a true mountain man tracker!" As the other hunters straggled back into camp they began their narrative of the events of the day. Eventually Alan got around to the tail of his conversion to my tracking methods. The other more skeptical and seasoned hunters, not knowing that I had previously planned this charade, began to snicker at his innocence. I put my arm on his shoulder and offered him the remnants of the bag of sweets that had helped to deceive him. "Oh, my gosh!" He grinned from ear to ear as he walked away shaking his head. "Raisinettes! Dang! I should have known!"

Most of the memories of that trip have faded, but even to this day, I don't have to say much to revive his memory of that embarrassing prank. "Raisinettes?" I quietly offer. His sheepish look is enough to know that the memory is still sensitive.

Out Cold

If there is a statute of limitations for doing dumb things, I'm hoping that it has expired so that I can tell you this story with getting in too much trouble. As an avid archer I am always looking for new ideas and new targets in order to increase my skill level and bring some excitement and challenge into the practice routine. The normal dull practice round consists of shooting arrows at a stationary target from 20,30 and 40 yard increments. This rather boring practice can be enhanced by competition with a fellow archer, or better yet a 3-D shoot with full life-sized targets, but the really fun method of honing one's archery and hunting skills, is to shoot at real live animals. This poses a rather difficult problem during the off season when shooting an animal would be illegal.

The invention of a little gadget called the rubber blunt has allowed me to cheat the system a bit and hunt without killing. Big, fat range cows are always a favorite target since they usually stand and take multiple hits, seemingly unaffected by the whack to their ribs by my rubber tipped 2216 Easton arrows. The next time you are eating ribs at the Long Horn Barbeque and you comment on the extremely tender ribs, you may have me to thank! Fellow archers have concluded that one must be selective in the types of targets to receive this thumping, since one careless Robin Hood sent his thin-skinned horse to the vet when his normally harmless blunting actually pierced the skin of the hay burner.

Many opportunities to fling blunted arrows at deer and elk and the occasional dim witted moose, have presented themselves through the years and I must confess that I have reaped a great deal of pleasure from that real life practice. In my warped sense of judgement, I have justified this practice since I figure that it gives the animals a lesson that may help them to escape a similar, but lethal fate at some future date. This story is about one of those times when I have questioned the wisdom of participating in this habit.

My good friend John and I had stayed an extra day in order to add some additional hunting time to a trip we had just taken into a favorite wilderness area. After we had packed out the two deer that Stan and I had harvested, we decided that if John and I stuck around for an extra day it might be possible to fill his remaining out-of-state deer tag. The plan was simple. Take a short evening hunt on horseback, then spend the night at the truck, hunt for several hours the following morning and head for home. I carried my well seasoned compound bow, since I still had a bear tag, as I rode along with John that evening through an area teaming with deer.

We rode abreast for awhile as we followed an old mining road up a cool, rocky canyon, then went single file as the trail narrowed to accommodate less traffic. We had seen many deer on the trip up the rugged draw, but had not seen any antlers. The trail eventually faded out, so we decided to turn around and start the trip back towards the truck. Soon after, I spotted a big, fat mulie doe standing near the trail below us. The next switchback would bring us to that location in a couple hundred yards, though from my perspective it was only about 50 yards to the unsuspecting deer.

Like a mischievious teenager looking for trouble, I stepped off my mountain pony and brought my blunted arrow to full draw. John had advanced several hundred yards in front of me, and was heading straight towards the doe, with a full view of her body, though he could not see what I was doing. I calculated the yardage and let it fly!

Guessing yardage under a variety of conditions is the down fall of many a would be Nimrod. Getting it wrong usually only leaves you empty handed and frustrated. I had aimed at a spot behind the front shoulder, but quickly realized as I watched the arrow's trajectory, that I may have shot a bit high. The arrow struck the unsuspecting critter right on the top of the head and dead center between her big floppy ears. She dropped like a sack of spuds without even a twitch to reveal that there was still life there. With horror, I said out loud to myself, "Oh no!,… Ohhhh, noooo! I killed her dead!"

By that time, John was approaching the lifeless deer, having seen her drop to the ground, after hearing the distinct thwack of the bow string. He said with a slight hint of disgust, "Ya killed her Palmer! Ya killed her!" I bounded into the saddle and raced down the switchback to the site of the assassination, all the while thinking of how I was going to explain this one to the game warden.

I pulled up behind John just in time to watch the once dead doe clamber to her feet, shake and stretch like she had just woken up, and walk away. "Whew!" I sighed. "Thought I'd killed her." She had been knocked out cold, like a stooge in the first round of an Ali fight. "Yep! Out like a light!" said John as he scratched his chin and shook his head. We both laughed nervously as we started our ponies towards the truck. With a regretful sigh I thought, "She's gonna need some aspirin in the morning!"

Mike's Pet Deer

Most people have a hard time getting close to anything in nature. My friend Mike seemed to take it a bit too far the other way. You should know up front that Mike is the kind of guy that is a magnet for disaster. If anyone could get hurt doing an activity it would be him, but he was always having fun.

One winter a small whitetail deer had gotten caught in the fence near his place on the mountain. When he discovered the terrified animal, he had attempted to free the poor exhausted creature. The strands of wire had become wound around its leg several times and in it's struggle to free itself, had only made it worse. When Mike got to the deer, it had practically severed it's hind leg at the joint, by repeatedly sawing it back and forth in it's vain attempt to escape this horrible trap. Since the wound was so bad, Mike concluded that the only way to free the deer would be to amputate it's tightly pinned leg. He decided that in order for the little yearling to survive it would take some doing. He pulled the skin down around the bloody stub and stitched it up.

The chicken coop became the doe's home for the next couple of months, as it slowly gained strength and healed up from the awful injury. One day in mid-winter, after a cold storm had dropped several feet of fresh snow, I decided to make a visit to their place to take some photos of the confined deer close up. Since I was a budding wildlife photographer, it was an opportunity that seemed to good to be true and I was anxious to take advantage of it. Since the crowded pen didn't make a great outdoor backdrop, we coaxed the small whitetail out into the deep snow, convinced that she wouldn't be able to go far and that I could get some great close up shots.

I began exposing film and was careful to hide the fact that the this brown eyed doe only had three legs. I was sure that the finished product would convince viewers that I had spent hours in a blind or stalking the critter sort of like the National Geographic guys. The clicking of the camera spooked the deer, and sent her lunging down the ravine away from us. She had seen daylight after being cooped up for the long recovery and was anxious to return to her friends in the wild. It became immediately apparent that though she had moved a considerable distance through the thigh deep snow, her limited energy was already spent and she could easily become a meal for the first lucky predator to happen upon her if we did not intercede and quickly return her to the confines of the coop. A later release date would at least insure that she would be able to move about without the encumbrance of the deep snow.

Mike waddled down through the deep snow to grab her just as she caught her second wind. Finally after a flying tackle that would have made Lawrence Taylor proud, he was able to pin the deer down for long enough to gain control again. Not knowing what else to do to get her back up the steep hill to the barnyard, he threw her up across his broad shoulders and headed up the hill. I had watched this whole escapade with interest and had managed to snap a few photos in the mean time. As Mike crested the top of the hill and drew near to my location, the wild little sweetheart began an earnest attempt to escape again and began to thrash wildly while still atop my fearless friend.

"Help me! Dang it,….. are you going to help me?" he frantically exclaimed. "You're on your own!" I countered, as he continued to take a severe beating around the ears that could only be rivaled by a full round in the ring with the likes of Mike Tyson. Somehow I managed to document the hysterical situation by continuing to snap photos as I shook with laughter. His frantic screams for help continued until he finally dropped to his knees to dump his persistent attacker into the fluffy snow bank. Still not seeing the humor in his predicament, he rubbed his head, still smarting from the stinging blows and muttered something about the kind of friends that he had. He then scooped up the deer again, careful to control the dangerous flailing hooves, and deposited the 3 legged prisoner back into the chicken coop.

I guess that's why friends are so great, because you can laugh and mock them while they are taking the beating of a life time and they will forgive and move on. Mike's pet deer eventually moved back into the wild and was seen several months later in it's natural habitat, evidently fully adapted to life as a 3 legged deer.

Big Buck

"That's a good one!" commented my experienced father-in-law. "It may be a lot of years before you beat or match that one!" he said, nodding with approval. The big mulie buck hung in the garage of our home in the small quiet town of Deer Park. The skinned carcass stretched from the ceiling to the floor even though the legs had been removed from the knees down. "You should have seen the look on people's faces as I drove down the highway!" I exclaimed with a proud grin. "Their head would jerk around like it was being yanked by a rope!" I explained to the veteran hunter how the hunt had unfolded and how we had loaded the massive deer onto my little Ford Pinto station wagon.

I had backed up to a bank since the deer was so huge. The three of us had difficulty pulling the whole stiff carcass off the bank and up onto the rack of the little wagon. We tied it on and proceeded toward town. When we left the gravel road and started down the highway, we became aware that what we were carrying was creating a lot of attention. The gawkers strained to catch a good glimpse of the massive antlers which stood up almost thirty inches from the ski rack. The tail hung off the back of the car while the deer's nose could be seen creeping over the front windshield. I had to admit that it must have been quite a sight to see! Even an inexperienced hunter could tell that the buck was almost bigger than the car!

We had left for Woodward Meadows early that morning and had arrived at our destination well before daylight. We stood around stamping the frosty ground and rubbing our cold hands together while our frozen breath rose above our heads. I explained to the other two hunters (my brother and a childhood friend), that I had been here before and had killed several deer here. We would spread out about one hundred yards apart and slowing hunt up the tall ridge, staying on the southern exposure which was more open. We decided to rendezvous at about noon, when we would reassess our strategy and hunt back toward the car for an afternoon hunt.

We said our goodbye's and "good luck"and started the slow sneak up the timbered ridge. The southern slope was scattered with large yellow pine trees that had grown tall and fat, towering above the grassy openings and brushy draws. The early part of the hunt was rather uneventful, even though we were tense with anticipation, stopping to carefully listen as squirrels scampered or dropped pine cones from the tall trees. My little brother was on top of the ridge to my left and periodically checked in with a quiet whistle and a wave. He was the Buck Fever King and I could tell that the anticipation and excitement of the hunt had consumed him. He snuck along like the Elmer Fudd character in the Hanna Barbara cartoon, fully equipped with all of the hunting paraphernalia.

As we reached the top of the first little finger ridge with the grassy top, I paused for a few minutes to take care of some urgent and pressing business. When I was finished with the paperwork, I picked up my 30.06 rifle that had been propped up against a tree and immediately spotted a large deer who was walking up the next ridge over. As soon as I saw the thick, swollen neck on the massive deer, I could tell it was a buck. "The distance must be a little more than two hundred yards," I mumbled to myself while raising the familiar Browning rifle to my shoulder. "Boom!," went the report of the large caliber rifle. I had aimed at the top of the deer's back, thinking that the one-hundred-eighty grain bullet would drop a bit at that distance, but had obviously misjudged the yardage and quickly adjusted. Boom, went the second shot, immediately after the first. The deer humped up as the shot found its mark and he disappeared from view.

My little brother had been watching me since I had reappeared from behind my makeshift outhouse and thought that I was shooting that fast just to tease him. He yelled down the hill to see if I was joking or if I had actually been shooting at a deer. "I got him!" I exclaimed with a smug smile. "He is a dandy too!" I said, smiling at the young boy, who was more excited than I was. "Let's go up and see if we can find him," I said while putting the gun back on safety.

When we finally got to the fallen deer, I straddled his wide body and grasped the antlers with both hands, exclaiming with wonder, "Wow! Look at that! He is huge!" We stood for a while just poking and prodding and running our hands up and down the wide set antlers, enjoying the excitement of the successful hunt. We weren't too eager for the work to start, knowing that it would be a long drag to the road down the thick brushy draw. We finally settled into the work mode, gutting the musky smelling buck that was obviously in full rut. It became immediately apparent that it would be a long day, since dragging the heavy carcass was about the same as dragging a horse. We grunted and strained while pulling the deer down the gentle slope, pausing only to catch a breath and wipe the sweat from our eyes. We toiled for several hours until we finally came to the old skid trail that the wood cutters had pioneered through the thick cedars. "I think I can drive my little car back in here!" I said optimistically, not sure if the low-rider would make it, without bottoming out.

I carefully steered the wood-paneled station wagon around stumps and through ditches, until I reached the spot where the big buck lay hidden. We struggled to load the heavy deer, tugging and grunting until it was securely attached to the ski rack. "Guess we wouldn't have fit it in the back of the wagon anyway," my brother said, fresh from his Hunter's Safety class where they had taught him not to flaunt the deer's head on top of a vehicle. "Guess not!" I said, glad that we had an excuse to display the trophy deer.

We drove a little slower down the highway with our precious load that made the Pinto wagon squat to the full capacity of its shocks and springs. Not slower because of the weight, but slower to allow the onlookers to catch an eye full as we paraded through the middle of town toward home. The heads continued to turn our direction as I pulled into the driveway, eager to show off my new prize.

Moose Magnet

The scruffy veteran grinned widely as he accepted my present and plopped the blue cap on his head. The large inscription was prominently displayed across the front of the stiff new baseball hat. "Moose Magnet" it read, in bright bold letters. We had just departed the closing office of the local attorney where I had acted as his realtor in purchasing a tract of land with a small cabin and I had given the hat as a parting gift. For some reason the local moose population had declared war on him which had caused me a great deal of amusement at his expense. He had recently had his second run-in with a female moose while walking his new property, and had been forced to take evasive action for the second time in the same year. His broad grin indicated his approval of the well earned title of "Moose Magnet".

His first run in with the awkward looking species had occurred the previous year near my home. He had been living down the road from me in a small camper until he could locate a place of his own. The land owners had invited him to "squat" for the summer on this vacant parcel and I had become aquainted with him sometime in the course of his stay there.

One day I noticed him hobbling around on crutches with a large white cast attached to his leg, so I pulled over to see how he was doing. He indicated that he had a broken leg caused by being trampled by a moose and began to tell me the story. He had obtained a small lawn tractor from someone which ran good but didn't have the mower still attached to it's undercarriage. He had been driving the tiny tractor up and down the road near our home that leads to a large tract of timber ground owned by the Boise Cascade Corporation. One evening as he was puttering up the dusty road toward the Boise gate, he was blind sided by a cow moose who evidently had perceived him as a threat. The riled mother moose proceeded to knock him from the tractor, fracturing his leg, and then stomped the little noisy tractor until it finally sputtered to a stop.

I could imagine what it must have looked like which brought a wide grin to my face as I listened intently to his tale. His bruised face and broken leg reminded me of the bandaged coyote from the old Road Runner Cartoons. "What did you do next?" I asked, trying not to laugh. It seemed rude at the time to be so amused at his misfortune, but the story had tickled my funny bone until I couldn't contain myself. I began to laugh uncontrollably while he paused for a moment, allowing me to get control of myself. He was rather encouraged by my amusement of his adventurous tale and began to embellish it a bit as he finished the story. He had been forced to hobble back to his humble residence without the mangled garden tractor, since the enraged moose had ruined it to the point that is wasn't driveable any longer. He had escaped to the safety of a nearby tree while he watched her snorting and stomping until she gave up and trotted into the woods. A nearby neighbor had come to his rescue and took him to the hospital. The little mangled tractor sat near his camper like a monument to his escapade. The tears of laughter had rolled down my blushing cheeks as his narration came to an end.

We laughed together again as he proudly perched his hat on his head.

Marc's Deer Hunt

The dampness of this cool October morning seemed to intensify the pungent outdoor aromas as my small companion and I crawled under the barbed wire fence to gain access to a parcel of land that was a proven whitetail deer haunt. It was a perfect morning to ambush an unsuspecting whitetail buck. I had been to this spot many times before, and by my previous successes, had been conditioned to believe that this excursion would be no different. The only variable to my previous hunts, was that my shadow, on this day, was my young brother Marc, who had insisted that he be allowed to come along on today's outing.

I held the bottom wire up as he wriggled his way underneath the sharp barbed wire. " Shhhhh!" I hissed, as his busy, adolescent feet trompled the pile of dry sticks next to me. " If you are going to come hunting with me, you are going to have to be real quiet"! His big blue eyes gazed up at me as he nodded in silence that he understood. "What a cute little bugger," I thought to myself as we continued our semi-silent stroll through the thick grove of fir trees.

Crunch, crunch! His clumsy little feet seemed to attract each and every available dry stick or leaf. "Maybe it would be better if you helped me by being sort of a bird dog," I whispered. "I will go up around that big grove of trees and sit down and in about 10 minutes you can start walking through this patch of woods towards my location." "That way you don't have to worry about being noisy and you can really help me out!"

I was sure that this inspired new strategy would work, and so continued to explain to him in a whisper, what was expected of him. "Just head that general direction in about 10 or 15 minutes and I will find you when you get here," I assured him. His worried look should have been enough to indicate that he was terrified to be alone, but my eagerness to try this new strategy seemed to make me oblivious to his doubtful posture. I patted him on the head reassuringly and headed for my stand on the other side of the dark woods. I sighed confidently as I slid to the ground next to a large tamarack to await the results of our ambush.

The time seemed to slip quickly away as my attentions were strained to detect even the slightest noise or movement. After about 45 minutes of waiting, I finally realized that my timid companion had not emerged from the thick woods. I rushed back to the spot that he would have originated from, hoping to find signs of his passage through the thicket. I found him standing there nervously, exactly where I had left him. When I asked why he had not traveled the short 100 yard distance to my stand, he replied that, "the woods awr too scawey and I didn't want to go thwough them!"

I smiled with mild frustration as I realized that this short jaunt, must have seemed like a mile through the dark woods in the Snow White fairy tale, to him! I don't know if Marc has ever been hunting since that day, but I'm sure that I won't forget his first hunt with me!

Pineapples and Hula Girls

The pomp and circumstance of the graduation ceremony came to an end as the forty-three graduates moved their tassels to the other side of their caps, signifying the end of twelve long years. At the end of the boring ceremony, the impatient and emotional crowd pressed closely, to congratulate their favorite graduates who stood lined up against the lockers down the long hall of the Pine-Eagle High School. The year was 1979, and I was one of those excited graduates who were about to be unleashed on the world. Some would be off to college and others out into the work force or military service, but I would be catching a plane the next day to fly to the Hawaiian Islands. Having never left the small town of Halfway, Oregon where I spent most of my life, it was exciting to think that I would be on a tropical island in less than twenty-four hours.

The tires of the big jetliner screeched as the plane lurched onto the long landing strip of the Honolulu Airport. I was grateful to finally be on the ground, since my equilibrium had been disrupted, making me queasy and uncomfortable. The muggy humidity and sweet smells of the tropical air, hit me in the face as I walked down the long walkway and entered the concourse of the busy airport. Several gorgeous island girls in grass skirts and bikini tops approached us and hung floral leis around our heads, officially welcoming us with a sweet "Aloha!" I smiled with excitement at the new sights and sounds of this international airport that seemed to be a melting pot for many cultures and types of people. The smell of the ocean wafted into the muggy concourse as I continued down the ramp toward the connecting flight to the little island of Lanai where I was to spend the next three months.

I was part of a group of teenage boys who had been hired by a mainland company called Youth Developmental Enterprises that had been supplying the Castle & Cook Foods company with laborers for the pineapple production on the small island. Many local natives also worked in the fields there, planting and harvesting the sweet fruits that grew on the prickly tall plants, but since there were never enough laborers available, we had arrived to fill the gap. Our small group boarded the small commuter plane and 'hopped' to the island of Lanai, which consisted of the little community of Lanai and was surrounded by acres and acres of pineapple fields in various stages of production. We rode from the tiny airport to our bunker-like dorm rooms in the back of a Castle & Cook pineapple truck with tall racks. I had signed on as a planter and my friend had been assigned as a picker. Since some of the fields we would be planting where not quite ready to go, I started out on a night crew as a picker.

The long boom of the conveyor belt, hung on the side of the big truck, which slowing crawled along the edge of the field, as we walked along behind picking the ripe fruit and dropping it onto the conveyor belt. We waded through the tall plants by the light of the bright boom lights, sweating and grunting as we examined the bushy plants for the ripe fruit, plucking it from its stem and tossing it ahead of us onto the moving conveyer belt.. Since the fields looked like a prime habitat for a variety of slithering creatures we always kept our eyes open, even though we had been informed that there are no snakes in Hawaii. An occasional rat could be seen scurrying down the long rows in front of us.

Soon I was assigned the job that I had applied for as a planter, and changed to an early morning shift that would end at about three o'clock in the afternoon. The chill of the early morning forced us to dress warmly for the truck ride to the open dirt fields, but it wasn't long before we shed our outer clothing as it became warm and muggy. The back breaking work required us to pack piles and piles of crowns (the pineapple tops) to the rows of mulch paper where we would use a small spade to insert them into the ground. Each day we would return from work looking like we wiped mud all over our faces, since the sweat and dust would cling to us like glue. The grueling work took it's toll on the less energetic workers, but since I had been accustomed to farm labor I took to it readily and soon began to plant more than the required amount to earn the base pay. The bonus checks came in increasingly larger amounts as I pushed myself to perform more and more each day. It became immediately apparent to my simple mind that the harder I worked, the more money I made. My claim to fame for this great adventure was that I became the third-fastest pineapple planter in the world, though they don't publish that in any books!

Almost every day after work you would find us at the beach, snorkeling and body surfing. One particular day we had traveled to the cliffs on the west side of the tiny island to explore the abundant wild life of the tidal pools found there. I clutched my mask and snorkel, tightly holding it in place, as I jumped feet first off the short bluff into the salt water of the Pacific Ocean. As I turned around to face the submerged rocks below the surface of the water, I came face-to-face with the gaping mouth and razor-sharp teeth of a huge Moray eel. My eyes got as big as saucers and I gulped mouthfuls of the briny sea water while frantically struggling to the surface to escape a confrontation with the grotesque sea snake. My body shuddered with the fearful thought of having one of these creatures attach itself to me with those long sharp teeth. On an earlier outing, I had been bumped into by huge Grouper fish as I paddled around the reefs with my mask and snorkel and had come to the conclusion that I was not really fond of the scary creatures that inhabited the dark shadows of the ocean. Put me in front of a grizzly bear any day, but not in front of a slimy sea creature! I clambored out onto the rocks to explore in a safer venue.

The small tidal pool in front of me was crawling with life and I began poking and prodding the various creatures found there. "Ah- hah!" I exclaimed. "There's a miniature eel behind that little rock!" I began poking at the little skinny snake-like-creature, hoping to get it to swim around a bit. All of the sudden, the vicious little guy jumped out of the water directly at my face, just missing me. The hissing little wicked creature bared it's teeth as if to warn me to stay away from it's kind. "I get the point already!" I thought to myself. "Mean little bugger!"

I spent many days at the cliffs or diving in the depths of the harbor for sea urchins, but the palm-tree-dotted beach was our favorite place to relax since there were always beautiful hula girls lounging around. We planted pineapples all day and gawked at the beautiful brown hula girls in the late afternoons! It was a grand life for an eighteen year old boy!

First Date

I had seen the gorgeous slender girl several times before and had admired the tanned long legs in her short cutoffs from a distance. We had been to several of the same church activities and had cautiously eyed each other. Finally the circumstances were right, and I asked her to accompany me to a late show for our first date.

The crowded car scooted down the highway, riding a bit lower than normal with the load of kids headed for downtown. The late show at the Fox Theater in Spokane was Rocky II, and we were on our way there with the car load of relatives. I had asked Sue out for our first date, which had blossomed into more of a group date, since a bunch of our brothers and sisters had invited themselves along to chaperon. We turned into the downtown parking lot and piled out. I walked to the lot entrance to slide our money into the appropriate slot in the orange box. Sue had followed me closely to the money box. With the crowd of siblings gathered close behind us, I looked for the appropriate slot to slide the bills into. I noticed that down the lighted street there was a street punk walking toward us yelling and carrying on, as if he were high on some drug that had severely altered his brain.

I turned back to the money box still distracted by the vagrant who by now had walked up behind our small group and began spouting some expletives and complaining that all of his problems had been caused by women. "How many men are there here?" I heard the wasted jerk say, as I spun around to see what was going on. As he spoke, I could see that he had reached into his jacket and was pulling out what appeared to be a handgun. Having just spent the last two years in New York and seeing much violence in the inner cities of Rochester and Buffalo, I was very aware that the intentions of the loser where anything but righteous. At that moment it was as if everything went into slow motion, and I struggled to wade through the group of kids to get to the attacker. My intentions were to get to him before he removed the gun from his coat, but he had already un-holstered it and was pulling it up to fire. I hit the large man in a hard tackle, my head and shoulders smacking him squarely in the middle of his broad chest like a great football hit, just as the gun fired two deafening shots over my head.

My first thoughts were that one or both of my brothers had been hit, which motivated me to quickly dispatch the criminal. The force of my full body tackle knocked the man to his back with a sickening thud, as I struggled to gain control of his nickle plated weapon. I fumbled desperately for control of the gun, knowing that I needed to get it away from his grasp before he was able to fire it again. I pushed his arm above his head while pinning him flat to the ground and kicked the shiny gun underneath the nearest car. The smack of fists against flesh could be heard as I attempted to pound the life out of the murdering puke. After smashing my fists into his face several times, I grasped his long hair with both hands on either side of his greasy head and began to smash his head into the hard pavement. All I could think of was that my brothers must be lying there dead, and I was going to take care of this idiot.

At that moment, the drugs he had taken must have given him Superman strength, because he lifted straight up in a sitting position, with me still sitting on his chest, quickly rising until he stood up on both feet. I suddenly realized how tall the man was since my fists where hitting him in the face and neck well above the level of my own head. By then, the slime-ball had decided that he had received enough abuse and turned to run. I stood on the sidewalk, panting from the vigorous exercise and began trembling when the adrenaline rush kicked into full gear. I wandered back over to the parking lot money box to finish the job that I had started. I had no sooner slid the wad of bills into the tiny slot, when I heard a loud profane outburst from the bruised and bloody attacker. "He really wants to get his butt kicked!" I thought to myself, now pumped up with the full strength of the adrenaline high. I turned toward the attacker for the second time as he exclaimed with an evil sneer, "I'm going to cut your guts boy!" The long steel of the once-hidden switchblade, flickered in the street lights as it snapped into the locked position. He slunk toward me with a menacing look. "I'm going to cut you! I want my gun back!" yelled the dope head, as he continued toward me with his long switchblade in hand. He continued a tirade of profanities as I circled just beyond his reach and threatened to kick his head in unless he vacated the vicinity. I continued to threaten him until his better sense finally took hold and he wheeled to run.

The stunned group of pre-teens followed closely as I ushered them quickly around the street corner to the long line in front of the movie theater. We stood in line for several minutes, recuperating from the violent assault which had left me out of breath, and with bleeding knuckles. The punk, knowing the turf, had circled around the short block, hoping to catch me off guard and began to approach us again in the line of movie patrons. My hot blooded red-head sister had seen enough! She began to scream at the approaching vagrant as I and my cute date herded the group past the ticket counter into the theater. The surprised lady at the ticket counter later was able to collect our tickets since we had pushed past her before she had collected our money. I quickly dialed 911 on the lobby pay phone and asked for the police.

As I sat in the plush seats of the theater in the darkness, I wondered if my beautiful bride-to-be would appreciate my violent behavior. The trembling of my hand soon subsided as our hands met in the darkness and clasped tightly. The whispers of our siblings went down the line like a domino affect, as they caught us snuggling in a relieved embrace. Their giggles revealed their delight at the developing romance, and that they had already begun to forget the troubles of the night. "That was a very scary first date," I sighed to myself, relieved that no one had actually been hurt. The next morning must have brought on a massive head ache for the attacker, since I was sore from the exertion of it all and yet, he had taken all of the abuse.

I had sufficiently impressed my pretty date, since all she could talk about when she walked in the door at home, was how I had gone back to pay the money for the parking fee, even under the extreme circumstances. "He's so honest!" she would coo. "And he's so good looking!" (I added that part!) Many years later we still talk about that first date and laugh about how I had won her over with my heroics. Twenty-two years later, even though we are both a lot older and grayer, she still thinks I'm sort of neat and I still think she's a hotty! That was an exciting first date! That excitement in our marriage has seen us through lots of good times and still continues!

Poof!

T he muffled sounds of frantic screams could be heard from deep within the fluffy snowbank as I stood on the tall porch peering down at the large dimple in the otherwise undisturbed snow. "Are you going to be good now?" I asked, giggling at my clever trick. The screams became more frantic as the little boy began to really feel the chilling effects of his predicament. I scrambled down the steps into the powdery white snow, reached deep into the puffy pile and plucked the struggling youngster from his frozen tomb.

My parents had left me to tend the house full of younger siblings, several of which had began to get on my nerves since they wouldn't acknowledge my authority and had begun to ignore my demands. After several warnings to the more unruly of the bunch, I had begun to devise a suitable method of torture to encourage his obedience to my demands. "I'll throw you into the snow bank!" I threatened. "You'd better put some clothes on or you'll freeze to death!" I counseled. It was dark outside and he had started the task of getting into his pajamas, but had become distracted and was now running around the house in only his underwear. "I promise that I will throw you off the porch, you little urchin!" I hissed with anger at his rude antics.

The new powdery snow fall had caused a large pile to accumulate at the edge of the high porch, which sat at the top of the steep bank of the partially covered daylight basement. It had continued to slide off the metal roof of the house until the fluffy pile had reached the bottom edge of the porch. The total depth must have been five or six feet deep and had only

164

recently fallen, making it a soft, but cold cushion for the rascally youngster. He screamed like a little sissy as I hoisted his scrawny naked body over the wrought iron railing and tossed him into the snow bank below. His wreathing body disappeared into the snow with a "poof" as he sank deep into his freezing prison. Since I was many years his senior, he had been no match for me as I had run him down and dangled him from the precipice. After listening to his frantic struggles to swim to the surface, I grabbed hold of his flailing arms and yanked his blue body to the surface. He ran into the house in tears, screaming something about "killing me till I was dead," and headed for the warmth of the fireplace. "That will teach you to mind me," I emphasized with glee. "Who's next?" I asked with a devious grin. The other, older, wiser boys ran for cover.

The prank had been so fun the first time that I quickly concocted an excuse to punish the wild little boy again. "Jimmy, don't!" the now humbled boy, squealed with horror as he struggled to twist free from my firm grip. "It will be fun!" I reasoned with the wriggling juvenile. Poof! His terrified screams, now muffled by the deep snow, could barely be heard from the depths of his claustrophobic nightmare. I jumped from the cold cement porch to his rescue, having felt a few faint pangs of remorse for my naughtiness.

By now the other younger boy, who had been watching with interest, had decided it was his turn to have some fun and had bundled himself up in his snow clothes. He stood waiting for his turn to be tossed over the railing, with an anxious grin. Poof! Another dimple appeared in the snow and another rescue operation began.

Oops!

The old blue Ford pickup skidded around the corner, kicking up a rolling cloud of dust and gravel, as we sped along the old mountain road looking for deer. My Grandpa had long since given up the strenuous exercise of hunting on foot, but had always taken me for short road hunts after school was out. Now-a-days this practice would be considered by most to be slob hunting and not ethical or legal, but back in those days it was a common practice and the roads we traveled were not highways or county roads, just old logging roads. The remote country of north eastern Oregon is cris-crossed with many miles of these types of logging access roads, many of which are now gated off and closed to motor vehicle traffic.

I thumped on the cab of the old dented truck and yelled, "Slow down Grandpa! You're going to fast!" "Damn it!" he would cuss, disgusted at his own inattentiveness. "Guess I'd better slow down and pay attention!" he would mumble in agreement. On some of the less-used roads, I would crawl in the back and Grandpa would drive along slowly until we saw something, then I could pile out and do a stalk of some sort. Most of the time, Grandpa would forget that I was back there and the speeds would gradually increase until I had to remind him. He had been a logger for many years and was used to covering the miles on these bumpy, dusty roads very quickly. If you've ever seen a logger's truck, you would know what I mean. Even the newer trucks get beat up and worn out very quickly. The truck slowed to a crawl as we approached the fork in the road ahead of us.

"Which way?" he asked, as if it really made a difference. "I don't care.

Let's take the right turn and go up Holbrook!" I yelled through the window. I was only sixteen, but had spent most of my life running up and down these old trails, either by horse or by vehicle. My choice seemed logical since we were running out of daylight awful fast and there was always a lot of deer up that Holbrook Road. The road didn't actually have a name, but that's what we always called it since the Holbrook ditch took off around the hill right where the road forked. I held on as the truck accelerated and turned up the hill around the sharp corner. "Grandpa! Slow down!" I yelled impatiently. He cussed again and shifted into a lower gear, slowing the long bed truck down immediately. We continued on up the narrow road for several miles knowing that our shooting time was almost over.

"Whoooooaaaaa!" I hissed loudly as I thumped impatiently on the cab of the truck. "There are some deer over there!" The truck skidded to a stop, with the thick dust cloud catching up to us and enveloping the truck. I caught my balance, quickly recovering from the quick stop, and piled out into the ditch next to the road. "I can't tell, ... it's really dark!" I whispered back into the open window. "I'm going to sneak over there and check it out." I informed the driver. He grunted with agreement, acknowledging my quick message. As I snuck the several yards through the clump of trees that hid me from the view of the alert deer, I kept my eye on the closest one which seemed much bigger than the rest. "It's a buck!" I exclaimed under my breath. I raised the well-used .300 Savage to my shoulder and squinted to see through the tiny peep sight toward the stationary target.

The muzzle blast flashed brightly in the dim light of the early evening, blinding me for a brief second as I struggled to see what had happened. The form of a deer dropped quickly to the ground as I strained to catch all of the action. The bulky four-point mulie buck bounded quickly away as I approached the spot where the big deer had been standing. "What the heck!" I exclaimed out loud. My eyes were as big as saucers as I watched the athletic buck race away to safety, and gazed down at the dead doe at my feet. The puzzled look on my face must have been a sight to see as I scratched my head and said, "No! It can't be! I'm sure what I shot at was the big buck!" I hollered over to the truck, "It's a doe! I killed the doe!"

Still bewildered at the strange turn of events, I quickly retraced my steps to get a better angle at where the deer had been standing and eventually realized that the grazing doe had been virtually invisible to me in the fading daylight. She had been standing directly in front of the broadside buck with her head down, giving the illusion that there was just one deer standing there. I had aimed to shoot without a second glance, in my exuberance to harvest the buck that had stood still long enough for me to take a shot. Usually the deer would hightail it into the security of the deep woods, when they heard the commotion caused by the skidding brakes of Grandpa's truck. This had seemed too good to be true, and it was!

"She's big and fat!" exclaimed Grandpa, who had eaten many does during the Great Depression just to survive. "Can't eat the horns, anyway," he counseled me in his efforts to console. I was distraught to say the least, having committed a horrible mistake that would be hard to live down. "I'll call the game department and confess to my crime." I thought to myself. "Maybe I'll only spend a couple of years in the State Pen!" We quickly gutted the fallen deer who had been shot cleanly through both lungs. Since there was no evidence that the bullet had been able to penetrate the second deer, we loaded the fat poached deer into the bed of the pickup and roared down the dusty road toward home.

"Oops! It's a doe!" said my mother, peering over the bed of the pickup at the deer carcass. "What happened?" she asked sensitively, knowing that something must have gone terribly wrong. I explained my predicament reluctantly as we hoisted the heavy deer to the gambrel to begin the skinning process. "It will sure eat good!" my mother exclaimed, knowing that the tender meat was much needed and preferred over the tougher meat of a big rutting buck. "No, you won't be able to eat it!" I explained, exasperated that no one else understood what I must do. "I have to report this to the Game Department!" I insisted with a hint of shame in my subdued voice.

Despite the objections of my hungry family, I reported the accidental shooting to the Game Department the next morning. "I'll come and pick up the carcass on Monday morning and then I'll stop by the school and get you out of class to talk to you," stated the stern officer. The bell of the school rang to dismiss the students for the day, and I stumbled onto the yellow school bus, wondering what had happened to the Warden. I had waited nervously for his arrival at school, knowing that this would bring unwanted attention and embarrassment to me. I was relieved when I arrived home to find that he had been to the house and had picked up the hanging deer carcass, but had not seen fit to look me up. Later in my life I realized that he must have had a good laugh, as he consumed the tender deer steaks himself.

The lesson learned was that things are not always what they appear to be, and don't be so eager to give up the tender deer steaks!

Osaga Tennis Shoes

The referee shook his head with disgust and stopped the match for the fourth time to allow me to put my shoes back on in order to continue the wrestling match in which I was losing by a large margin. As a gangly sophomore I was still growing into my sprouting body and was being beaten soundly by the more muscular Junior. The gold colored, split leather low tops had slipped off my feet several times during the awkward match, embarrassing me and the referee, but offering some comic relief and distraction from the fact that I was being beaten so soundly. The referee's impatience with the situation, manifested itself when he finally said, "tape those boats on your feet and buy some real wrestling shoes for the next match!" My sympathetic coach, smiled as he quickly wrapped several strands of the white athletic tape around my ankles. "There that ought to do it!" he exclaimed with amusement. "Now get in there and wrestle hard!" he stated encouragingly, knowing full well that I was out-classed and would likely get pinned again.

I hustled back to the center of the mat, stumbling when the toe of my size twelve shoes snagged the thick mat and sent me staggering. The only-slightly-amused zebra, shook his head again as he gave a sharp blast on the whistle to signal the start of the last round of the match that had seemed to last an eternity. The final whistle ended my misery and I stumbled off the mat again, staring down at my taped-up Osaga tennis shoes that had caused me so much trouble and embarrassment.

When I had first seen the cool shoes on the rack at the clothing store in Baker City, I knew that they were destined for my feet. "Wow, cool! Hey Mom, look at these! This is what I want!" I exclaimed, pleading a little because I had seen the price tag and knew that they were more than our limited budget might allow. We had traveled the sixty-mile distance to the more populated town in order to purchase our yearly supply of school clothing and had just now gotten to the shoe department. I was excited about the radical split leather design of the foreign-made shoes, and continued to pester my mother, who had continued on to inspect the other, less expensive shoes. "Let me take another look," conceded my frazzled mother, who had been carefully choosing each item. "You'd better get the size twelve, since you're still growing," she advised. "They're really big!" I argued, not wanting to look like a dork with water skis. "Well, if you want those shoes, they'll have to last you a while," she explained with patience. I reluctantly plopped the larger size shoes onto the overladen shopping cart, hoping that I would grow fast and that the shoes would soon fit.

My size ten-and-a-half tattered Nike's dropped to the floor of the station wagon, as I slipped them off and reached for the sweet-smelling shoe box. I inhaled the fresh smell of new leather shoes, as I pulled the crumpled tissue paper away from the new shoes and slipped them on my sweaty feet. "I guess they're not too bad," I thought, trying to convince myself.

Those frightfully large shoes did cover a lot of miles and didn't get discarded until they were worn out, but I never did grow into them. My feet never grew a centimeter after that day, though my scrawny body did continue to mature into a fine specimen. The extra long tennis shoes could have been used for water skiing, except that we didn't have a boat.

I unwound the athletic tape from the handsome golden shoes and wondered who in the heck had talked me into buying these fancy split leather Osaga tennis shoes. "Osaga. Must be Japanese." I mused. I turned my attentions back toward the activities on the wrestling mat, soon forgetting all about my urge to water ski.

Shasta

The little orange and white puppy squealed and grunted with enthusiasm as she fought to find an available nipple on her prone mothers plump udder in competition with her energetic siblings. "I'll take that one," said my wife, who had decided to purchase a replacement for my dog that had met a tragic death a few months earlier. "They are still suckling, but have started eating puppy chow and are ready to be weaned," assured the owner of the dwindling litter. "They've had their first shot and have been wormed," the owner exclaimed, anxious to reduce the litter by one more. "Great hunting dogs!" prophesied the wearied salesman. Little did he know how true that statement was. Nor did he have a clue of the legacy this little dog would leave behind.

"I'll call her Shasta!" I finally exclaimed, happy to have settled on a name that didn't sound like something a child would call their stuffed teddy bear. The heads of my young bright-eyed children nodded in the affirmative as the wriggling little Brittany Spaniel responded to the name. I filled in the blank spaces on the AKC registration paper and the name became permanent. My wife smiled with satisfaction as I accepted this fine present that seemed to salve the wounds left behind from my previous loss.

The once immature pup quickly grew into the stature of the classic pointer that typifies this breed. After many training sessions in the fenced back yard of our quaint little suburban home and many practice trips to the local woods, she was ready to take afield for her first real hunt. Though still a pup, she had grown in stature physically and mentally and was as hunters say, "bird crazy." The natural style and pointing abilities of the breed were apparent as we searched the stubble fields and weed patches in the rolling wheat country of Eastern Washington.

The first rooster cackled as he rose quickly above the tall grass and flew toward the open wheat field. Shasta stood at attention as my semiautomatic twelve-gauge belched lead and the plump pheasant crumpled, falling with a muffled thud. "Git the bird!" I encouraged the willing retriever. She quickly closed the distance and pounced on the scrambling wounded bird. "Good girl! Bring it here!" I requested enthusiastically. My heart swelled with pride and satisfaction as I watched the

young pup attempt to carry the large bird toward me. The heavy bird was more than the thin youngster could carry aloft, so she re-adjusted her grip by grabbing the big rooster by its colorful ringed neck and continued toward me, her prize dragging the ground between the thin gangly legs. After that first day afield she continued to blossom into an extraordinary hunting dog, constantly improving and surprising me with her willingness and fantastic ability. We spent many glorious days roaming the hills and glens, hunting the many varieties of game birds available such as pheasant, grouse, quail, huns and chukkers.

One time on a cold December day she pointed and retrieved a full limit of grouse, quail, and pheasant, all the while dragging a belly swollen in full term pregnancy. I still have the vision of her sparkling eyes, glistening with the lust for the hunt, while she crossed the ice-choked creek over and over again, dragging her enlarged udder across the snow and ice as she enthusiastically struggled to search out our prey. That night she gave birth to twelve healthy puppies without missing a beat!

One day after slaughtering a covey of blue grouse that she had discovered all up in the same tree, I was trying to get her to leave the site, having killed all of the birds in view. Me and my two partners had killed nearly a full limit each at that one tree, which would explain why she could still smell the enormous scent cone around the tree. I dragged her away from the spruce tree time after time, in an attempt to convince her that there were no more birds. After her frantic yelps had continued for some time, she broke loose, went back to the tree, put her front feet up on the trunk and looked up as if to point. I finally put my head against the tree trunk and looked up through the thick branches of the tall tree. Sure enough, there sat a lone grouse like a statue. The bird dropped to the ground after the final shot and Shasta walked away from the tree, finally satisfied that her job was completed.

Another time while on a lunch break during a pheasant hunt, I had leaned up against an old fence post to rest and had watched intently while she nosed around in the snow oblivious to the fact that we had stopped hunting for a few minutes. She continued to move back and forth with her tail quivering the way that it always did when she was on the hot scent of a bird. She locked up stiff just a few feet from me, pointing to a bump in the snow with all of the enthusiasm of the real thing. I ignored her for a minute, thinking that she had just gone crazy. "There isn't a bird there you stupid dog!" I muttered with a mouthful of a peanut butter sandwich. I walked over to her, while shaking my head in disbelief. "Here, I'll show you!" I sputtered with a full mouth. She looked up at me with her glistening eyes, never moving a muscle off of her classic point, one foot up, nose down and pointing forward, and with her stubby tail quivering with excitement. "There's no bird there!" I insisted. Her eyes followed me, but she never moved, as I walked over and gave the snow a swift kick. Up came a pheasant hen that had evidently hidden under a small clump of bent-over grass the night before and had stayed there, safely tucked under the grass tuft and the newly fallen snow. I never doubted the expert after that day. "She trained me to hunt!" was the story I would tell over and over.

One day in the last season of her life, we were attempting to make a short hunt in one of our usual spots and were hampered by the exceptionally deep snow and bitter cold. I had put on my snow shoes in order to keep up with her, even though by this time in her life she had slowed a bit. She had learned to control her rambling in order to save energy and would make methodical short loops in front of me, instead of the wild energetic spurts of younger years. We traveled down the creek bed which was swollen to the brim with rushing water that had broken the ice from most of its course, except for the rim of ice around the edges and the slow places. She yelped as the ice broke beneath her feet and she plunged into the frigid waters. I listened intently to the commotion, knowing that she had done this many times before, but I soon became concerned when her yelps became frantic. I rushed forward toward the creek bank in order to see what was happening below me. She had tried to pull her weakening body up onto the ice at the edge of the fast-moving water, but had been unable to do so and was now clinging desperately with her front claws to the slick slab on the creek bank. I leaned forward and talked to her encouragingly, but could see that she would be unable to save herself this time. Weakened by her advancing age, and the cold water, I could tell by the diminishing sound of her desperate whimpers that she would not be able to last much longer. I leaned my shotgun against the fence, quickly removed one snowshoe and slid part way down the steep bank to offer the snowshoe as traction. As she tried to get a paw up onto the snow shoe, she slipped back into the swift water and started to sink. Frantically I leaped into the chest deep water to rescue my faithful companion. Grabbing her with both hands, I tossed her, with a grunt, to the steep bank and sunk back into the icy water. I tried to remain upright as the swift current caught hold of my remaining snowshoe and sucked me into the middle of the stream. Unable to detach the snowshoe, I finally realized that I would not last long if I didn't get out of the frigid water. I struggled downstream until I could pull myself up the bank by grasping the tall grass and brush. Returning to the scene of the incident, I found Shasta lying where I had tossed her, shivering with cold. I quickly replaced the loose snowshoe, scooped up the freezing wet dog and my shotgun, scrambling for the truck as fast as my energy would allow.

While writing this story, I could think of many stories like this that would describe to the readers what kind of dog my Shasta was, but have only penned a few of the highlights. The next springtime after this last story, she had withered away to a former shadow of herself and I was forced to put an end to her wonderful life. I bawled like a baby as I placed her lifeless body into the shallow grave near my home and shoveled the moist dirt around her. It would be a long time before I could bring myself to try another puppy. The most recent pup's lineage shows Shasta as it's great-great-grandmother. I'm not sure my heart can take another one, but I'm gonna try! Her twinkling eye and lust for the hunt shows in her grandson. Maybe she's smiling from her hunting grounds in her new life!

Susan Returns

Though this story is not actually true, it is very likely that it could have happened at our house. One day while having a game night together as a family, we were asked by my son Nathan to write a short story in two minutes, after picking a topic from a hat. He had selected topics and had placed them in the hat earlier in the evening. This is the topic I drew, and the story I wrote that night. My wife thinks it makes her look mean, but I liked it enough to include it in this book!

The toys flew everywhere as the little boys and girl ran for cover, with fear and trepidation showing on their little chocolate covered faces. The smallest boy made a shrill squeaking noise as he propelled his nimble body into the small space between the bed and the cluttered floor.

His thoughts raced back to earlier in the day, when his mother had said, with a stern voice, "Don't pick in the cake! It's for the church social." The second-to-the-oldest child, a portly little guy, had been the clean-up man. He had scrambled for the hall closet, only after cramming the last two pieces of delicious chocolate cake into his mouth. His nostrils hissed loudly as he struggled to breathe while gulping down the last remnants of the stolen delicacy.

The door squeaked as it opened, and the angry mother surveyed the now-quiet scene. Susan had returned.

Randy Kills the Duck

The cousins sat cramped in the small car, excited about the opportunity to get away from the boring adult activities of the family reunion. Though all were adults, we were anxious to hang out in a less formal environment and act like we did as teenagers. Even though we lived miles apart, we all thought alike, and had brought our favorite plinking rifles along, just in case we had the chance to break away from the women folk sometime during the long weekend of family activities. The guns lay side-by-side in the rear of the little Subaru station wagon as we motored down the narrow paved road toward the little city dump. The dump was our favorite plinking spot, since there were always lots of glass bottles and cans to shoot at without worry of having to clean the mess up. We would line up hundreds of discarded glass bottles of various sizes and shapes, along the bank of the dump site and then burn up boxes of ammo as we each took turns emptying our clips.

Along the route to the dump was a large year round pond that was long and wide, being surrounded by nothing but sagebrush and rocks. The water hole was home to a variety of wildlife, such as muskrats and ducks and other aquatic creatures, but wasn't deep enough to sustain fish, and became rather stagnant in late summer months. It had become my habit to slow down and scan the water's surface from the road, since I had harvested many muskrats with my .22 long rifle, shooting them from the old road. All of our instructors at Hunters Safety had taught us never to shoot at water, since the bullet can ricochet off the water's surface and end up somewhere other than the intended target. Since the pond was surrounded by nothing but miles of sagebrush, we had ignored the stern warnings and found it rather fun to shoot at the water targets since you could always see exactly where you were hitting, the large "splunk" of the bullet creating a large water spout.

"Hold up!" I spoke up from the passenger's side. "Check out the two ducks out on the pond." The cousins hadn't had the pleasure of this shooting gallery quite like I had, and were anxious to continue on down the road toward the dump. The car rolled to a stop on the edge of the road bed and I piled out. "Hey Randy, see if you can shoot next to the duck and scare it off!" I challenged my older cousin. "See if that new scope can do the trick." I continued to goad him. "I haven't sighted it in yet," he said with doubt, knowing that we would be able to see exactly where he was hitting. "Don't hit it! Just scare it!" I said with confidence. "Just shoot next to it, so if it ricochets it won't hit it." The active outdoors man was always a good sport and always up for a challenge. He climbed out of the car and retrieved the small bore rifle from the back. "Okay, a little to the left....." his voice trailed off as he peeked through the scope.

The sharp crack of the rimfire rifle broke the silence and the poor little mud duck fell dead. "What the heck did you do that for!" I said with disgust. "I said to shoot next to it! Not to poach it!" The bewildered look on his face was like a kid that had been caught with his hand in the cookie jar after everyone else had gotten away with it. "Aaaa, a, I really was aiming about a foot to the left!" he acknowledged with chagrin. "Guess I need to sight it in!" "Guess so!" we teased, as we climbed back into the foreign car to continue our fun. "Good shootin' Tex! Ya nailed er clean!" I continued to tease.

Pautzke Eggs

The General Store parking lot was a flurry of activity as the busy crowd rushed to prepare for a weekend of outdoor activities that would culminate with the big fireworks display that Sunday night. My mind was far from the thoughts of these 4th of July festivities, since I was preparing to take a pack trip to the south fork of the Flathead River in the notorious Bob Marshall Wilderness of Montana's Rocky Mountain range. We would leave in a couple of days on the 4th of July and would be missing out on all of the usual boisterous festivities of the Independence Day celebration.

As I entered the store with careful thoughts as to what items were left to purchase on my seemingly endless list of possibles for this upcoming trip, I waded through the maze of merchandise and people, heading in the general direction of the fishing supplies. The years of being "too busy" to fish had taken it's toll on my stash of gear. I was prepared to totally re-outfit my supplies so that the arduous horseback trip deep into the prime Montana wilderness would not be wasted on an un-prepared, had-been-fish-slayer.

As I wandered down the many aisles of fishing gear, most of which was foreign to me, I started to have second thoughts about my previous career as an avid fisherman. Had I really been as good as I thought I was? Were there better, more sophisticated devices to entice those big fat rainbow natives to my frying pan than the simple Spruce fly or the good ole' hook, sinker, and salmon eggs that I had used so successfully in the past? Maybe the years of neglect to my fishing activities had allowed me to slip into a technology stupor that had left me in a long-past-time-warp, of which there was no return. My doubts increased as I continued my search for something familiar to me. The rows and rows of new reels made me feel like my old IBM Selectric Typewriter next to a Pentium PC with Microsoft Word Perfect. I wondered if my ancient reel, which sounds sort of like an old International combine, would be up to the task.

In a confused and puzzled, yet deliberate and hopeful mood, I hurried along each aisle, scanning each shelf for items that were familiar to me. As I rounded the corner of the bait aisle, my eye caught a familiar sight. Salmon eggs! I fumbled through the many varieties looking for just the right one. Awe!.....the blue cap attracted my gaze and I reached down to pick it up. Pautzke Eggs! What a find! A flood of friendly memories began to wash over me as I fondled the short glass jar with the dark blue lid. Grandpa Pope had always used Pautzke Eggs. My eyes began to glisten with moisture as I dropped the small jar of salmon eggs into my basket. As I rounded the corner to the checkout stand, a smile crept onto my face. A familiar voice echoed in my mind, "Pautzke Eggs, . . . you can't do no better!"

Rerun Prays

Some of my best friends in the whole world have been my pets and I've had several through the years that were quite special. Some people may think that animals can't talk or understand emotion, but this story illustrates the opposite.

When I saw the newborn colt, my eyes widened and I approached for a closer look at the beautifully marked Appaloosa. "Wow, he's really neat looking," I said with a tone of reverence. "Eight hundred dollars!" said the part-time bus driver, who ran his small horse ranch in the day and drove the school bus in the evenings for the local sports teams. "Sold!" I gasped, with the realization that my wife would probably kill me for spending that much money on a horse, when we had been just barely scraping by and didn't even have a fence to put the horse in. "He is absolutely gorgeous!" I exclaimed when I returned home to face the wrath of the 'keeper-of-the-purse.' "He's just what I've been looking for and is the color that I've always wanted!" I said, straining to plead my case before the stern mother. "Come on! Let's go look at him and you'll see what I mean!" I continued. Needless to say, the colt was bought, but remained at the ranch until he could be weaned. He spent the next four or five months running the pastures, suckling his mother and being shown off in the local horse shows, winning many trophies and ribbons for "Best of Breed."

The colorful colt grew in stature until he reached a height of about sixteen hands and weighed about thirteen hundred pounds. He quickly learned to carry a rider and took to it willingly, with an attitude to please.

After many trips to the mountains and after-work rides, he became a rather accomplished and obedient mount, responding readily to leg cues and verbal cues, above and beyond the normal run-of-the-mill trail horse. Through the years Rerun and I had been through many tight places and hair-raising experiences which are common to the mountains, causing us to form a strong bond of trust between us. My whistles would bring him running to my side, ready for anything that I had in mind that day, and this day was no exception.

I had been asked by the local bishop of our church to perform a program for the youth at our 'Father and Son Camp-out,' which was an annual over-nighter consisting of fathers and their sons and grandsons. The bishop had heard of my parade exhibitions where I appeared as a mountain man in full authentic dress, and suggested that I could use something like that to make an impression on the boys. "I'll appear as Porter Rockwell," I said to the kind cleric, "and will come in shooting and hollering!"

The day arrived and we began our preparations for the evening performance. The big horse whinnied and ran to my side with eagerness, sensing that we would be going to somewhere more fun than the confines of the pasture. "Hup!" I blurted in the normal fashion while tossing the lead rope up over his neck. The obedient horse jumped up into the trailer and sidled into his usual position for the trailer ride to the mountains. After kissing my pretty wife goodbye, my son's and I piled into the old suburban and drove away down the dusty road, eager for the chance to be together in the woods.

I drove down the road, nervous for the evenings performance, wondering how my trusted pony would react to the crowd of people and the new environment. We had never done anything quite like this before. I knew that he would trust me and that I probably didn't have to worry about getting bucked off or anything like that, though the thought was a nagging worry somewhere in the back of my mind.

The stunt would require that we ride up to the fireside, surrounded by a multitude of boys and men in the dark, while shooting a pistol and yelling loudly. Everything that we would be doing was a new experience for Rerun and would be a spooky environment even for the most "bomb proof" horses.

The darkness fell around us and the radio crackled, "We're about ready for you." "Just a few more minutes," relayed the messenger. "Roger that!" I replied in affirmation. "We're about ready." Overcome with the nervousness of the moment, I paused for a few minutes in the darkness of the forest and knelt for a few words of prayer, hoping for some assurance from a higher power that all would be well. As I knelt in the dirt clutching the loose reins in my hand, the trusting horse stepped quietly toward me from behind. As he heard the words of my prayer, pleading for all to go well, his ears twitched forward and I felt the soft nuzzle of his nose come to rest on my shoulder. His head remained there throughout my prayer as if to assure me that he understood and that all would be well. I rose to my feet with tears glistening in my eyes, and affectionately rubbed the neck of the big gelding while holding his head next to mine. "Thanks!" I whispered to my trusted companion. "I needed that!" I muttered another prayer as I rode off into the darkness toward our task, thanking God for such a fantastic, faithful friend.

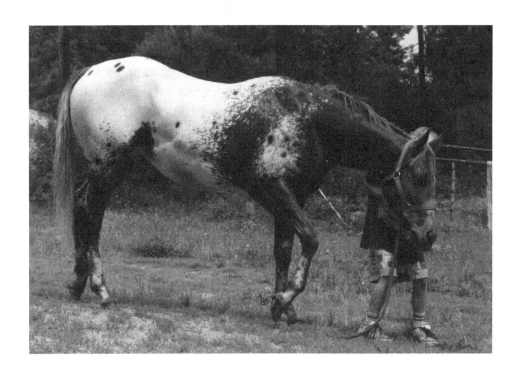

Dad Reese

The little wiry man hobbled to the door, opening it wide like the courteous door man at a fancy hotel. "Howdy!" he exclaimed with a big grin and boisterous attitude. "Come on in Susy! You git better looking every time I see you! Who's the scalawag tagging along with you?" he said, inviting me and my wife into his humble home. My wife Sue was one of his favorites and had been in his home many times as a youth, since she had been high school friends with his youngest daughter. Earl was referred to as 'Dad Reese' by the many youth that hung out at their home. Though somewhat rough around the edges, he was well liked by most people that walked into their country home. His demeanor was open and friendly, though sometimes a bit more honest than some were comfortable with. "You sure have a big butt!" he was rumored to have said to one of the teenage girl friends that was visiting his daughter.

The short and slightly built man had been very vigorous in his youth and had developed quite a reputation for his rowdy antics. "Everybody would lock their doors when the Reese boys came riding into town with guns blazing!" he would brag with a smile. The twinkle in his eye was enough to make one doubt that story just a bit, yet he was sincere enough to seem credible. He would hobble around on one leg and a cane, rarely using his wooden leg that allowed him to walk somewhat normally. He had lost one leg in a hunting accident, when a shotgun had gone off in a duck blind, damaging the leg severely enough that it had been removed a little above the knee. He could be heard bragging about the gun fight he'd been in that caused him to lose his limb.

We entered the modest home and sat down for a visit that would normally last several hours. You couldn't visit Dad Reese without staying a long time. There were always stories to tell that we hadn't heard before and always some new gun to be admired or tested. Birdie was Earl's sweet wife who would just grin when he started in on one of his great tales. She had been his faithful companion for many years, loving him through thick and thin. The wrinkles in her beautiful face were a testament to many years of an exciting life with her vigorous companion. She smiled again as he invited me into his bedroom to check out one of his latest toys, and turned her attention to my wife, who she had developed a strong bond with through the years. I ducked my head to enter the bedroom through the short threshold, and sat down next to the one-legged-man on the edge of the short bed.

"Check this out Jim!" he said with excitement. He had reloaded many rifle cartridges for me through the years and had done some special reloading for himself. He had loaded the cartridges for his .44 magnum pistol with powder and then had packed the open end with common toilet paper, turning them into blanks. "Watch this!" he said with a mischievous grin. He pointed the handgun toward the low ceiling and pulled the trigger. Bang! The explosive report of the large-caliber pistol, created a dusty cloud of shredded toilet paper that instantly filled the little room, causing us to squint and cough. "Cool!" I said with a nod of approval. "Do it again!" I tempted. "Nah, ma will get upset if I do it too much," he explained as if he had done the stunt before, testing her tolerance level.

"Are you guys okay?" came the sweet timid voice through the closed wooden door, after several minutes of silence. "Yes, we're fine!" we both exclaimed with a giggle, sounding more like a couple of mischievous teenagers than a couple of adults. Birdie's patient coaxing encouraged us to "grow up" and join the women folk for some normal interaction.

Earl is much older now, struggling with the ravaging effects of old age on his worn out body. He rarely leaves the wheel chair now, but occasionally has the energy to snag a passerby at the ankles with the crook of his cane that normally hangs uselessly on the side of the wheel chair. His usual vigor for life is almost extinguished, except for the bright twinkle in his sparkling eyes. "Dad Reese,…." someone will begin to say, speaking about some interaction they have had with the crusty old man. They continue to reflect on his colorful life, repeating his nick name with a sense of love and admiration for the loving old codger. "Dad Reese." The name has a friendly ring to it!

Dedicated to the memory of a real American cowboy. Earl John Reese passed away July 19th, 2005. Part of his eulogy read, "Our birth is but a sleep and a forgetting, The soul that rises with us – our life's star, hath had elsewhere it's setting, and cometh from afar. Not in entire fogetfulness and not in utter nakedness, but trailing clouds of glroy do we come from God who is our home."

William Wadsworth – author

We will miss you Dad Reese!

Rodeo in the Driveway

The clank of the pickup and horse trailer coming up the road brought me to attention, since I had been waiting for them to arrive. I had invited my dad along for a short half day ride up the mountain behind my house. He had recently decided to purchase a horse and pair of mules in order to accompany me on my yearly pilgrimage to the mountains and had taken me up on my offer so that he could get in some riding time. This wasn't his first time on a horse, but he hadn't ridden since he was a kid and was a bit anxious about taking up the sometimes-dangerous-hobby at his age. This was to be a good practice session for the recently purchased horse and the newly trained mules. Bill, the big gray horse, had been purchased from a local reliable cowboy, who had assured him that the horse was "bomb proof" and had been down the trail many times before.

The 'flea-bit' gray stepped out of the trailer, cautiously looking around the yard as the new owner tied him to the side of the trailer. The two big mules jumped from the trailer, wide-eyed and bushy tailed, looking like they had just seen Beulah's ghost (see the story, "Beulah Goes To Hell), which turned out to be a good indication of what our morning was about to be like. My horses stood calmly tied to the hitching rack staring across the mowed grass of the huge yard, curious about the newcomers, and waiting patiently for the upcoming ride. It was obvious that the spooky twosome had become a handful for my father, so I strode across the lawn to give him a hand. The tall dark jenny mule nearly yanked his arm out of the socket on her way to escape some unseen ghost, leaving him wrestling with the stocky brown john mule that had recently returned home from the trainers.

After a couple of hours of catching and re-catching the riled jackasses, we had given up hope that we would ever get down the road with the whole crew and finally decided to take the stocky one and leave the other one in the corral. When I approached the newly trained mule with the regular saddle blanket, he exploded with fright and attempted to jump over the chest-high hitching rack that was built out of an eight-inch-thick fir tree strapped to a pair of railroad ties. The athletic knot-head was brought short of clearing the horizontal pole, when he hit the end of the tied lead rope and came crashing down in the middle of the hefty cross pole. The thick tree snapped like a toothpick under the heavy lunging animal, bringing the pole and the mule to the ground. We struggled to free the thrashing idiot, and finally ended up cutting the lead rope in order to keep him from hurting himself further. He ran off across the yard like he was being chased by the Headless Horseman, with no indication that he had learned anything at all at the expensive trainer's corral.

After catching the terrified animal and attempting briefly to saddle him once again, we gave up and totally abandoned the idea of taking the two frightened long-ears, up the road. It had been our intention to put some hay manties on the mules for the practice they and my dad would need for the upcoming trip to the mountains, but after several hours of nonsense, we had finally decided to saddle up the riding horses only, and take a short ride. We had started at seven a.m. and now it was nearly noon. "This isn't helping to convince me that mules have anything over a horse!" I exclaimed with exasperation. I had cured my idiotic mule, Beulah, with a bullet to the head, and was sorely tempted to do the same with these two basket cases.

Bill the horse, had stood looking on at the rodeo, waiting and wondering when it would be his turn. He pawed the ground, anxious to be heading up the road, while my dad strapped on the new high-back saddle and fitted the new bridle to his large head. The horse stood still while the stiff older man stepped nervously into the stirrup, but exploded into a bucking fit before Dad's leg had cleared the leather of the new saddle. For some reason the usually calm critter had decided that he wanted a turn at being a rodeo horse, having watched the example of his corral-mates. My dad flew sideways, never really getting a seat, and landed with a loud thud on his back on the rough surface of the gravel driveway. I watched with amazement as the 'bomb proof' horse bucked across the driveway like a saddle bronc at a professional rodeo. Each jump seemed to top the next as he bucked and bucked and bucked. My sixty-four-year-old dad seemed oblivious to the show his horse was putting on, since he lay still, stunned and groaning in pain from the harsh impact of the tough landing.

"Well, ya didn't make it the full eight seconds!" I said, trying to bring some humor into the tense situation. "It sure looked cool, though! Wish we had it on tape!" I continued to mock, not knowing that he really was down for the count. The 'flea-bit' gray finally stopped bucking and now stood still, puzzled at what had just happened. We never did figure out an explanation for his sudden madness. He had never bucked before and has never bucked since, but that day he could have qualified as the Rodeo Horse of the Year!

We all escaped permanent physical injury that day, even though my dad's backside turned a pretty black-and-blue color for several weeks. My dad would have a hard time trusting his new stead for a long time after that day since he had not been a willing participant in the impromptu rodeo. The two mules have moved on to more experienced hands and Bill's new trail mates are a pair of old trusted Jennies that have seen many years of experience on the trail. Bill continues to act like he is a 'bomb proof' horse, even though his passing dream once was to star in a professional rodeo.

Scented Socks

One of my favorite activities is to spend time in the mountains hunting the elusive elk that roam the high alpine meadows and dark timber of the west. While I do enjoy hunting other species, I have always been particularly fascinated by elk because of their aggressive and vocal mating habits. It is amazing how easy it is to fool even the most wary of bulls when they are in the full swing of the rut. The downfall of many a monarch has been their temporary insanity caused by raging levels of testosterone at the peak of the breeding season. I have seen many species fall victim to this natural phenomenon, including humans.

One such incident involved my long time friend and hunting partner, John, who was to be married the Saturday after his return from this particular hunting trip. He had known his bride-to-be for many years, but had only recently kindled this whirlwind romance with her, since both had been married previously. The smitten single dad had committed to this trip prior to his engagement, and though he seemed preoccupied by the thoughts of his new life that was still in the birthing stages, he started the trip with his usual enthusiasm. The long horseback ride placed us deep into the pristine wilderness and smack dab in the middle of some of the best elk hunting in the world. The timing was such that it coincided with the rut cycle of the elk, which became very obvious as we began to hear the trademark bugling sounds echoing from the steep canyons.

After several days of intense hunting we decided to take a day off to wash clothes and catch up on sleep. We had been teasing John about his impending marriage, making irreverent comments like, "Looks like you are in the rut! Your neck is already starting to swell!" "We should hog tie you so that you don't show up at the wedding on Saturday! That would really put you in a pickle!" After several days of this verbal abuse, he had started to loose his composure and began to show obvious signs that he was ready to go home. His usual passion for the hunt had lost it's luster and was being replaced by the yearning to be with his sweetheart. He had already expressed his desire to tag one of the other elk that someone had killed so that he could leave early.

As we sat around the camp that day, occupied by various domestic chores, he was sitting in the tent rummaging through his clothes bag for a clean pair of socks, when he let out a little groan that caught our attention. It sounded sort-of-like the sound a big bull makes when he has finally had enough of the courtship and is ready to get down to serious business. His smile stretched from ear to ear as he held a small "post-it" note aloft for all to see. "It's even scented with her perfume!" he said, with a love sick yearning to be somewhere else. He stuck his flared nostrils deep into the roll of socks where the scented love note had been hidden, breathing long and deep in order to take full advantage of the faint, sweet smell of his soon-to-be lover. That was it! He was really a goner from that point on! His love sick antics seemed out of place in a camp full of filthy whiskered men that only had hunting four-legged variety of 'deers' on their mind. It was almost sickening to watch, but with some understanding of his predicament, we began to ease up on the ribbing we had been giving him.

He reminded me of a rank bull during the rut that had caught wind of a cow-in-heat and immediately became a raving lunatic, following the scent like he was being led around by a nose ring. Until his early departure a day or two later, he was pretty much worthless for anything except daydreaming, which he did between sniffs on his wadded up socks, that had become his new little snuggle toy.

On his way out of camp that last day, he waved goodbye, rounding the corner out of sight, anxious for the new wife and new life that awaited him at the end of this long trail. Who would have guessed that scented socks could have that much of an effect on a full grown man!

The Principals Office

The cold metal chair seemed hard and uncomfortable as I sat perched on its edge, fidgeting with the zipper of my jacket. I could see the gray-haired Principal pointing his finger and talking sternly to my classmate through the window of the closed office door. Though his words were inaudible through the solid oak door, I could tell that he wasn't pleased and that the young freckled faced boy was getting a good old-fashioned tongue lashing. His flushed cheeks betrayed his controlled anger as he pointed to the large wooden paddle that adorned the office wall, making sure that the visual aid hadn't gone unnoticed by the somber youngster. I continued to fidget in my undesirable seat, since I was next in line for an appointment with the experienced administrator. The strict playground monitor had kindly scheduled this appointment with the principle, assuring me that he would want to see me, even if I was not interested in visiting with him.

"Sit still and don't move!" urged the prim-and-proper secretary, who sat busily typing behind the desk next to me. I had tried to excuse myself to go to the bathroom down the hall, when the alert prison guard had thwarted my weak attempt to escape. I sat on my hands to hide the fact that they were trembling in fear. This was my first trip to the principle's office, though as it turned out, would not be the last. I was a third grader, and had been too shy up to that point in my educational career, to cause any trouble at all, let alone get sent to the office. I had gazed through the other side of these office windows before, on my way down the long corridor, gawking with interest to see who occupied the lonely chair in which I now sat, and wondering what awful crime they had committed to deserve this status. I ducked my head with shame as I saw the passers-by straining to check out the occupant of the chair in which I now resided.

The boy wiped his tear-stained eyes and brushed past me, relieved that his turn was finished, but annoyed that I was there to witness his emotional breakdown. I shuffled into the brightly lit room reluctantly, at the cordial invitation of the obviously annoyed Principal. I studied his carefully groomed hair, slicked back with the wet look of Brylcream. "A little dab will do ya!" The familiar jingle from the hair product commercial came to my mind as I eased my rear end down on the edge of my new chair. I continued to stare at his well designed 'whoop-de-do', which is what we called the intentionally flared tuft of hair that decorated the front of his well-manicured hairdo. He sat behind the big desk in front of me, leaning back as he placed his hands together behind the slicked back head of hair and glared at me for what seemed like an eternity. "Well Mr. Palmer, …do you want to give me your version of the story?" he asked with mock sternness. I stammered a brief, but plausible explanation of the scuffle I had just been involved in, never taking my eyes off the stiff 'whoop-de-do' that adorned his slick head.

"He started it!" I whined convincingly. We had been pretending to play baseball at the worn baseball diamond on the edge of the playground, when I had hit a home run with my pretend bat, smashing the pretended ball clear over the head of my opponent, who claimed to have caught the invisible projectile. The ensuing disagreement had turned to fist-ta-cuffs, neither one of us backing down from our claims of greatness. The alert playground monitor had grasped both of us by the shirt collar as we rolled around in the grass, punching and hitting as violently as any third-grader could. Yanked to our feet by the gray-haired spinster, we had been dragged against our will down the long hall to the office, where we had awaited our fate at the hands of the dreaded Principal. "I'm not going to use this paddle on you today," he explained, "but the next time you visit here you will see it in action!" he warned, trying to keep up the straight face. He knew that I was normally not a trouble maker, and was pleasantly amused that I had been feisty enough to have had this disagreement with my classmate. "Get out of here!" he stated bluntly, "don't let me see you in here again!" he said with a slight smirk. I slid quickly to my feet and ducked around the corner to the long dark corridor. "I wonder if he really would use that big paddle?" I thought, as I rounded the corner to my classroom door.

It was a long time before I made my next visit to the principles office. This time I was a senior in high school and was there to explain why I had egged the County snow plow from the window of the school bus. It was a different Principal, but the familiar slicked back hairdo made me wonder if it was a requirement for the job. "The Principal will see you now!" said the helpful secretary as I shuffled reluctantly into the brightly lit office. "Mr. Palmer..." began the stern principle. I stared at the 'whoop-de-do' and thought about my very first visit to the principle's office. The paddle that hung on the wall behind him caught my attention. "Could it be the same..." my thoughts trailed off as I gave the annoyed administrator my full attention.

The Round Table

This story is not about the knights of King Arthur's Court, but rather, about 'nights at the round table' that belonged to my Grandpa and Grandma Pope. The stories told around this table would become forever cemented into my memory banks, along with the memory of the many days and nights spent playing Scrabble or Canasta. I can still savor the rich smells and sights of the plenteous good meals that were served at this table through the years. The table was really just a simple round dining room table with four matching wood chairs. The edges had been worn smooth through it's years of use in the dining room of the humble single wide mobile home. The toothpick and napkin caddy would usually be situated in the middle of the table, but would be removed when a serious game of Scrabble was in session. Grandpa always sat with his back to the wall, facing the front door and my tiny Grandma would always sit at his left, perched atop her pillow to make her a bit taller.

There was in the adjoining cupboard, a stash of coloring books and crayons and play-dough, which could only be brought to the table after it had been carefully washed and dried. All of the twenty-one grandchildren and many of the fifty-plus great-grandchildren have taken their turn around the table, creating some wonderful art project of which Grandma would always praise even if she couldn't really figure out what it was supposed to be. My earliest memory must have been when I was just three or four years old since I remember being packed to the car by my father after having spent an enjoyable evening around the cozy table.

The table was always where the real action took place! Sure we spent some time lounging on the short sofa or the living room floor, but that was down time. Anything that was anything, happened at the table. I remember the monster-of-a-catfish that Grandpa brought home one night when I was still too young to accompany him on his night fishing excursions to the Snake River. The massive old fish lay across the table full length from side to side, with even a bit of the slimy tail hanging off the edge. The ugly whiskered catfish got filleted right there where it laid and then later returned to the table as tasty cuisine.

The brutally competitive games that were played there until the wee hours of the morning (in most cases), allowed us to visit, but mostly to listen to Grandpa and Grandma reminisce about the "good ole days." Grandma would sit in her usual spot nearest the kitchen, knitting some project that would go to the newest baby in our small town or family, while Grandpa would sit in a "Yoda-like-fashion", with his hands draped across his pudgy middle and recite story after story from his youth or logging days. The stories would really come to life since he had been able to sufficiently polish them at the round table, telling them over and over again. I've been accused of telling a good story and must confess that I learned my trade as an apprentice to a master, while sitting around the smooth edges of that little brown table.

One cannot talk about the table without talking about the voluminous amount of good food that has been served there through the years. The smell of fresh brewed coffee would permeate the air as we consumed piles of fried bacon and eggs and toast on our way to an early morning fishing trip. Mounds of potatoes and meat and salads, or stacks of little round tender pancakes smothered with butter and syrup would cross the smooth surface of the table whenever we were around, but my favorite memory was the green salads. Everyday after my rigorous wrestling practice would get over, I would stop by Grandma and Grandpa's house on my way home across the little country town. Grandpa, concerned that I get enough vitamins in order to maintain my strength, would always have two huge green salads sitting on the table when I got there each night. These were no ordinary salads! It must have taken him a significant amount of time each day, because they were carefully arranged in the large wooden salad bowls, with several varieties of dark green leaf lettuce, tomatoes, grated red cabbage, spinach, broccoli and cauliflower and fresh peas. It would then be topped with a mountain of rich dressing and croutons and bacon bits or sunflower seeds. I would rush up the porch stairs and through the door each day, dropping my gym bag near the door and slide to a stop in my normal place at the familiar round table. We would sit there munching on the luscious greens together, like a couple of old milk cows chewing their cud, with only an occasional grunt of satisfaction or comment about the good flavor. This continued through my senior year in high school. It wasn't until much later in my life that I came to truly appreciate this gesture of love.

It was at this table that I learned of the time that Grandpa would have to shoot deer out of season during the Great Depression just to survive and of the old log cabin homestead were Grandma's family got their start. I learned of hard times and good times and funny times. I learned where I came from and what attributes of goodness that I would like to have in my life. I heard the old married couple argue and curse at each other, but always care for each other. I saw good times and bad times around the old table. Family reunions caused by joyous occasions or sad occasions would always bring us around this familiar circle.

I can still hear the echo of Grandpa's rich voice saying, "Yep! That's a good salad!" And I can still see the old round table surrounded by the wonderful people that made it famous. Ask any of the Grandchildren about the old table. They would all have stories to tell of the "nights of the round table."

Red Fish Cave

R emember when you were a little kid and were fascinated by hidden treasure or secret passageways and concealed hideaways? While some just dream about such places and things, others live the adventure and have the bright memories to prove it.

One such place for me was a well hidden cave located in the deep, echoing canyons of our nations deepest gorge, Hells Canyon. My younger brother Kim, had taken a field trip to Red Fish Caves, which the U.S. Forest Service had sponsored for his freshman class, into the spectacular Hells Canyon, to see some of the many petroglyphs that are evidence of previous civilizations who made these deep canyons their seasonal homes. Since we had lived on a remote farm that had been used as a Nez Perce tribe summering grounds, and had found many arrow heads and obsidian flakes as remnants of that great race, we had been conditioned to appreciate the historical value of such precious finds.

The scrawny freshman recounted his visit to this remote cavern, explaining that some native American had evidently stumbled onto this well hidden cave entrance and had wintered there, or at least stayed there long enough to have painted the likeness of some red fish on the cavern walls. Now a designated National Recreational Area, Hells Canyon is a deep rugged wonder of nature, carved out of the rocks by the rushing waters of the Snake River many centuries before. The salmon runs and mild climate of the river bed must have attracted the early residents to this area for the voluminous amounts of fish and the convenience of the mild winters. The story of this ancient hideaway seemed to excite the adventurer in me, and we soon made arrangements to travel the short 20 mile distance from our home in Pine Valley to view this new discovery.

Anxious to see what Kim had so eloquently described, we parked near the river and quickly hoofed it up the trail that wound up the steep draw. After an exhaustive search of the entire ravine, we still had not found the entrance to the cave and I was starting to experience a great deal of frustration with my younger sibling, who had been to the site just a week before.

"How can you forget the location of a place that you have been too so recently?" I said with a fair amount of disgust. My brother, while talented in many other areas of life, had not been blessed with the same accurate internal compass that I had somehow been graced with. The innate ability to find my way around the mountains, especially to a place I had previously been to,  had gotten me out of many a pinch as I had explored the local hills as a young curious adventurer. The frustration that I now felt with my brother began to motivate him to search even harder.

"I know it's right here somewhere!", he exclaimed sheepishly. "It's a totally hidden entrance!" His baffled look conveyed his frustration as his young eyes scanned the rugged terrain. We crawled around the corner on a small ledge that led downward towards a brush patch. "It's got to be higher!", he moaned. "This little ledge has had some traffic on it, this could be it," I offered helpfully. "Hey! Here it is!" he suddenly exclaimed. "I knew it was here somewhere!", he sighed with relief. As I slid down the last 10 feet of the skinny ledge, it widened suddenly into a landing pad big enough for several people to stand and I realized that we had made it. "Amazing!"

I thought to myself. "Who ever found this cave originally, must have done it by pure accident!" "This is cool!" The opening of the entrance was so well hidden that we had to be literally standing at the entrance to see it.

I knelt at the entrance to examine the likeness of a large fish painted in some kind of faded red stain, and wondered what the ancient occupant must have meant to portray. "Looks like a spawning salmon." I said thoughtfully. "Let's go inside!", my rejuvenated brother blurted. The rank pungent odor of rodent droppings permeated the damp air as we cautiously entered the cool darkness of the mysterious cavern. Thoughts of creeping things entered my mind as my imagination began to work overtime. "Must be rattlesnakes and bats in here." I reasoned. "What if we run into a cougar or bear resting in here?" I thought as I tried to regain control of my creative thought process.

The forehead-high-entrance began to narrow to the point that we had to wriggle through a long passage-way like an earthworm. "So this is what it feels like to be born!" I chuckled nervously. It was a tight fit even for two slender teenage farm boys. "Wouldn't want to eat my lunch inside, then have to try going back out that hole." I continued my nervous joking. The skinny passage-way continued for just long enough for me to develop a good case of claustrophobia, then widened gradually until we could stand up again. Soon it opened up into a huge echoing cavern that could have fit a house. "Wow! Look at those big stalactite and stalagmites!" we breathlessly exclaimed in unison. This was some neat stuff! These are the types of Tom Sawyer like adventures that boys are supposed to have!

We continued our careful and thorough examination of the expansive caverns, traversing each little nook and cranny, up and down and sideways, until we were completely satisfied that there wasn't any more to see. The main passage-way had narrowed to the point that the pancakes I had for breakfast were not going to allow my slightly enlarged belly to pass. "Well, that's about as far as we can go." Kim pronounced as he turned around to make sure I was still behind him. "Yep! Let's get out of here," I agreed.

We traveled back towards the light like a small band of hobbits from Middle Earth, yearning for the light of day after their trip through some underground dwarf city. As we stumbled blindly to the bright entrance, the hot summer sun reminded us that we had returned to the reality of Hells Canyon. "Didn't see any snakes or bats." I stated disappointedly, like that would have made the trip more authentic or something. It had been a grand adventure, and we promised to return again soon.

I have traveled back to that special dark hideout many times since that day. Of course I did remember exactly how to get there, I remind my younger sibling. Each time I make the strenuous hike to the cave and pass the red fish petroglyphs, I am awed by the thoughts of the past occupants and what their lives may have been like. Many years have passed, and I wonder now if my forty-three-year-old-pudgy-middle would allow me to pass through the 'birthing canal,' as we dubbed the claustrophobic-narrow part of the cave.

The last time I was there, with my family and several of my brothers, I was disappointed to discover that the entrance had been gated by the Forest Service in an apparent attempt to discourage vandals from damaging the icicle-like lime deposits that have taken so many years to form. I scanned the make-shift visitor's log that consisted of a worn, yellowish sheet of paper and a stubby pencil, stuffed into a rusty tin can that had lain there for years. My mind was flooded with a rush of great memories as I saw my name scribbled on several entries. "Remember the time we brought our girl friends up here in the rain?" I quizzed my now balding, still scrawny, brother Kim. "Ha! Didn't our flashlights accidently go out back in that big cavern?" he gleefully reminisced. "Those terrified beauties sure did hold us tight in the dark!" I said with a teasing grin. My wife of many years jabbed me playfully and said, "let's go give that a try!" We wriggled through the cable mesh barricade and began the adventure all over again.

Texas Heart Shot

Texans are known for doing everything BIG or usual or fantastic. Like the man from Texas who was heard saying, "acres and acres and she's all mine!" "Your ranch?" asked the visitor. "Nope. Ma sweet wife!" drawled the Texan. The following tall tale, while absolutely pure truth, is one of those "Texas like" stories that I have had a hard time getting people to believe.

I was hunting in a party of older, more experienced men, who had been hunting together for many years and had many a story to tell themselves. My new father-in-law had brought me along on this late buck hunt mostly because of my enthusiasm for hunting. In the bitter cold of the pre-dawn darkness, he introduced me to the guys as we stood around waiting for several late arrivals. He explained that we would be hunting an area that had produced many large bucks in the past. They had caught these old monarchs on the exposed southern slopes, as they migrated out of the deep snow into the more mild climate of the Horse Shoe Lake area. Like they had done many times before on this late November hunt, they began the methodical chore of installing tire chains on all four tires of the two rigs that would make the slow trudge up the mountain. "Not too many deer in here," one of them explained. "But if you see one, it is likely to be a big buck!" His tested theory later proved to be prophetic. The late arrivals skidded into the rendezvous and the introductions continued.

The low whine of the four-wheel-drive rigs was muffled by the knee-deep-powdery-snow, as the convoy chugged up the old mountain road to the drop off point. The well planned drive would require several of the more mobile hunters to work down hill from the top of the snow cloaked hills towards the clearing at the bottom where several shooters would be on stand, waiting to ambush the unsuspecting deer as they were flushed from their hide-outs in the thick draws above. I quickly volunteered to be one of the "bird dogs", since I was the new guy, many years their junior. The old guys had spent a lot of thought devising this hunt, and I didn't feel right about taking advantage of the preferred stands. "It is best to start at the bottom of the pecking order and work your way up the seniority ladder with hard work!" I said to myself as I sat at my starting point waiting for daylight.

The rising sun, though muted by the threatening clouds, began to illuminate the woodlands, as I started my slow stalk down through my assigned drainage. It wasn't long before the sweat began to roll and I realized that the deep snow would make this hunt more difficult than I had anticipated. A slow moving stalk was what I had in mind so that if I did come across a deer I would have time to get a shot before it moved away towards the point of ambush. Since there was virtually no evidence that deer had been in the area since the last snow fall, I quickened my pace so that we would have time in the day to change our location to a more profitable venue. I arrived at the ambush point at the same time as the other "drivers" and heard similar reports from them. We clambered into the cold vehicles and began our ascent to a new location. I had climbed into my father-in-law's Chevy pickup so that he could ferry me to the top of a different drainage to start the drive over again. As the reliable old green truck plodded up the logging road, we conversed about the lack of deer sign and expressed hope that our change of location would produce more sign than the last.

"Just wait here for awhile till you see the other truck come by," he explained. "They need to drop off the other guys so that you can all start down at the same time," he continued. I waved goodbye as he drove back down the road, and looked for a soft place to sit while I waited. I walked to the edge of the ravine that overlooked several long open ridges and settled into the fluffy snow to wait for the other guys. In an instant I realized that there was a deer standing under a tree several ridges over, so I brought my binoculars up to get a better look. The magnified view through the binoculars revealed that the deer's large body was adorned with a magnificent rack. My heart rate rapidly increased as I fumbled to inject a cartridge into the chamber of my open-sighted Browning 30-06. While raising the well-used rifle to rest on my knee, I began to mumble to myself something about getting the deer to turn so that I could get a clean shot. After several minutes of waiting, which seemed like an eternity, I decided that this deer was big enough that I was not going to let it get away. "I'll try a Texas Heart Shot!" I thought in exasperation. (For you green horns, a Texas Heart Shot is when the bullet enters in or near the anus and travels through the body and into the heart of the prey). "That is a long ways over there!" I muttered outloud to myself. "That has to be at least four hundred yards across there!" I continued out loud. I steadied the rifle and settled into a firm stance for the long shot. I continued to talk to myself while raising the sights a little, as I re-evaluated the distance to the still stationary buck. He was still facing straight away from me, with his head lowered as if in a sleepy stupor. "Sure wish he would turn," I grumbled, still sighted in on the backside of the massive deer. "That's a long ways over there!" I repeated to myself confidently. "I better raise it up a bit more," I whispered as I raised the sight to the top of the deer's antlers. I breathed in a deep gulp of the chilly air and held it, while carefully squeezing the cold trigger of my trusted weapon.

The loud report of the semi-automatic, shattered the stillness of the quiet ravine as the 180 grain bullet found its mark and the unsuspecting deer dropped to the ground like a sack of spuds. "Well I'll be darned!" I exclaimed out loud, still continuing my conversation with myself. I lowered the smoking gun and reached for the binoculars. "He dropped right there! Hasn't moved a muscle!" I breathed with a sigh of relief and exultation. I emptied the chamber, placed the gun on safety and began my laborious traverse, up and down and up and down until I reached the farthest ridge where the big buck had dropped. The massive buck lay sprawled where he had fallen with no sign that he had even kicked out in the normal spasms of a dying animal. I quickly gutted the deer and started the long drag to the designated meeting place in the meadows below.

"Texas Heart Shot!" was my confident reply to the queries of my jealous hunting partners as they asked where I had hit him. "Over four hundred yards!" I stated with a slight smirk, to additional questions from the doubting hunters. Bagging the large buck had gained me instant recognition and acceptance from the gang of seasoned out-doors-men and had given me yet another fantastic tale to tell. Later evidence would reveal, after boning the carcass of the deer, that the bullet had entered at the base of the tail just above the anus, passed directly through the heart and had lodged in the bottom of the brisket. "Yup, a true Texas Heart Shot!" I would later be heard to say. This story was destined to be told enough times to become truly polished!

The Barrel

The little town that I lived in as a young boy was really much better than it's name. Halfway, Oregon received it's name simply because it was literally "halfway" between two other towns that have long since faded and all but disappeared. Halfway is a sleepy little town nestled in the middle of Pine Valley, a lush green haven, sandwiched between the Wallowa Mountains and the high desert of the Snake River breaks. My father had moved us there in order to take a job on my grandfather's logging crew when I was approximately 4 years old.

We lived in a modest single wide mobile home on a large corner lot at the end of a quiet, side street of the small burg. My days were spent playing on the large corner lot with my prim-and-proper sister Kathy and my younger red headed sister Lori and our mangy mutt named Whack. The dog's name was a compromise between the name Black and Whitey. The only thing I really remember about the poor pup was his stupid name and the fact that he got ran over by a car at a rather young age. We buried him somewhere in the yard behind our tiny home.

Many of our activities were rather uneventful but occasionally we would do something that would shake up the quiet neighborhood. Our house must have been the talk of the whole block, since most of our neighbors were older folks who were not used to so much action. The fact that I was the only boy, sandwiched between two sisters, may explain the fact that I was usually at the forefront of the trouble we caused. The local volunteer fire department became rather familiar with our address and my name in particular.

The day that we played with matches and started a fire in the tall dry grass behind the house, brought the whole eager fire department down on us, but was nothing in comparison to the day that we scared my mother to death.

We had been playing in the dusty gravel of the driveway and had decided to play a trick on our gullible mother by pretending that my sister had been ran over by a car. Kathy was really the instigator of this annoying prank, but as usual I received the bulk of the blame. She had laid down at the edge of the street and instructed me to go tell mom that she had been run over. It probably wasn't really a stretch to get our mother suckered into our charade, because I had already ran over my sisters legs once when I was left unattended in a running vehicle as a toddler and had managed to slip the car into drive and ran over Kathy's legs as she played on the ground in front of the car.

This time, my great acting job may have gotten me nominated for an Oscar, except that we lived in Halfway, not Hollywood. Convinced that her five year old daughter had been thoroughly squashed by a passing vehicle, the frantic young house wife nearly tore the thin door off the mobile home as she barreled through the opening, screaming like a banshee. She rushed to the side of her seemingly unconscious daughter with the concern that only a mother can appreciate, finding her limp body at the edge of the narrow side street.

Moms sometimes have a weird way of showing that they love you, and this was no exception. The whipping that we received when she realized that she'd been the victim of a well executed prank, was in direct proportion to her love for us, but her anger was tempered a bit by the tremendous relief she felt in knowing that we really weren't hurt, so she at least spared our lives.

Some weeks later, after the memory of this event had faded, we were back at our usual mischievous diversions and seemed hell-bent on continually topping any previous event. At the side of the house were several small metal drums that had been converted from their previous use, into garbage cans. In an effort to escape the pending punishment that awaited me for some crime that I had committed, (I can't even remember said crime at this writing), I had decided that the neat little barrels would make a safe hiding spot for this young-four-year-old trouble maker. Looking both directions to be sure that no one had detected me, I slipped quietly down into the old oil drum to hide until the impending doom had passed by. I was prepared to wait it out for the long haul, but soon realized that no one had even been aware of my wrongdoing and that my long concealment had been for naught. As I tried to stand up to hop out of the tiny barrel, I immediately realized the gravity of my predicament. I was stuck! My vigorous wriggling only aggravated the situation as the barrel soon tipped onto it's side and rolled from side to side. After struggling silently for some time, I soon became rather panicked and had to swallow a large chunk of pride before I could clear my throat enough to yell for help. My girlish screams went unheeded until my mother finally realized that those weird sounds didn't belong to our noisy little dog, Whack. She pretended not to laugh as she began a series of attempts to free her troubled offspring. Finally exhausted by her valiant efforts to free me, she surrendered and recruited the local volunteer fire department. With horror, I realized that the loud wailing sounds of the fire station siren were for me and I tried to crouch deeper into the barrel with no success.

The captain of the local department who also happened to be our neighbor, shook his head with dismay as he realized that it was me that had caused him to be disturbed from his afternoon siesta for the second time in a couple of weeks. The "jaws of life" had not been invented yet, so the inventive welder began to cut the barrel from top, to bottom, with a giant sized tool that looked like a pair of bolt cutters. I hadn't had so much attention since my head had emerged from the birthing canal, so I was relieved when the pressure on my boney knees was released and I could scramble from the once-tight-spot to freedom.

"He's really a very good boy!" I could hear my apologetic mother explain, as I retreated to a safer hiding place out of the lime light. "He's never really done anything like this before." she said, sort of convincingly. "I'm sure he is a good boy, ...when he's asleep." the departing fireman murmured as he climbed into his antique red truck and drove away. My mother still insists that I was a perfect little boy, but I think that maybe she is starting to suffer the first affects of "old timers" disease.

The Big Nightcrawlers
Are in the Cemetery

I pulled the stiff green slicker tighter around my neck as I bent over to scoop up the slimy brown worm. The rain dripped off the end of my nose as I dropped the crawler into the heavy bucket. The light of the dim flashlight revealed that the bucket was about half full of the slithery worms that I sold at our family store as fish bait. "That's a lot of worms!" I thought with satisfaction as I stood tall and stretched my sore back. Picking up nightcrawlers wasn't the easiest work in the world, but sure was lucrative for a young teenage boy. There was at least thirty dollars of worms in the five-gallon bucket, which wasn't bad for an hour of work. Bending over with rain dripping down your neck in the dark, isn't exactly fun, but brought great dividends for a young entrepreneur. "I would sort and package them in the morning." I thought to myself as I peeled off the dripping rain coat and headed off to bed.

The job was trickier than one would imagine. Most people have squashed worms on the sidewalk after a night time rain storm, but have never actually hunted for the sometimes elusive worms. It requires that you bend over with a flashlight in one hand, with the other poised to pounce on the extended fat night crawlers. The ideal conditions would be after dark, during a good soaking rain when the worms emerge from their flooded quarters, which is where the big worms get the name, nightcrawlers. After the ground is sufficiently wet, they will appear out of their small borrows to lie on the cold wet grass. If you were lucky enough to catch a mating pair while attached to each other, you could double your rewards. The slower the stalker went, the more crawlers you could catch, since they are very sensitive to the ground vibrations and would dart, like lightning back into their holes. Sometimes when the brown skinned worms got a head start into their tiny home, it took some patience to gently tug until they would relax enough to pull them out without breaking them in half. It was important to sell good healthy worms in order to get repeat business from my regular customers.

As is natural for anyone, I was always looking for an easier way to collect the worms, but had yet to find a substitute for the old fashioned backbreaking labor of the night time hunt. My grandpa had a gadget that consisted of three rods stuck deep into the sod of a watered lawn, and was attached to a power cord that would literally shock the worms to the surface. After plugging the worm prod into the outlet, the worms would immediately begin to appear in their struggle to escape the uncomfortable electric current. This method could be done in the daylight hours which seemed appealing, but the worms never really recovered from the shock and wouldn't last more than a couple of days without dying. This bad side effect excluded this method for the worms that went to the store cooler for resale, since quality was so important to the fishermen customers.

I had my favorite spots for hunting the nightcrawlers, which obviously were the places that consistently produced the most. The lawn at our home always was the easiest, but since we rarely watered, I could only do it after it rained. The lawn at the grade school was good during the dry summer months, since the sprinklers would always be set up somewhere to assure that the spacious lawn stayed green. But the best location of all was the local cemetery. I worked once a week at the park-like grave yard, mowing around the rows and rows of headstones with a hand mower or weed whacker. Since the repetitive trips around the well-kept grave yard had desensitized me to the spookiness of the morbid place, I was only a little uncomfortable with the thoughts of collecting worms there. Many of the headstones had the names of people I had known, and as I traveled mindlessly behind the gas powered mowers, I would daydream about the lives behind the names.

One night my friend and I decided to spend the night picking up nightcrawlers in the cemetery, since we had mowed the day before and the sprinklers had been on that whole day, making conditions ideal for our night time work. We arrived after dark and turned the sprinklers off since we had a key to the utility shed where the large pump was stored. We bent over and began our tedious work. "Wow, look at this one!" I gasped with wonder. "It's as long as a snake!" I exclaimed, as the thick nightcrawler dangled at arms length in the beam of the new flashlight. Even though I claimed that it wouldn't bother me to be in the grave yard at night, I had purchased a bright new flashlight, just to be sure I could see better in the dark. The bucket was soon nearly running over with the magnificently chubby nightcrawlers that seemed bigger than anywhere I had previously gathered them. We returned to the shed to turn the sprinklers back on and to lock up before heading for home, while continuing to look over our shoulder with apprehension, as we walked to the truck.

"Of course they're bigger in the cemetery!" my grandpa said with a laugh when he heard about our bounteous take. "Why do you think that is?" he said, with a serious face. Since it never occurred to me until years later that the worms weren't really feeding on more than the rich soil of the grave yard, we steered clear of the cemetery from then on.

I guess that human nature always gives us the illusion that things that are harder to get, or out of our reach, are bigger and better than what we feel is the norm. It seems that life is always like that old clique, "the grass is greener on the other side of the fence," and my newest clique, "the worms are always bigger in the cemetery."

Thanks, I Needed That!

Have you ever heard that aftershave commercial where the guy slaps his face with after shave and says, "Thanks, I needed that!"? Well, this story is something like that, only it didn't have anything to do with aftershave.

It all started back in the mid 1980's when I had been serving as a Boy Scout leader and had talked our troop of boys into traveling to Oregon to do a 50 mile backpack trip into the Eagle Cap Wilderness. This particular group of boys was full of athletic jocks, with a few nerds mixed in for good flavor. They were a good bunch of boys, that really liked being together, and liked the outdoors. Though most of them had done some camping, none had ever done anything quite this adventurous.

As we prepared for the trip, we had done quite a bit of coaching as to what types of items to bring (equipment, food, clothes, etc.). One boy, in particular, was somewhat of a misfit and struggled with his attendance at our regular meetings. Consequently, he was a bit on the short end of the stick, when it came to being properly prepared. I had made several telephone calls to his foster mother, in an attempt to oversee his inventory of food and equipment. Even though I had been very specific as to the types of light-weight food to bring, he still showed up at the last minute with a bundle of heavy cans.

Like a pack of excited school boys, rushing the doors at the last bell, they were off to the races as we headed up the Imnaha River on the first leg of our journey. By the end of the second day some of the shine had worn off, as the reality of the high altitude and the law of gravity had set in.

The boy came to me that second night to inform me that he had lost his can opener and defiantly asked to know, "What I was going to do about it." I told him that I wasn't going to do anything about it, since it had been his choice to pack cans. I was kind-hearted enough to show him how he could open the heavy cans with a pocket knife.

The third day brought out the 'complainer' in most of them, and I soon learned how Moses must have felt, as he led the murmuring children of Israel into the desolate Sinai desert. Grumbling under their breath, they toiled and trudged uphill all day, navigating the winding, root infested Cliff River trail. As we sat around the campfire that night, watching the moon's reflection in the beautiful cold water of Crater Lake, the boy took me aside for the second time to inform me that he had now lost his pocketknife and would no longer be able to open his heavy cans of food. His once defiant, "what are you going to do about it?" was more like a plea for help than a challenge. My initial cold- hearted response sent him away to ponder the error of his ways. Later, when I caught him trying to open his food cans, by smashing them with a sharp granite rock, I relented and lent him the small can opener that I had neglected to reveal to him. His humble, "thank you", was enough to make me realize that he had learned his lesson.

On we trudged, making short work of the scenic 5 mile hike to Pine Lakes. (*By now you are wondering what all of this has to do with the topic of this story, but if you hang in there, you'll see that the shorter version couldn't have been as much fun!*) Pine Lakes was our heaven! We lounged around for two nights and the better part of two days, just fishing and fishing and fishing.

The boy came to me on the fifth day, wanting to know if he could borrow some fishing supplies since he had lost all of his lures. He had repeatedly casted into a downed tree that was a haven for a whole school of very visible fish. It had been driving him crazy, since he had yet to catch a fish, but had not had his hook in the water long enough to catch one. He had been too busy trying to untangle his snagged lures from the tree branches, that had been the safe haven for the tempting school of brook trout. I refused his request for replacements since he finally admitted that most of his and his tent mate's fishing tackle now appeared as decorations to the underwater tree, that now seemed to qualify as a Christmas tree.

Since his fishing career was now over, he took over the duties as the fish watcher. We had created a live well in the small stream next to our camp in order to save all of the fish we had caught to carry out on the last day. It now teamed with fish that scurried back and forth, desperately looking for an escape route. His job was to keep them in, by building up the little rock fence around them. He seemed to really take to the small task, and soon developed an attachment to his slimy herd.

The thunder could be heard in the distance,as we hurriedly packed up our gear to leave, that last morning. Since the approaching dark clouds threatened to dampen our spirits, we had decided to pack up the fish on a long stringer and head for the truck without cleaning them. The boy insisted that it was his duty to carry the fish that he had so carefully tended for the previous 24 hours, so he tied the heavy load of slippery brookies to the top bar of his now lightweight pack. It was quite a site to see from behind with over 60 pan sized fish dangling from the same stringer! What happened next is what made reading this whole story worth it!

At the first small stream that trickled across the well-worn-mountain-trail, the boy stumbled and fell to his knees, which brought the slimy load swinging quickly to the front of his smelly pack, whacking him smartly across the face. Furious and sputtering, he grabbed the smelly mess with both hands and threw it around behind him with all of the energy he could muster. The familiar wad continued its orbit around his head until it smacked him with it's full force on the other side of his face. The heavy impact, of the slimy wad of fish, caused him to drop to his knees again, in a cussing fit. He mumbled something about those, "#&^#$&&@ fish, anyway!"

As I rolled in the meadow grass gasping for air between the convulsions of laughter, I thought of that aftershave commercial and wondered why he hadn't been quick enough to say, "Thanks, I needed that!"

Skinny Dipping

First off, let me say that my wife is probably going to kill me for writing this story, since it may have to involve some level of confession, which may also include her participation in some of the included events. This story is for those of you who have skinny dipped, for those who have tried but chickened out and those who are just flat out exhibitionists.

For those of you readers who would be too naive to know what this practice is, please be assured that it has absolutely nothing to do with anything skinny! The dipping part comes in when the naked participant jumps in and then right back out, usually because of technical difficulties caused by the water being too cold.

Recently on a pack trip to the famous Bob Marshall Wilderness Area, I was sitting on a driftwood log sunning my naked white body after taking an icy, but refreshing dip into the rushing waters of the river. I lay there quite relaxed, spread eagle, while trying to dry off enough to put my clothes back on, when my startled wife who had been fishing down the stream, came walking by. "What the heck are you doing?" she hissed with her best version of the disgusted voice. "Givin' you a good look at a real mountain man!" I returned with my sharp wit. I think much quicker when I'm naked, you must understand. "Want to join me?" I continued, since I was still naked and thinking quicker every moment. My bubble was burst when she walked away shaking her head and mumbling something about me being a crazy old coot. "Besides someone will come by and see you!" She yelled over her shoulder. "That will scare them off!" I said, still in the quick-witted mode. She didn't join me that time, but I wouldn't say that she never has!

Some of you will never admit that you have tried skinny dipping, since there probably were no credible witnesses. Like the time at the pond by  the old State gravel pit, when I actually got my wife to join me in the water after dark. Now mind you, no one ever saw her actually take her clothes off, but she really was naked! Now remember that I said something about credible witnesses, and she will always say that I was a liar and people that know her, actually believe her version over mine. There was that other time at the lake, in the middle of the day when we both jumped out of the boat and well, lets just say that the old swimming trunks got hung on the side of the boat. I'm not sure that constitutes as really skinning dipping since we didn't actually jump into the water while naked.

Have you ever seen a great waterfall or deep clear pool of water and had the unmistakable urge to jump in naked? This year on a hunting trip with a bunch of crusty old geezers, I had made several comments to the boys about a really cool water fall I had seen that day that would be a great skinny dipping spot. These comments just brought looks of disgust down upon me. And there was the slow running stream that ran right by our camp that had deep clear pools of water with clean sandy bottoms at the corners where the stream changed its meandering course. "This water just screamed at me to strip naked and run and jump in," I explained to them. Again, I receive blank and disgusted stares. Of course I know that these great guys are either just good actors or they have already tried this, and know about the 'dipping' part. They have probably already experienced some of the technical difficulties of skinny dipping, or have dipped and screamed and scrambled from the icy water when it has turned them blue in a matter of seconds.

You see, skinny dipping is just a romantic fantasy that has no basis in real life. Thinking about it is really the great part, not the doing. The doing is either too cold, or too sandy, or something else...anything else, but romantic. And if you are thinking about solo skinny dipping, well...that is just plain boring, and besides you would have no credible witnesses!

Snipe Hunt

Some of the best pranks I have pulled through the years have been at someone else's expense, usually causing them some major source of embarrassment and discomfort. The snipe hunt has always been one of my favorite pranks to play on the green horns. My friends and I had worked out the details of many snipe hunts before, taking advantage of all the new little Tenderfoot Boy Scouts until they had all been initiated properly into the small troop of rowdy boys. This prior experience had prepared me for the chance to really pull off a good one.

I received a call from one of my school teachers one summer evening, after working in the hay fields, who informed me that there had been some unspent money allocated for a guided horse back trip to the mountains for any student who wanted to go along. It would be a three day event requiring the participant to have access to a horse and their own bedding. Other than that, the trip would be catered by the local pack station. Upon arrival I realized that much to my pleasant surprise, the only boys to attend were me and one other boy. The other fifteen participants were girls. Not just any girls! These were most of the best looking girls in the high school! "How could you go wrong on a trip like this?" I thought with a smile. "Fifteen pretty girls and two boys! And we get to ride horses and go to the mountains!" These were a few of my favorite things that they forgot to mention in the Sound of Music song.

The ride up the long trail was uneventful and we arrived at Big Camp on the Imnaha River in time to set up a good camp and picket the hungry, tired horses. After the second day of fishing and laying around camp, we began to be bored and to scheme up ways to play pranks on the group of girls, who for the most part were unaccustomed to life in the wild and were very naive about the woods. We had made the comment about going snipe hunting that evening and quickly realized that only one of the girls had ever heard about snipe hunting. At the opportune moment, we took the informed girl aside to include her in on the great prank we had planned. I and my companion would pretend to take a long hike late in the afternoon and wouldn't return until well after dark. We would make a loud pronouncement of that fact so that each girl would sucker into our well-thought-out plan. Our female accomplice would take each girl unto the woods for their try at the snipe hunt. She had carefully explained to them that they would stand by a large tree where the snipe trail came past and hold the gunny sack open while thumping on the trunk of the tree with a stick to attract the mating male snipes. The thumping noise would simulate the noise the female makes when they are looking for a mate. "The long beaked birds only come out at night!" she had explained to the innocent participants. "The birds will run down the trail and right into your well placed sack," she explained with a straight face. "When you feel the bird wriggle in the gunny bag, you need to close it up and reach into the bag quick enough to throttle the bird." she continued with her careful instructions.

"Why are you taking that shovel up the hill?" asked one of the naive, sweet girls, when I started up the hill for my evening hike. "Oh, it looked like a good walking stick!" was my swift reply. She nodded, satisfied by the ridiculous answer and walked back toward the other girls. What they didn't know was that my friend and I would lay in wait up the trail and would be putting the wriggling snipes into their bag as they thumped on the tree. Without a flashlight, "which would scare away the snipes", the girls would never see us.

Evening came and soon we heard the thumping on the tree which signaled the start of this fun prank. The tree had been carefully selected, not because of the close proximity to the fake snipe trail, but because the horses had been tied here for several hours and there were plenty of piles of the fresh green road apples laying around. My 'walking stick' was now used to shovel a hefty pile of steamy horse dung into the bag while hiding around the other side of the huge tree trunk. The screaming girl reached into the bag, elated that the trick had worked well enough to attract a snipe, then squealed with disgust with the realization that she had just choked a handful of gooey green poop instead of a male snipe. Initially we thought that the trick would only work once, but when each of the girls had been pranked, they had wanted in on the gag, so that the remaining participants would suffer the same embarrassing fate as they had. As they filed back into camp one at a time, they excitedly recounted their adventures and that they had caught a snipe in the bag, but it had gotten away. "The trick must be to really grab fast and squeeze hard once they're in the bag," they would seriously comment, while the other girls bought their phony story. "Eeeeeouuuuuuugh! Gross!" each girl would squeal when they realized what they had grasped onto. "Don't tell the others!" would be our prompt response, which was not really necessary since they all wanted to dupe the others in the same fine fashion. The night wore on as each girl took their turn at the snipe tree.

We all had a great laugh at the gross snipe hunt, but none would admit what happened when we got back to civilization. I'm not sure if they were embarrassed, or if they planned on suckering someone else into going snipe hunting. What a great snipe hunt!

Wild Ride

The day dawned on a cold cloudy day in November. This was a day that had been anticipated for several weeks since we had to wait for dad to get a day off to take us hunting. We had heard from the local gossip circles that someone had spotted a herd of elk the day before near the confluence of the 4 streams that ran down through the pristine Pine Valley. Though we had combed the woods in all of our favorite haunts, we had fallen short of our expectations and had only been successful in harvesting one cow elk out of the 4 available tags that we had drawn that season. That last day of the season dragged on like an itch that couldn't be satisfied. Acting on the tip that had been provided by our dubious sources, we had centered our search for the elusive wapiti in the high desert topography that is typical of much of Eastern Oregon near the breaks of the Snake River drainage. While seeing many mule deer scampering out of the brush choked coulees as the day dwindled away, we had yet produced any evidence of the reported elk herd. As the approaching dusk progressed, while driving along a gravel road, resigned to our failure, we spotted the ghosty herd traversing across the top of one of the distance sagebrush speckled hills, towards the timber on the north slopes facing Pine Creek. I was about to leave the state for several years and would not be able to hunt during that time period, so I was highly motivated to fill my tag with one of the tasty critters. Since I was the only volunteer willing to attempt the distance with such a short period of daylight left, I headed for the mountain-top at a full run with my trusty open-sighted .30-06 Browning and with what I thought was a pocket full of shells.

I ran for some distance down a deep draw and turned left up a smaller draw that I figured would lead directly to the small herd of dallying creatures. As I crested the hill that led out of the head of the open draw, I saw that the object of my long stalk was still holding at the crest of the hill approximately 400 yards to the north. While still gasping for air, I sprawled on my belly in the snow, to get a steady rest for my trusted semi-automatic. Long since stripped of its scope due to malfunctions caused by multiple falls, the rifle settled into it's familiar cradle as I brought the sights to rest on the first un-lucky critter. The loud shots echoed to the canyon floor below as my audience strained to observe the action from their lower vantage point. I had seen one elk tumble to the earth after one of the six shots so I was confident that my tag was filled at last! Through the rapidly diminishing daylight, I signaled to my father and siblings that I had been successful.

I started my trek up the hill to the slain elk, as darkness began to envelope me completely. I had just enough daylight left to realize that I not only had one dead elk, but two others down that were still very much alive. The lower back had been broken on both so that they were not able to flee. After realizing that I had emptied my pockets of available ammo, I was faced with the task of a more intimate form of killing, my hunting knife. I went to the one on the steep hill, since my initial attempts to get close to the other one had met with frustration and failure. I just couldn't get close without getting struck by flailing hooves.

As I approached the young antlerless elk, I realized that I could get on the uphill side with no apparent danger of being flogged to death. My idea was to straddle the elk and slit it's throat to put it out of it's misery. As I climbed aboard the elk, I grabbed it's ear with my left hand and with the other hand attempted to slit it's trembling throat. When the elk began to run down the hill propelled by it's still-able-front-legs, I was still attached to it's back and began a wild ride down the mountain, clinging to it's back while desperately stabbing at it's throat, trying to end this nightmare! The horrible sucking sounds of the breath coming through the newly created holes, soon ceased as the life ebbed from the floundering elk. The dead yearling slowly crumpled in a lifeless heap beneath me. Needless to say, after this exciting trip down the mountain, I had 3 elk to fill the 3 available tags, and an unbelievable story of a wild ride!

The Circle of Life

Many times in my life there have been opportunities to defend the fact that I am a hunter and a gatherer and have taken the life of many of Gods creatures. It never has been a blood lust thing, just a desire to be out in the wild and to enjoy the occasional elk steak or pheasant breast. I have often made the comment to friends that when I see a deer jogging across a field, that my mouth starts to water, just thinking about the tasty back straps or sirloin. Though devoid of a desire to kill just for the sake of killing, I have to admit that I have not thought much about the life of the critters that I have killed and eaten other than to see them as a tasty morsel or to admire their beauty. I have however, felt a twinge or two of remorse, when my actions have caused an animal to suffer unduly. It is a great pet peeve of mine anytime I have had to observe the waste of any of God's creatures without cause. I have never allowed my children to kill the little tweety birds or anything for that matter, without using it to sustain life. "You kill it,… you eat it!" I have said to them many times. I am pleased whenever I see that they have taken that lesson to heart.

On the way to a family reunion recently, after going many years without hitting a deer with my vehicle, I plowed into a young deer with the grill of my pickup. There was silence in the car for a couple of seconds, until my young 4 year old son, who was sitting in the seat next to me, piped up in a matter of fact voice, "Dad, you kill it,… you eat it!" I did feel remorse for the loss of this precious little life, especially knowing that it would go to waste in some landfill somewhere in Stevens County.

This incident was brought to my memory one morning as I traveled down a country road, clipping along at a good pace until I saw a pair of Valley quail with a bunch of tiny youngsters gathered at the side of the dusty road. I slowed, but was too late, as one of the little ones smacked into my windshield and rolled lifeless to the road bed. "Dog gone it!" I exclaimed with an air of sadness. "What a waste of a wonderful little life. The poor little guy didn't even have a chance to live a life." I shook my head and pondered the results of my actions. "I should have slowed down sooner," I thought to myself. "Dang it anyway!"

I continued down the road in my now sober mood, thinking of life and death and things. I slowed the car to pull over into the weed filled driveway of a property that I had just listed for sale. One of the benefits of my career as a Realtor was that I had the opportunity on many occasions to be in the outdoors. I had traveled to this country location to take photos of a large parcel of wooded property that was a real wildlife haven.

As I stepped over the short wire gate and proceeded onto the weed choked property, I heard the distress call of a male valley quail. "Funny," I thought, "that I had just been thinking about the small quail I had squashed." I noticed that the small family of quail had taken refuge in the tangled limbs of a stunted pine tree to avoid the attack of a large red tail hawk that was watching with intent interest to see if he was going to get quail for lunch. In my life as an avid bird hunter, I had witnessed many times as a hawk or owl would swoop down and snatch a fleeing game bird right out of midair, so I was well aware of the life and death struggle that was taking place at the small pine tree. As I stepped between the hawk and his would be prey, I waved my arms and said "shoooooo! Get out of here!" The disappointed predator spread his large powerful wings and flew off into the morning sun.

I smiled broadly as I realized what had just happened. I had just saved the life of a quail! Maybe I had righted a wrong. I had taken one life and given one life in return. "The circle of life!" I thought as I reverently bowed my head and walked back to the truck.

Spider in Church

Reverent as a church mouse, I sat at the head of the small congregation in the old school house which now served as our church building. I was sitting at the front of the small gathering of Saints at the cloth covered table, officiating as a Priest in the sacred ordinance of the Sacrament. My shyness had often been mistaken for quiet reverence, since as a young boy I would sit silently looking neither to the left or to the right, frozen in fear that someone would discover me and look in my direction. The shyness had long since been replaced by a thoughtful, heartfelt respect for Deity and the sacred symbols of the gospel covenants.

The table bearing the emblems of Christ was situated in plain sight directly in front of the rows of old theater pews. This had become my normal seating arrangement during the first portion of the main church meeting since I had been called to serve in that capacity.

Distracted by the lure of outdoor activities as any teenage boy would be, I sat pondering my summer activities and became oblivious to my surroundings as the opening hymn was sung by the faithful, but diminutive congregation. Any movement was kept to a minimum because our location had the same effect as being in a fish bowl. The generic opening prayer had ended and I sat quietly listening to the Officiator's list of announcements.

All of the sudden out of nowhere, a huge gray spider dropped out of the sky and landed directly on my knee. The wriggly monster must have been as big around as a quarter! With a stifled, panicked yelp, and a quick swipe of the back of my hand, I launched the grotesque eight legged creature into

228

space as I jumped quickly backwards in my metal chair. The loud noise and quick movement instantly attracted the stern gaze of most of the serious church goers. Since no one else had seen the spider, I figured that I should just pretend that nothing had happened and dutifully began the preparation for the ordinance, all the while frantically searching for the beast that had violated me. To this day when I participate in the sacrament or sit quietly in church meetings, I always keep my eyes peeled for flying church spiders that drop out of the sky.

After spending it's early years as a small country schoolhouse, the durable building was converted to use as a church. It is situated near the tiny burg of Jimtown at the north end of Pine Valley in Eastern Oregon. It served as a church for many years and has spent the last twenty years or so as a personal residence and still stands to this day. If only those walls could talk!

Wheat Burgers

If you have smelled and hefted and gobbled a big juicy burger from the local drive-in, then you probably will be as repulsed as I was by the thought of eating something that is as far from the artery-clogging, chin dripping, taste of real beef, as Bill Clinton is from the "real deal." My mother, though sweet as a honey-dipped roll, was in her faze of being a health food fanatic and had become rather annoying with her insistence that we follow her lead. The times were a bit lean, since my dad was starting a new business venture and hadn't had a regular paycheck for a while. He would come home to his nest full of fledglings, who sat around the kitchen table waiting for the scant meals, like a nest full of hungry baby birds. If the food hit the table, it was immediately consumed. Our poor dog, Kip, would have starved to death if he had to rely solely on leftovers for his sustenance, because there weren't any. Now, don't misunderstand me, it's not that we ever really went hungry, but sometimes it just wasn't necessarily the type of food that a teenager would do back-flips for. We had begun to dip into our food storage, which had been set aside for such lean times. It consisted mostly of hard, red winter wheat that had been stored in airtight fifty gallon drums.

My mother would sprout the wheat, by soaking it in water until it was swollen and heavy, and would then leave it to germinate in glass jars that sat on the window sill of the dining room. The soaked seeds would begin to show the green sprouts of life in just a few short days, and would then be prepared for consumption in a variety of creative ways. Of course you could always just eat them plain out of the jar, which my mother said, "would make you grow tall and strong," or they would be ground up into a mushy wad of gluten and green stuff that would be seasoned and fried, turning it into a vega-burger. I could eat the fresh baked bread that was smothered in real home-churned butter, but the wheat burgers were hard to swallow. The round, plump patties looked surprisingly like a real beef burger, but the taste was awful. Now, I suppose, if it wasn't touted and presented as a real hamburger, one would realize that it is just a bunch of wheat sprouts and expects the taste of such, but when it is disguised as the real thing and falls way short in the other important categories, such as taste and smell, then it becomes a surprise each and every time. I ate my fair share, but saved most of the left overs for my siblings, since the dog wouldn't eat the chewy-wads-of-whole-wheat-goodness either.

Mom is still sort of a health food nut, never really moving onto another faze, but she hasn't tried to fry up a juicy wheat burger since those lean times on the farm. I still tease her about her choice of cuisine, even though my doctor says wheat burgers would lower my cholesterol and help me to lose some weight. I wipe the dribble of burger juice off my chin and think about wheat burgers...NOT!

The Sled Race

The sledding hill was a long steep stretch of road about ½ mile long that was treacherous with a vehicle, but was heaven on a sled. This portion of our mile long driveway started above the curve and continued straight down the steep hill until it gently leveled out near the bus stop. This worked in our favor during winter months especially when we were late for the school bus and needed a faster way to get there. The old runner style sleds rarely got used because they would slice through the thicker snow and stop, but the snow conditions on the sledding hill were more than ideal which motivated us to dust off the sleds and wax up the runners. It had snowed and was very cold, turning the recently ploughed road into a fifteen-foot wide luge track. Normally the road either had too much snow or been scraped down to expose the gravel making it difficult to navigate with one of the sleds, but conditions on this day were more than ideal, since it happened to fall on a holiday when we didn't have to be to school for several days.

We ran excitedly down the road to the point where we could start coasting down the hill toward the sharp corner, the cold frosty breath rising above us with each puff of air. "Make sure no cars are coming!" cautioned my ever vigilant sister. As the oldest, she had become like a little mother hen to the rest of her younger siblings. "Wait till we look around the corner!" she yelled to me as I took a running start and belly flopped onto my long sled. I had spent a great deal of time carefully waxing the shining steel runners, and was anxious to try them out. "Wheeeeeeeeeee

Hawwwwwwww!" I yelled as the sled quickly picked up speed, causing me to tip slightly and skid sideways as I rounded the sweeping 90 degree corner and shot across the bridge and down the steep part of the hill. I swallowed the lump in my throat and tightened my grip on the handle bar as the sled zipped down the hill causing the white landscape to become a blur. "YeeeeeeeeeeHawwwwww!" I squealed with my prepubescent voice, gulping the frigid rushing air. When the sled reached a speed far beyond my comfort zone, I slammed the toes of my newspaper filled hand-me-down boots into the icy roadway in a futile attempt to slow my out-of-control progress down the road. As I reached the portion of the road that leveled out, I steered the sleek sled sideways into a skid and came to a stop. "It's awesome!" I yelled back up the road to my more timid younger siblings. I could see their dark figures rounding the corner above me and watched with a wide grin as they picked up speed until they came zipping by me with wide eyes and tight grips on their smaller sleds.

We hurriedly trudged back up the hill, anxious to give it another try, pleased that we were in for a day of fast thrills and spills. After several more white-knuckled trips down the slick luge, I said with a grin, "let's try a rat race! That would be a blast!" The initial thrill had worn off a bit as we had become used to the swift speeds and had learned how to stop safely before reaching the bus stop. So now seeking new thrills, we started down the hill in a race that would be a combination drag race and crash derby, or a "rat race" as we now dubbed it.

Unexpectedly blinded by the snow churned up by the sleds in front of me, I dropped back a bit, adjusted my hat down across my eyebrows, dropped my head and let 'er rip! As we rounded the corner one of my brothers crashed into the snow bank, grunting as he came to an abrupt stop. Now gaining speed rapidly, I quickly caught up with the next racer, crashing into the rear of their sled, causing them to veer quickly to the side and slow down. Without slowing a bit, I soon came within reach of the next sled, grabbed tightly onto the steel runner, yanking it quickly sideways. The sprawling rider tumbled into a cloud of snow dust, crashing into the hard snowbank with a thud. I waved goodbye and continued speeding down the road. With my jaw clinched in determination I lowered my head again in order to streamline myself and pick up as much speed as possible, in order to catch up with the remaining competitor. Just as we neared the finish line, I reached for the runner of his sled and yanked, causing the rider to tumble sideways, allowing me to barely finish first. "No fair!" yelled my distraught neighborhood friend. "That's the rule we agreed to!" I insisted. "Well, then let's go try it again!" he challenged. We wrapped our ropes around our waist, stuffed our cold hands deep into our pockets and trudged quickly back up the hill. "New race!" we announced to the other disgruntled racers as we approached the top of the hill.

The Toilet Seat Incident

Much has been spoken and even written, about the following described event, among my family. Most of which may or may not be true. Since I was the only one there to witness this unfortunate episode, I will attempt to tell it like it was and set the record straight.

The hunting camp was a buzz of activity that morning as I trudged up the hill to take care of some serious business at the makeshift outhouse that my son and his friend had cobbled together. We had given them the assignment upon our arrival at our usual camping spot, to take the brand-new toilet seat that my cousin had provided and construct a latrine that would service the camp of hunters for the entire week and a half. Compared to the usual arrangements, this was like going to the bathroom in the Marriot Hotel.

The two teenagers had thoughtfully patched the latrine together, using the shiny new seat, some baling twine and about a half a roll of duct tape. They had precariously perched the front of the new white seat atop a short slender stump that they had created by trimming a young tree that seemed to have grown there just for that purpose, then had tied the rear of the seat to a horizontal pole that had been meticulously lashed between two spruce trees. The duct tape had been used to attach a plastic garbage bag around the front of the seat to avoid the possibility that the user would accidently urinate on his own shoes. (A woman would never have thought of this strategy since it physically just doesn't apply. Just like a man can't understand the need to lower the toilet seat when he's done.)

The completed project was really a site to behold, though it had a fatal flaw that would later be my undoing and is the subject of this ridiculous tale. The carefully crafted device looked more like a crude spaceship than a toilet, but it had served its purpose well, offering some degree of comfort in the rugged environment of the wilderness.

We had decided to break camp that morning and I had been given the assignment to take down the crude outhouse after I had taken care of my business. "I was going there anyway," I had explained to my companions, as I tucked the last roll of paper under my arm. "If no one else is ready to use it, then I'll just take it down and cover it up when I'm finished," I informed them. Oblivious to the impending doom that awaited me, I sauntered up the hill like a little kid that had procrastinated his duty until it was almost too late. I slowed my gait just a bit so as not to appear too eager to get there, just in case someone had been watching me walk up the hill. Most people would understand the urgency involved but still it's a private matter and one that I was reluctant to share.

As I lowered myself onto the well-used throne, I could see that our timing for abandoning this location was impeccable, since the once-empty-hole in the ground had been completely filled with eight days of used groceries. "Not much of a hole to fill in." I mused, as I relaxed after my push to accomplish the business at hand. I shifted my weight in order to complete the paperwork and had gone back for one last pass, when I suddenly heard a loud popping sound and felt myself plunging toward the stinky mess below. With horror I realized that the composite toilet seat had finally reached the limits of its endurance and had snapped in half. The camp full of slightly overweight hunters had stressed it beyond its endurance since it had only been supported on the front and back. My fall seemed to be in slow motion as my life passed before my eyes in what must have been just a split second. "This is not happening!" I thought frantically.

It is amazing how fast the human brain can process information in a crisis. Falling into a full latrine, backwards with your pants down, ranks right up there with a host of things that should happen to someone else rather than yourself. My lightning-speed-imagination gave me a quick glimpse of what my fate was about to be, which motivated me to react with cat-like reflexes in order to save myself from this awful doom. My jerky reaction looked like an unseated bull rider touching the back of the bull with his free hand, as I arched my back away from the stench and thrust my free hand out to grab anything available in order to break my fall.

The slow motion abruptly came to a halt as my hand found traction on the stub of a low hanging branch. I was elated that my fate had now taken a turn for the better, but also immediately realized that my hand was impaled on the sharp broken branch that had saved me from a much worse outcome. Now precariously poised horizontally above the sewage it became a rather athletic maneuver to return myself to an upright position. With legs together and my pants still down around my ankles, it was becoming increasingly difficult to hold myself aloft, so with a grunt and a super human effort, I sprung to the side of the hole and gasped a sigh of relief.

It must have been quite a site to see as I stumbled into camp with my pants half zipped and with blood pouring profusely from my new wound. "No, I didn't get attacked by a grizzly bear! It was the toilet seat!" I sheepishly explained. The roar of laughter that ensued gave me an indication that this event would become the fodder for many jokes at my expense.

My brothers are always pleased to take advantage of such episodes in order to make any attempt possible to exercise revenge for my many pranks at their expense. As I suspected, the toilet seat incident has not yet faded from their memory banks.

The Air Is Thin Way Up Here

I'd like to think that I'm an honest sort of a fella, so must confess at the get go that this story is written not only to entertain the reader, but to give an old fashioned ribbing to my long time hunting partner, Stan. I met the burley logger for the first time at a Junior High football game in which our son's shared a role on the same team. His sideline antics were the first clue that I was gonna like this guy! Finally, a fan that was as enthused about football as me! Somehow we bumped into each other and got to talking and realized that we had a lot in common. Some months later we arranged to take a horse pack trip into the Pasayten Wilderness of north central Washington. The adventures of that trip seemed to cement our budding friendship into a bond that has seen us through lots of good times and some bad.

Our favorite trip each year has become like a pilgrimage to Mecca for a Muslim. We scheme and plan and polish the previous years tales until we have come full circle and it's time to go again. Though somewhat embarrassing for Stan, this story has to be told. It would be such a waste to leave it only in our campfire circle.

It was our second year to this pristine high altitude heaven. We had packed deep into the Eagle Cap Wilderness of northeastern Oregon's Wallowa Mountains to a place that we had previously discovered to be filled with healthy herds of the elusive Wapiti or Rocky Mountain Elk. Hunting elk had become a favorite passion, along with all of the camping and horse packing that is associated with such a remote excursion. Stan was a relatively new convert to the sport of archery, but had become rather proficient with his compound bow.

After several days of combing the open meadows and dark timber of this high alpine drainage, while sitting on a high bluff glassing the opposite side of the canyon, I discovered a hidden basin that had been previously undiscovered by our hunting party. As I glassed the multi-terraced terrain from my lofty vantage point, I realized that there was a herd of grazing elk concealed in the highest meadow below the rocky crags of Red Mountain. The massive antlers of the big bull were barely discernable from my distant perch across the wide canyon. When I reported this sighting over the campfire that evening, and announced that I would be attempting to hunt there early the next morning, Stan reacted enthusiastically and said that he would go with me.

Before the rooster would crow in the lowlands, we were headed down the trail with a fine horse under each of us. When we reached the distance meadow that we had determined was directly below the high basin, we parked our trusty mounts and started the long, gut wrenching climb to the mountain top retreat, hoping that our prey would still be in the vicinity. As we entered the lowest of the plush alpine meadows, the pungent odor of elk urine began to revive our hopes that the crafty animals would still be there. Soon we realized that there was more texture to this haven than I could discern from my vantage point of the previous day. We stealthily continued our search, all the while climbing higher and higher, until we reached the highest level of the hidden basin. We peeked over the lip of the beautiful high meadow and with disappointment saw that it was devoid of what we had come all this way to find.

As we stood at the edge of the park-like meadow, that had the appearance of a well groomed golf green, my eye caught a glimpse of a small movement. "Could it really be?" I thought. "Yes, it is!" "Stan, look over there! It's an elk bedded down!" Quickly we both dropped to our bellies, hoping that we had remained undetected. We quietly whispered in short, excited breaths, the ideas that each had about how to get close enough for a shot. We decided that if one of us could belly crawl around the small basin to the tiny clump of trees directly uphill from the bedded cow elk, that it might be possible to get within archery range.

After a short deliberation, Stan won the coin toss, and he started his lengthy crawl towards the clump of spruce trees. I had decided that in order for me to be in a position to help move the animals closer to Stan, or to be in a strategic position in case they spooked, I would have to travel about 1/4 of a mile downhill and then back up into the other end of the long meadow. Just as we parted, the silence was broken by an ear shattering squeal that was the signature mating call of a majestic, dark-caped bull. "Wow! There are more elk here than we can see," I thought to myself, as I quickened my pace to my appointed position. "When I get into position, I will bugle and that bull will either come towards me, or run right over the top of Stan!" I continued to mutter to myself as my round- about route brought me into position for the ambush.

I bugled as planned, and started my sneak towards the top of the hill which led into the bottom of the small basin below Stan's hideout. Much to my dismay, when I crested the hill and looked out onto the empty meadow, not an elk was to be seen. After several minutes of disappointing silence, I saw Stan hoofing it across the opening towards me. As he drew near, his short anxious breaths indicated that he had seen some action and I had missed it all!

"What the heck happened?" I asked with a grin. "Awe, ahhhh, well, aaah, geez! Dang it! Awe!" The sputtering logger began a stammering session that would rival any two year old's description of his presents on Christmas morning. "I had him this close….. he was huge! I could see the whites of his eyes he was so close," were a few of the short sentences that I could understand as his tirade continued. His callused hands shook like a leaf as he raised his arms to mimic the size of the massive rack that he had been just a few feet from. His quivering voice continued to explain that the big bull had gone up there!

He pointed to the shale slides above us as he explained that the bull had taken some of the cows and escaped up the shale slide and over cliffs that would have made a mountain goat think twice. As he excitedly continued to explain his version of events, I deduced that the elk must have winded me from below and had walked single file right past Stan. As he shot his unsteady arrow into the dirt at the feet of the nearest elk, he had lost all composure and stood there with his mouth open, watching multiple targets moving past him in single file.

By the time I got to him, the elk fever had totally consumed him and he was reduced to a quivering mass of jelly! His pitiful condition brought me close to tears, as I consoled him between the convulsions of laughter. I assured him with a wide grin that this type of behavior would eventually be controllable if he stuck with it. I continued to console him between giggles, "must be the thin air,…. the air is pretty thin way up here!"

The Bear And The Log

For many years in the State of Washington, baiting had been a legal and an accepted method for hunting the elusive black bears that are so prevalent in this thickly wooded northwestern State. Though contrary to the beliefs of many a would be tree hugger, this practice was far from a sure-fire method to harvest a bruin. "Like shooting a dog off a dish!" I used to say, before I had given the hunting method a real try. "What a lazy way to hunt," I would exclaim in my ignorance.

I had decided that this was the year that I was finally going to get serious about harvesting a black bear. I had a lot of experience hunting many other varieties of wildlife, and in fact had encountered many black bears in the wild, but had never really had the desire to hunt and kill one until now. After many days of attempting the "spot and stalk" strategy, I began to wonder why I had run into many bears accidently, but now that I was hunting them, was having a difficult time getting even a glimpse. After a friend made the suggestion, I reluctantly agreed to give baiting a try. "Donuts and sweet things is what you need," was the suggestion. At the time, I happened to work at a grocery store and had access to the discarded meat, produce and bakery goods that were not fit for human consumption.

I loaded my well-used Datsun pickup with the stale grocery products, and drove to a remote location within 30 minutes of my home. I had previously scouted this location and had figured that I needed to pack the smelly goods into plastic buckets so I could carry them about ½ mile into a thick cedar draw that had yielded a multitude of bear sign. Everyday for a month or so before the hunting season started, I would make the repetitive drive and hike to my baiting location.

It wasn't long before I got a hit and the bait began to disappear on a regular basis. It became rather obvious that there were multiple bears taking advantage of this free lunch. I began to experiment with different types of bait and soon came to realize that just like people, bears had different tastes. The favorite was fresh meat trimmings and then the bruised and dented produce, like apples and grapes and peaches. Potatoes and onions and lettuce were rejected, while watermelon and cantalope were just barely tolerated. While beginning to enjoy the intrigue of this grand experiment, I was anxious for opening day so that I could halt this "lazy" hunting practice and finally get some rest. In reality, it had begun to be a real chore to pack the produce laden buckets to my stand site everyday. I sheepishly admitted that it surely wouldn't be a lazy man's preferred method. I would soon realize how difficult this task could really be, as opening day came and went without even seeing a hair of the shy beasts.

I had taken the effort to sprinkle flour around on the ground at the encouragement of a baiting veteran, in order to accurately assess the size and diversity of the bears attending the daily feeding. I would show up at all different hours of the day without any success. It wasn't long before I realized that my 'sure thing' would take more scheming than I had originally planned. After deciding that the bears must have been using my bait as a midnight snack instead of a daytime meal, I began to experiment with ways to interrupt their schedule, hoping to catch them in the daytime.

I began to cover the delicious piles of grub with huge piles of sticks and debris and had found a heavy log to hold the rest of the brush in place. My misguided theory was, that by covering the bait, it would take much longer to access and consume the chow and would give me a better chance of sighting a bear in the daylight hours. It took me awhile to catch on to what was happening, but it eventually dawned on me that the heavy log that I had been using to delay the feast had began to be relocated to a further location each day. I would come into the bait and see that the sticks and debris, along with the large log, would be totally removed from the site each day. It was as if this particular bear was frustrated at my antics and had decided to take matters into his own hands.

Each day the massive log would be a little further from the pile than the day before. I would drag it back and install it at the top of the aromatic pile each day. Each successive day the log would continue to be further away, until finally it disappeared altogether. I searched a wide perimeter around the bait pile looking for the log, but it was no where to be seen. The huge bear had decided to eliminate this nuisance once and for all. I never did even catch a glimpse of a bear at this bait site and finally admitted defeat. The bear with the log had beat me at my own game!

There's a Hair in My Maggots!

I reeled backwards away from the dead horse carcass, overcome by the fumes of methane that had saturated the air. I held my breath until I could escape the nauseating smell, as I walked quickly away from the rotten mess and into the fresh breeze. While holding my rubber-gloved hands aloft, like a brain surgeon getting ready to operate, I wondered what the heck I was doing with my hands deep inside the rotting carcass of a dead horse.

I had been supplying maggots to the local bait shops, who in turn sold them to fishermen for fish bait. My supply had been cut short and I had been looking for a quick fresh batch of the squiggly white skin worms in order to meet my obligations to the merchants. The business was extremely lucrative, but the money did not come without a huge price. The business required that I allow meat scraps or dead animals to rot in the sun and attract flies until they had laid a multitude of tiny yellow eggs on the yucky meat. I would then cover up the meat barrel and allow the fly larvae to hatch and to grow into plump little maggots. That was the easy part! Next came the rubber glove and clothes-pin-on-the- nose job!

If you worked quickly, it was possible to scoop handful after handful of the wiggling maggots into a bucket before they retreated from the light toward the bottom of the barrel. Normally if the lid was closed they would all be at the top of the barrel until it was exposed to light. It was a tricky deal, because if the lid was on too tight, the fumes would kill the maggots, and if the meat was too close to the top, they would all escape before they could be captured. I would then take the bucket full of the squirming mass of baby flies, and dump them into cedar sawdust to clean the smelly gunk off them. After allowing them to swim through the sweet smelling cedar, I would separate them from the dirty sawdust and dump them into a fresh batch. Then began the tedious process of dishing them out tablespoon by tablespoon into their separate containers. Two or three tablespoons of maggots per container with some new fresh sawdust would complete the

tiny package. They would then be kept refrigerated until they could be sold, keeping them dormant and postponing their metamorphosis into a fly.

This particular day, I had traveled to a friend's farm to check out the status of the decomposing horse and had been delighted to find that the maggots were ready to go. I had found that the largest mass of the white larvae was located inside the rib cage of the huge animal. Not realizing that the decomposing gases would be so concentrated, I had sucked in a lung full of the gas and was nearly overcome. Normally I could breath through my open mouth without smelling the yucky goodies, but this time was different. As I stood far off from the carcass, recovering from the inhaled gases, I contemplated the stupidity of my part-time occupation and decided then and there that there had to be easier ways to make money. I shook my head, puzzled at my idiocy and thought how silly and morbid it must look for a full grown man to be dipping fresh maggots out of the belly of a rotting dead horse carcass.

The maggot growing business would have to be done by someone else from now on, even though I had made a lot of money at the enterprise. I had been asked how I could stand to handle the smelly little worms, and would reply by explaining that the maggots aren't smelly, the rank stuff they crawl around in is smelly. "In fact," I would say, "it is not uncommon for me to eat a bowl of maggots every once in a while for breakfast!" "A little milk and sugar and they're not bad!" "It's like eating a bowl of rice." I would continue. "I tried a bowl, the other day and didn't get sick until I found a hair in it! Ouuuuuwww, yuck! There's a hair in my maggots!"

Under Pants in the Checkout Line

Some things just ought to be buried and forgotten so as to not dredge up the same sensitive feelings as the real event caused, but if this story can bring a smile to the reader's face, I guess it would be worth the pain of remembrance. I must say that the following repressed memory is number one on the 'top ten list of most embarrassing moments' for me, so hopefully you will fully appreciate it.

The Pine Mercantile was like the old time general merchandise grocery and hardware stores of the old days. It was a full blown grocery store with produce, dairy and meat department, but also had on its shelves clothing and guns and other miscellaneous products that would keep the local residents from having to travel the long winding road to Baker City. Situated in the sleepy little town of Halfway Oregon, the quaint little store's economics often closely reflected the ebbs and flows of the unstable local economy. In an effort to increase the meager income produced there, which was the soul income for our family of 15, it was a requirement that we try to be the 'one stop shopping' center for the local population which consisted mostly of cattle ranchers and loggers.

My list of many duties was to keep the coolers full of milk, pop and beer, mop floors, cut meat, check groceries and generally anything that was required. This day started like most others with me and my older sister opening the store with my father. After doing the normal opening procedures and settling into the assigned duties of the day, I took my place behind the counter of check stand number one. I was to be the number one checker for the first shift of the day and my sister was the backup. The morning went well and nothing happened that would forewarn me of any impending danger. I nodded to Mrs. McKim and continued to check groceries for other customers as she entered the front, grabbed a shopping cart and headed out of sight.

It was an unusually busy morning, which started to cause me some nervousness and agitation since as a typical, flighty teenage boy, I would rather have waited quietly in my supposed- authority-position with my checker apron on, than have to do any real work. I was barely keeping up with the long line when I reluctantly called over the scratchy intercom, "Checker please!". It was then that Mrs. McKim, who was a rather large women, ambled up to the checkout stand pushing her bulging cart into my line. My eyes darted back and forth between my immediate customers order and hers. I could tell that she had really loaded up. "Must have had a paycheck," I thought to myself. I had learned early on that the economics of our customers often immediately manifested themselves through our checkout lines. I finished the previous order and tugged the overloaded cart into place.

With my older sibling now in place behind me, it became sort of a contest to see who could punch the buttons on the old registers faster. I was doing very well, until I encountered a severe problem. Towards the bottom of the cart, was a pair of very large women's panties that my portly customer had found in the dry goods department of the all-purpose store. I had not doubted my fathers wisdom of expanding our line of goods, until approximately that moment. I continued to pick up items all around the large wad of silk, until the dreaded moment when I realized that I would have to pick them up. Hesitating briefly, I took a deep breath and gingerly picked them up. I hoped that my friendly customer could not see the horror that must have shown on my face as I fumbled to find a price tag on the bolt of cloth before me. I had never before touched a pair of women's underwear, let alone examined them so thoroughly. In a last vain attempt to find the price and continue my once fast pace, I held the lingerie up and with both hands stretched them out full length. My face increasingly filled with bright red blood as the tension mounted. I realized that the width of the monstrous panties was almost the full span of my outstretched arms. Still not finding a price tag, my panic came to full blossom and I started looking for an escape route. It seemed as though my head would explode with all of the blood that was being pumped there! When I lowered the embarrassing item in preparation for my escape, I caught a glimpse of the sympathetic house wife's slight grin. That was it! I dropped the panties like a hot potato, lowered my head and darted around the corner. Like a bawling range calf cornered in a catch pen, wide-eyed and frantic, I rounded the corner of my sisters check-out stand, muttered for her to take care of it and sprinted for the backroom. I was well on my way to the safety of the cooler, before she finally realized the gravity of my situation.

One good thing about that day, I guess, is that it made every other possible embarrassment, pale in comparison. I shuddered to think about it again as I wrote this. I hope you have appreciated my sacrifice!

The Big Rock

The boulder was about as big as a Volkswagen Bug, being a little rounded and smooth on top, which made a great perch for me to sit on. I held my fishing pole between my dangling legs and gobbled my baloney sandwich. My grandpa and cousin were standing directly below me, warming themselves by the fire we had built to fend off the cold on this blustery spring day. The boulder I was sitting on was embedded in the loose gravel bank above the more level river bank. The water was high since the dam was releasing a lot of spring runoff over its steep spillway. The murky water below us was turbulent and treacherous. My grandpa had warned me several times to keep away from the bank, saying in a stern voice, "If you fall in there, you'll never come out again!"

We often fished from this location since there were a lot of big fish lurking in the boiling waters below the turbines of the Brownlee Dam. The fish that got sucked through the whirling turbines would end up as chopped up little pieces, much of which would be consumed by the big lunkers that lay below the dam. This was our first outing of the year, since the weather had been cold, too cold for a young boy to tolerate for very long at a time. Grandpa had thought ahead and had brought a stack of dry firewood, knowing that us youngsters would be more occupied by the fire than fishing, which usually meant fewer tangles and hence, less work for him.

My cousin Randy who was several years older than I, fussed around with the fire below me, attempting to chop some of the larger pieces of wood into faster burning kindling. I tossed the crust of my mostly finished sandwich to the fish, and tightened the slack in my line to see if I'd had a bite. It didn't take any skill to fish that way, since the fish would swallow the bait whole before we would notice any action at the end of our line. The rough waters would constantly wiggle the end of our pole, until we would just give up checking.

I rose from my perch, awakened by some warning voice within me. "Get off the rock!" was the prompting. "Get off the rock now!" it came again. Startled a little at this undeniable communication from some unseen power, I quickly stepped off the large granite boulder. At the instant my weight shifted onto more solid ground behind the mammoth rock, it shuddered as if it had come to life, rolled from its resting place, and crashed down the steep embankment into the all-ready-treacherous river. My alert grandfather, turned quickly toward the booming noise, with a look of horror on his wrinkled face. "Are you all right?" he questioned with concern. My reply was slow, since I was still shocked by the violent crashing noise and the huge splash of the rolling boulder. "I'm okay. It just scared me!" I said, with a trembling voice. My cousin had moved up the river a bit, and had returned when he heard the commotion. "I was just right there below that rock chopping wood a minute ago!" he muttered, glad that he had a short attention span and had moved on to more exciting things. We continued fishing for a few minutes in silence, then having somehow lost the desire, pulled in our rigs and headed for the old brown Buick. The fish could wait till next time.

I have pondered the meaning of the events of that day, many times, and have wondered what purpose God might have saved me for other than my normal mundane life. I'm not complaining! The alternative sure doesn't appeal to me. My wife and children think so too! The big rock could have changed my life forever. Maybe it did.

The Chase

Sundown was sort of a rescue pony, coming to us for free because of his breathing problem. They said it was because he had been foundered before, causing health problems that made his breathing difficult and gave him stiff joints. He was a quite good looking horse being a black and white pinto and was about the size of a small Arabian. When he first came to our house, he was in very bad condition and would do nothing but mope around all day with his head down. It didn't take us long to figure out that he was extremely gentle and willing to try most anything, so we would saddle him up almost daily and push him to the limits of his short endurance. It wasn't long before he snapped out of his stupor and began to enjoy life again. Soon he was loping around the pasture like a young colt, and was willing and able to do most any activity we asked of him.

We took him on several pack trips to the mountains and learned that even though he couldn't run very fast, he could out walk most any horse around. Once he hit his pace, most other horses just couldn't keep up, so he spent most of the time in front as the lead horse. After several years of this type of activity, he became one with me and we trusted each other in most circumstances. An example of this was when we went elk hunting one day on horseback.

It had snowed about a foot that evening, so we decided that the next day we would saddle the horses and ride from the house up East Pine Creek until we cut tracks in the snow, then we would get off the horses and hunt. The horses were very excited as we trudged up the snow-covered road, any sounds being completely muffled by the soft new snow. Our mounts soon settled into the steady pace and continued to toil through the wet snow for about an hour. We decided that we would leave the road for awhile and turned up the hill to travel along a timbered ridge, hoping to find some new sign in the undisturbed snow.

All-of-the-sudden several elk jumped from their beds and ran up the hill ahead of us. Since we had not seen enough of them to properly identify the sex, we decided that we should chase after them until we could get a better look. The hunt was for bulls only, so it would be important to get a good look. I had heard that a horse could outrun an elk over long distances, so I was anxious to give it a try. My trusted mount caught wind of the pungent elk odor and soon figured out what his job was. He began to follow the scent and the tracks, like a blood hound, picking up speed as well as excitement for the chase. We began a slow lope through the timber, jumping over logs and crashing through the brush closely following the fresh trail left by the departing elk.

The circling elk, soon began to travel straight down the hill, which led us to a steep bank above the road that we had traveled up earlier in the day. I wondered how we would get down the steep gravely slope and climbed down from the saddle to take a closer look at a safer way around. Encouraged by the willingness of my trusting mount to continue this long chase, I hooked the reins over the saddle horn and slid down the long embankment on my rear until I came all the way to the bottom and slid out onto the road. I encouraged the steady horse to follow my lead, and to my surprise he quickly followed. He dropped his rear end to the ground and slid to the bottom like a little kid on the playground slide. The sparkle in his brown eyes revealed that he was still up for the chase, so I grabbed the saddle horn and pulled myself back up onto the sweaty horse and continued on down the trail in hot pursuit of our prey.

We did eventually catch up to the elk, proving the theory that a horse can out run an elk. I have had the opportunity to prove this theory several times since then and have not been disappointed. Sundown continued to be a faithful and willing companion until his untimely death several years later, when he broke his neck at the end of a picket line, having been pursued by some wild animal that had spooked him. I cried that day, broken hearted to lose such a great friend. The rescued horse had somehow been given a second chance at life and had lived happy and healthy until the end. I have owned many good horses since then, but will never forget my little pinto. When I think about him, I always remember that day of the chase. What a great friend and what a great day!

The Turning Point

Standing at the top of the podium, I leaned over to allow the First Place medal to be placed over my head. The take-down tournament had been a grueling event with wrestlers competing from Single-A schools on up to Triple-A. It was gratifying to me to be recognized among so many great wrestlers as the best-in-the-region at take-downs. It wasn't the first time I'd come away with First place and wouldn't be the last, but I had made a goal to never get taken down again and this specialized tournament was proof that I had realized a level of proficiency that may allow me to be able to realize that goal. Just a few short years before, I had struggled to just keep from getting pinned, let alone actually win a match.

I had started my wrestling career as a sophomore in high school, after a battle with the politics of the basketball program, when I decided that I would like to try a sport that was one-on-one. At least on the wrestling mat, wether you won or lost, you would at least know it was you that had control of the outcome, without relying on some teammate. I certainly wasn't any good at it in the beginning. I struggled to control my awkward, growing body that weighed about one-hundred-thirty-five pounds soaking wet. It was disheartening to lose every match, but I stuck with it, improving a little each time, until the turning point when I finally had enough of the losing and decided that it could be different.

I remember spending a great deal of time scanning the physical attributes of my more muscular opponents, then deciding the outcome of the match before I had even entered the ring. It never dawned on me that even though we weighed exactly the same, that I could have an advantage just with a change in attitude. It was a gradual change at first, starting when my uncle Tim had visited for awhile and had spent some quality one-on-one time mentoring me. He had been a state contender in the heavy weight division and had been giving me some pointers that seemed to perk my interest in learning more. I noticed that the new moves gave me an advantage over some opponents. I had begun to become a technician at the moves, practicing them over and over again until I could do them against even the best wrestlers. By the time the actual wrestling season rolled around, I was ready for some real action.

Several matches into that next season, I caught myself playing the mind games again and decided that I wouldn't let that happen again. The muscle-bound red head, walked out onto the mat, stretching and flexing and strutting his stuff. His cocky, but confident demeanor and physical presence, had totally psyched me out. I stared across the mat, with jealousy. "Why wasn't I that strong and that cool?" I thought to myself. We shook hands at the whistle, beginning a struggle that would teach me a great lesson. I had decided of course, that because of his appearance, he would naturally be better than I. The take-down came as a surprise to me, as he fell for my set-up like a sucker fish to a big fat worm. The ref signaled that I had won two points for the take down, and the struggle in my confused mind began. "But he's better than I!" said the little voice that had sized-up the muscle-man. He countered my take down with an immediate reversal, which proved that the little voice must be right. "See! He's better and stronger than you, just like I thought!" continued the wicked little voice. "No!" I said firmly to myself. "I will not lose again!" I mouthed the words to myself, sounding half convincing. The next two points went to me as I scrambled behind him, finishing my switch. "Hey, maybe you're right!" said the little voice. I threw the Half Nelson like lightning as he lowered his head, opening himself up for the move. He was on his back in an instant and I sucked up the slack in a flash, to begin my bulldog-like-death-grip, for the pin. He had not spent much time on his back in his illustrious and successful wrestling career, which motivated him to struggle violently, panicked at his predicament. He flopped around like a fish out of water, until the whistle blew and the ref's hand slapped the mat, signifying the pin. "Yes!" I hissed, as I jumped to my feet to accept the win. "I wanted that one!" I thought with satisfaction. "That other little voice is a goner!" I thought, as my hand was raised to the crowd for the win. "This feels much better than losing!" I mumbled as I strode over to the scoring table to sign the win card.

The next match was going to be more difficult, since the wrestler had been seated second in the tournament and had been a state contender the previous year as a sophomore. The little voice started its relentless campaign again. "He pinned you in about thirty seconds last year, remember? You can't overcome his strength or experience!" the voice reminded me. "Go away!" I said to myself, rebuking the negative thoughts. "I will not lose again!" I said convinced at my new-found-power. I overheard the confident former champion say to his coach as I walked past his small crowd of supporters, "This one is in the bag! He's the one I pinned last year in the first thirty-seconds!" My jaw tensed into a determined clinch, as I stomped away to prepare for the upcoming match.

The little voices had been totally extinguished by the time the whistle blew and the match began. I dove instantly for the take down, catching the overconfident wrestler off guard. The referee had barely had time to signal the take down points, when the unsuspecting athlete raised his knee to stand up. My speed was almost blinding as I scooped him into a cradle and rolled him immediately to his back. Panicked, that he could be in such a helpless position, he kicked and fought valiantly until he broke my strong grip and scrambled to his belly. Now realizing that he was behind by five points, he began an increased effort to dislodge me from my superior top position. Deftly countering each move with lightning speed, I remained in total control throughout the remaining minutes of the match.

The crowed roared to their feet with deafening applause, excited to have witnessed the big upset that no one had been expecting. The referee grasped my hand firmly and raised it high in the air, while whispering to me, "What a great upset! Nice job young man! You'll have a great wrestling career!" I walked to the scoring table, still trembling from the exertion and scribbled a vague resemblance of my signature. The little voices were gone and all I could hear was the roar of the excited crowd. I had turned the corner. It was a new beginning, with a whole new outlook. I was a winner!

Even though I did lose a few close matches in the next two years, I was able to finish those last years with a 50-win, 5-loss, record. I have witnessed that same change in many young wrestlers that I have coached since then. I recognize the look in the clinched jaw and the determined focused eyes, as their heart and mind convince the body to do their bidding. The turning point is always a great day!

Hot Springs

A good long soak in the hot mineral laden waters of a good hot spring, is one of my favorite things in the whole world. A few hours in the relaxing waters can remove months of stress and anxiety and leave me listless and happy, like the drugs my doctor gave me after my shoulder surgery. The hot tub at home comes close to this bliss, but doesn't quite have the same atmosphere of a destination like Ainsworth Hot Springs in British Columbia, Canada. Situated high on the hill overlooking the Kootenay River, the famous soaking spot attracts people from all walks of life and from far away locations. For some, it's like their religion, which is apparent by their almost reverent demeanor as they perform their soaking ritual and ice water plunge with quiet precision, as if they've done it many times before. They flock here like pilgrims to the Holy Shrine in Mecca, only with sandals and towels in tow.

My wife and I have been to this place many times together and several times with all of the kids. The horseshoe-like cavern goes deep into the mountain, which is like going into a cave complete with stalactites and stalagmites in waist-deep water that is very hot. The steamy corridors of the sauna-like cavern are dimly lit by a string of lights placed strategically to allow some dark corners for the religious soakers to bask uninhibited in the radiant thermal heat that comes from deep within the earth. Each end of the tunnel originates at the warm sitting pool next to the cold plunge. Only the most religious soakers enter the icy waters of the cold plunge. It is a rather exhilarating experience which serves to shrink up anything that has become baggy in the warmer waters. Then there is the regular pool, which my kids have enjoyed from an early age. We usually travel to the spot in the colder season of the year, when the snow is sometimes falling as we frolic in the warm waters of the pool.

This reminds me of some secluded hot springs that we used to visit in my youth. The amenities are not so nice as Ainsworth, but the water and the mineral part were awesome. It has something more to offer besides the comfortable amenities of the more public hot springs though, in that it does offer total privacy which at times has encouraged some attendees to shed their inhibitions and clothing, as my sister-in-law found out one day when they surprised a naked hippy enjoying the hot water of the thermal spring. Years ago, someone with ambition had placed an old cow trough in the path of the flowing hot water which has with time, become encrusted with the brown, slimy mineral deposits associated with any hot spring. To access the remote bathing spot, one must swim or boat across the Snake River and hike a short distance up the gently curving ravine, to the hot springs. It never attracts the more prissy types because of its rustic nature and because one must thrash through several hundred feet of snake infested prickly weeds to get there.

My best memory of this place was when my wife and I and several cousins and my aunt Bev, decided to ditch the more somber visiting session of a family reunion and travel to the river for a dunk in the hot springs. Luckily we had brought along several float tubes which helped out the weaker of the swimmers as we crossed the wide expanse of water to the weeds on the opposite side. After the long soak in the slimy mineral water, we plunged limply back into the colder waters of the Snake and began our long slow swim back in the dark. The full moon reflected off the water as we swam along visiting in the relaxing natural environment. We clung to the tubes and slowly kicked along while enjoying the good company. We laughed together as we collapsed on the opposite bank, limp from so much relaxation. I've dunked in lots of hot tubs and hot springs, but that is by far the best time I've ever had.

The Great Catch

One of our yearly traditions has been the annual Turkey Bowl on Thanksgiving Day, which is a full fledged tackle football game minus the pads and helmets. The only major injuries we have sustained through the years have been an occasional broken nose or hand or ankle. The minor injuries have been many and splendid, such as bloody noses, split open heads, bruises, scrapes, sprains and bruised egos. There had been several attempts through the years by less rugged individuals (that means wimps) to change the game to the tamer version of flag football. Since it always had ended up as tackle anyway, that idea soon faded, as did the instigators of such madness. Whether rain, sun, sleet or snow, we have played on. Several years we have played in up to a foot of snow. One such year the snow had come in several spurts and had blanketed the field with about one-and-a-half feet of the powdery white stuff. Since only the hard-core players had dared to show up in such weather, the teams were limited to six or seven players per side, which necessitated a change in strategy. It became more of a passing game without much blocking or rushing, any forward progress being severely hampered by the deep snow.

We played at a field that under normal conditions was a youth soccer field and was considerably shorter than a regulation football field. On each end there were metal soccer goal posts upon which a net could be attached when in use. The poles were made out of steel pipes about four inches in diameter, standing about eight feet tall, and were slid down into slightly larger pipes that were flush with the ground in order to be able to remove them when not in use. Somehow they had been left in place, which worked well for our game since they now became the markers for our makeshift end zone.

The game had been rather heated with both sides scoring several touchdowns. Even though the field conditions had gradually improved as the snow became packed down, the players had become slower, tiring quickly in the deep snow. On several consecutive plays, I had duped the defense into thinking that I had tired completely and that to guard me one would only have to play shallow defense. On the next play, I started with a short slant, then turned quickly and headed long. As I neared the vicinity of the end zone, I turned to see how the play was developing and realized that the quarterback had seen me dart past my defenders and had thrown a long bomb toward the end zone. Keeping my eye on the ball, I continued up the field, hoping to run under the lofty pass without falling down in the cumbersome snow.

The next several seconds were as if they were in slow motion and seemed to last forever. I had visions of making a "Jerry Rice" catch in the end zone, which motivated me to sprint even faster in order to elude the defenders that had now double teamed me. I struggled to catch up with the football which seemed to have been thrown a bit long. I looked back at the ball, straining to stretch my stride, reached out and made the most spectacular catch you have ever seen! Jerry Rice would have smiled to see such an athletic fete! What happened next would have made the top ten of the World's Funniest Sports Bloopers if only there had been a camera running.

As I cradled the pig skin next to my chest to assure its safety, I turned back down-field and with horror, realized that the once-slow-motion-action had all of the sudden sped up to normal real time. Directly in front of me was the solid steel soccer post. My life passed before my eyes as I realized that there was no time to slow my momentum before impact. Closing my eyes, I instinctively tightened my grip on the football. A resounding thud rang across the field as flesh met steel. "Uuuughhh," I grunted as the force of the impact knocked the wind out of me. My body hit the pole bringing it to an abrupt halt, but my feet continued on past the pole until they were several feet above the ground and parallel to the ground. I dropped in a heap to the cold snow, with the instant realization that I may never sire children again. The brunt of the impact had been absorbed by the sensitive tissues of my nether regions. "Touch down!" someone yelled in the back ground. "He actually hung onto the ball!" "Hey man, are you all right?" Now what a silly question to ask someone that is struggling to breathe and has his testicles where his Adam's apple should be! "Check out the bent pole!" another team mate exclaimed. "It's bent at a 45-degree angle!" said another. I lay on the ground for several minutes, writhing in pain but with the football still gripped tightly in my hands. "What a great catch!" I thought to myself. "But it sure hurts!"

Wilderness Dash

"**L**et's have a race through the mountains that will be a stretch for all of us," I thought as I sat pondering something that would be a fun but challenging family event. We had grown up with the Wallowa Mountains as a backdrop and had visited its high altitude haunts, many times. I was always looking for some excuse to head to the mountains, since I was a self-proclaimed mountain man and enjoyed camping in the rough terrain more than the average person. After struggling for a few days trying to think of an appropriate name for the venture, I proclaimed with excitement, "We'll call it the Wallowa Mountains Wilderness Dash! We'll make tee-shirts and the whole bit!" It was to be a commemoration of sorts, to Chief Joseph and his band of resilient natives, who had been driven from their homes in that area. The small band of Nez Perce had covered a lot of ground in what was now known as the Eagle Cap Wilderness, so I thought this difficult race through their home turf would be a fitting tribute to such noble and tough people. The tee shirt logo has a drawing of the mountains and Chief Joseph.

After much preparation and forethought, we arrived at the starting point at Wallowa Lake, dropped off by our wives, who kissed us goodbye, wished us well and headed the four-hour drive around the mountains to where the finish line would be. The race was to be started and completed by teams of two which would even out the odds a bit, since some of my younger siblings would probably try to run the entire fifty-mile distance and they were now stuck with someone much older than they. The teams were to have plotted a course, written it down and must travel that exact course for the entire time or face disqualification. The dark clouds overhead made me question the wisdom of such a venture, since we would be traveling over some of the most rugged mountain passes in the country. The weather at such high altitudes can be unpredictable at best. Our gear included a fanny pack with survival and first aid equipment, some energy food and a light jacket. My survival kit has always included a wool stocking cap and gloves, which I used several times later in the trip.

We hit the sign at the trail head which signaled the official beginning of the race and trotted up the well-worn trail on the east side of the West Fork of the Wallowa River. The quick pace soon slowed to a fast walk as we struggled to keep up with our younger partners. After several miles into the race, I had pulled a groin muscle severely, and was struggling with the pain, knowing that the race had just begun. I popped a few pain pills and started manually lifting my leg by grabbing the pant leg and lifting with each step. The drugs worked well and I soon settled into a pace that would continue for many hours and many miles. "These young chaps may have a fast start, but can they go the distance?" I chuckled to myself.

The trail soon found its way out of the timber, as we gained significant elevation and we started up the long rocky switchbacks of Hawkins Pass. The sun had gone down making the already gloomy day seem even darker and foreboding. As we reached the dizzying height of the summit, the wind had begun to howl and the slight sprinkling of rain had turned to snow. I was glad for my many hours of survival training which had prompted me to put on my warmer clothing and slip a black garbage back over my head as a makeshift rain slicker. This protective barrier of thin plastic shielded me from the wind somewhat and we continued on over the brutally harsh environment of the high mountain pass. Now on the leeward side of the mountain, the effects of the wind and blowing snow had vanished as quickly as they had appeared.

Now freezing because of the soaking rain, my companion and brother, Stephen had begun to suffer the first slight effects of hypothermia, becoming a little disoriented and sluggish. We stopped at the place the packers call 'head camp' on the head waters of the Imnaha River and built a huge warming fire to dry out and take a snack break. Now approximately halfway through the long grueling marathon, we had lost sight of the competing team who were ahead of us. We started back down the trail toward the next intersection in the well-maintained trail at Cliff River.

Our competitors had chosen a route that seemed longer to me, but a little less difficult than our choice had been, so when we turned right at the intersecting river, they kept going straight. We saw their bobbing heads disappear down the trail by the light of their flashlights. Little did we know that we would not see them again until at the very finish line. We had hoped to intersect another less-traveled trail that winds through the thick timber down from Norway Basin at Fly Creek, but all visible evidence of the trail was gone. It had evidently been abandoned shortly after my last trip down the rough trail many years before. Since our hope of finding and traveling that path was frustrated, we continued up the Cliff River Trail to Crater Lake and then to Pine Lakes and then all the way to our Grandpa and Grandma Pope's front door, which is where the race was to officially end. Since our originally plotted path had changed, we had traveled approximately four miles extra in addition to the fifty miles we had planned.

As we stumbled in pain toward the final last steps of the race, we noticed our competitors, Kim and Eldon standing there watching us. A sinking feeling came over us when we realized that we had been beaten by our brothers, but were elated to find out that Kim had blown his knee out and had been carried from the Pine Creek Pack Station by vehicle. "We won after all!" I exclaimed to my worn-out baby brother. There was some controversy after we discussed our little side trip, but the decision was finally unanimous that we had won the prize which consisted of an authentic Nez Perce shield decorated in the native American fashion.

We have had two additional races since then which have been eventful as well. Each could be an interesting story all to itself, but it will suffice to say here, that I and my partner or partners have won each of these long grueling dashes through the mountains. The second race was the one where I received my Indian name, "Talks with Elk." My wife was dubbed "Wailing Woman of the Mountain" and my hallucinating sister was dubbed "Crazy Woman Touched in the Head" for obvious reasons. You can tell we had a lot of fun with it!

The last one ended up being sixty-four miles, traveled in less than thirty-two hours. Two close family friends participated in that race, one of which had chided my wife for telling him that 'by the time he got to the finish line he would be taking little tiny baby steps.' He had laughed heartily at that tidbit of advice, thinking that he was tougher than a girl. My wife and sister had been my partners for the previous race, beating out the other team by more than seven hours and had experienced the brutal physical hardships of such an outing. Needless to say, my dear tough wife had the last laugh. Matt came to the finish line like a whipped pup, one little painful baby step at a time. We laid around in pain for a day or so, from the soreness of the abused muscles, but the sweet taste of victory once again acted as soothing salve.

The Wilderness Dash has not had any willing participants for the last couple of years, but may have some new challengers with the rising generation. I may have to revise the rules to allow horses for the old guys, if I'm to stand a chance against some of these young bucks. Don't tell them that though because I don't want them to think they have some sort of an advantage because of their youth. Remember, old age and treachery win, over youth and vigor every time!

The Toboggan

The morning finally came that I'd been waiting for! I was convinced that Santa Claus had come, but it was a family rule that no one could go into the living room until Mom and Dad were awake, so we waited patiently at the foot of the bed for them to rub the sleep out of their eyes. We would line up, youngest to oldest, and march down the hall together, descending on the brightly wrapped presents like Mormon crickets on a wheat field. As we rounded the corner into the living room, my eye caught sight of something big and shiny. The new toboggan stood in the corner of the room all by itself decorated, only with a big red bow. The beautiful sled seemed to call to me, begging for me to take it for its first spin.

The varnished-wood-finish brought out the natural grain of the beautiful wooden sled, making it glisten in the lights of the Christmas tree. It was about six feet long and two feet wide, with the sweeping curve of the wood forming the front and with rope handles hooked to the sides. It was a thing of shear beauty! "Let's go sledding!" was my first response. My mother suggested that it was too early in the morning and that we should open all of the other presents first. I resisted her suggestion but was brought into line by the stern look of my sleepy father. "There will be plenty of time for that later," he explained, trying to be patient with my pestering. We opened up all the wrapped presents and then bundled up before heading out into the cold.

The deep powdery snow glistened in the bright sunlight. It was a perfect day for the maiden voyage of the long toboggan. The runner sleds were useless in the deep soft stuff and had been stashed against the shed for a time when conditions suited them better. We dragged the heavy, new sled to the top of the longest hill and pointed it toward the bottom. We could see the fence of the lower pasture far below, but never even considered that it could be a danger to us. It was several football fields away and we had never even gotten half that far on our best ride on the other sleds. The summer float tubes now doubled as big bouncy sleds, but were useless on this hill unless the snow was very deep. The hillside was fairly open, but started getting brushy the farther downhill we would travel. The sharp short thorn bushes would rip at our clothing as we sped by on our tubes or saucers.

My hand came to my forehead to shield against the bright light of the afternoon sun that gave off little heat since it was so cold and the clean bright snow reflected the light so well. I squinted to look down the hill that hadn't been touched since the new snowfall. "Let's give er a try!" I shouted with excitement to the waiting line of passengers. "I think we can all fit!" I suggested, since the sled was longer than anything we had seen and we wanted to see what it would do and how many it could hold. I got in front and my neighbor slid into line behind me, anxious to go. All of the small children piled on behind, until the wooden sled was filled to capacity with the menagerie of bundled up passengers. "Okay, here we go!" I shouted as the last passenger gave us a shove down the hill and jumped on the back.

The speed was a little too exhilarating, especially for the poor sucker in the front, which was I! I hadn't counted on the powdery snow being kicked up into my face, taking my breath away and making it impossible to see where we were going exactly. "Lean left!" I yelled as we whisked toward a big stickery brush pile. I soon learned that it was unwise to stick any body parts outside of the profile of the fast-moving sled, since I had been whipped soundly by some of the passing brush. I swallowed the large lump in my throat that was caused by the thrill of the ever-increasing speed. We pummeled down the hill, gaining speed all the way like a runaway train. Several of the smaller children had tumbled off the back when we had become airborne over one of the lumps of snow that we now identified as rocks. "We will never be able to stop at the bottom!" I thought with horror. My excitement to try the new sled had vanished, now that I realized that this ride had become more than I originally bargained for. "Lean left!" I yelled again, as we barely missed some buried object that stuck partially out of the blinding white snow.

"Put on the breaks!" I screamed, above the sound of the rushing wind.

"There are no brakes!" yelled the neighbor in my ear. My heart was now in my throat, choking me as the terror of the out-of-control situation consumed me. The slick bottom of the shiny toboggan did its job as we continued to whisk down the slope past our normal stopping point. The frozen powder pelted my stinging red face as the front of the speeding toboggan bounced over the lumps and bumps, kicking the snow up into my face and taking my breath away. Even though we had reached the bottom of the steep hill and the sloping terrain had leveled out a bit, our momentum pushed us nearer and nearer to the lower pasture. Since I was struggling to see, being nearly blinded by the stinging powder, I didn't notice the fence until it was almost too late.

"AAAAAAHHHHHHH! Watch out for the..." my words broke off as I ducked to avoid getting clothes-lined by the sharp barbed wire of the lowest strand on the sagging fence. Since my feet had been jammed into the hooked front of the sled, with passengers crammed on behind me, I was unable to free myself from the inevitable wreck. The wire skimmed my head, knocking my stocking cap off, then caught the unsuspecting boy who was next-in-line, at about shoulder height. I closed my eyes tight, bracing for the impact as the screech of rusty wire being ripped from its staples, shattered the cold air and made me cringe. "This is bad! This is really bad!" I said to myself over and over again, afraid to open my clenched eyes, even though we had lurched to a sudden stop. "Ooooooohhhhh!" groaned the neighbor, once he had caught his breath. "Do you still have your head?" I questioned cautiously, afraid to look at the imagined carnage. Luckily, his thick padded coat had shielded him from the devastating effects of the strand of wire. Since it had hit him squarely in the chest, the impact had been distributed in a manner that had allowed the sled to continue under the fence with me still attached but left him sitting on his rear, but still hooked to the rusty wire. All of the other lucky passengers had bailed out one at a time from the back of the long sled, as we had picked up more speed than they were comfortable with.

We lay groaning on the cold snow for several long minutes, taking inventory of our body parts to assure that we were all intact. Part of the shine had worn off the new toboggan that day and though we did use it to shuttle items back and forth to the sledding hill, we never did have another ride as thrilling as the first!

about the Author

If you ask him to explain why his experience is overwhelmingly country, he will tell you that he should have been born in the early 1800's as a crusty old mountain man. He swears that his wife Susan convinced him to come to earth in this day and time instead, and excuses his many trips to the mountains and his obsession with the mountain men, to this affinity for an earlier time in history. Born in John Day Oregon and raised in Pine Valley Oregon, James R. Palmer Jr. currently has a successful career as owner and Associate Broker of a real estate firm near Spokane Washington and is the proud father of 6 wonderful children. He has been a construction worker, grocer, pineapple planter, farmer and horseman. He lives on his 33 acres in the woods with his wife, children, 5 horses and 3 dogs.

Printed in the United States
By Bookmasters